CENTRAL EUROPE

The Fox
of the North

BY THE SAME AUTHOR

BIOGRAPHIES

Clausewitz
Zapata
The Hussar General: The Life of Blücher
Moore of Corunna

OTHER WORKS

Peace for our Time
Blood, Toil, Tears and Sweat
The Peninsular War
A Day's March Nearer Home
The War in the Desert

The Fox of the North

The Life of Kutuzov, General of War and Peace

Roger Parkinson

David McKay Company, Inc
New York

Printed in Great Britain

Contents

Illustrations

Between pages 116 and 117

1 a. Field Marshal Mikhail Illarionovich Kutuzov, from a painting in the Borodino Museum. (*Novosti Press Agency*)

   b. Alexander I. (*Novosti Press Agency*)

   c. Field Marshal Count Alexander Vasilievich Suvorov. (*Radio Times Hulton Picture Library*)

2 a. The Empress Elizabeth and her court at Tsarskoe Palace outside St Petersburg. Painting by A. Bennis. (*The Mansell Collection*)

   b. Austerlitz, 1805. From a painting by Gerard. (*Radio Times Hulton Picture Library*)

3 a. General Prince Peter Ivanovich Bagration. (*Novosti Press Agency*)

   b. Field Marshal Prince Mikhail Barclay de Tolly. By Vendramini after de St Aubin. (*Radio Times Hulton Picture Library*)

   c. General Count Levin Bennigsen. After a drawing by Cook. (*Radio Times Hulton Picture Library*)

   d. General Sir Robert Wilson. (*Radio Times Hulton Picture Library*)

4 a. M. I. Kutuzov at the command post on the day of the Borodino battle, painted by A. Shepelyuk, 1812. Photo by M. Alpert. (*Novosti Press Agency*)

   b. Napoleon at Borodino. Painted by Verestchaguine.

Maps

Preface

To the Russians, Kutuzov is a hero similar to Britain's Wellington and Germany's Blücher. He fought the French at Austerlitz and led the Russians against Napoleon in the terrifying campaign of 1812, so well described by Tolstoy in *War and Peace*; he symbolized the spirit of the Russian people during the Napoleonic struggle. Later generations venerated his name. Stalin presented Kutuzov as an example to be followed in the conflict against Hitler; Russian fortifications in 1941 for the Battle of Moscow were built on exactly the same sites as those used by Kutuzov's forces in the Battle of Borodino against the French.

But outside Russia Kutuzov has been largely ignored. Foreign historians have often belittled his achievements or have echoed his enemies, describing him as incompetent, lazy and dissipated. This is the first full-length English work on Kutuzov, yet even apart from his military career he offers much scope for the biographer – his individuality, his experience of the Russian court and aristocratic society, his relationships with the ordinary men and women of the Fatherland, even his bear-like hulk and twisted, war-torn face. This fascinating character also presents a challenge for the writer: Kutuzov wrapped himself in mystery, and he well deserved Napoleon's name for him, which provides the title for this book.

I express my thanks to the following for helping me accept this rewarding challenge: Mrs Anne Hughes, for her enthusiastic and skilful translation from the Russian; the Russia and Soviet Studies Department, Lancaster University; Mr Alan Palmer, for his expert advice; the National Book League and the staff of the London Library; my wife Betty, for her French translation and all other painstaking work in our partnership – and for helping me to see the enigmatic Kutuzov as I believe he really was.

I

Mother Russia

(1745–1773)

On the night of Thursday, 20 August 1812, Russia's newly-appointed commander-in-chief was asked by his daughter: 'Do you really hope to defeat Napoleon?' Mikhail Illarionovich Kutuzov answered: 'Defeat him? No.' Then he added: 'But I hope to deceive him.' Hours later Kutuzov rode from his St Petersburg home to face Napoleon Bonaparte and the invading French Grand Army at Borodino, and thereafter to prove the accuracy of his reply to his daughter in the fearful campaign of 1812.

Austerlitz in 1805 and Borodino in 1812 – perhaps the two greatest battles in the Napoleonic Wars. On both occasions the clash took place between the main French and Russian armies; both times the respective regiments, totalling as many as 250,000 troops, were commanded by two men who never met each other face to face as individuals, but whose duel provided the most fascinating episode in the Napoleonic upheaval.

Napoleon called Kutuzov 'the sly old Fox of the North'. To Kutuzov, his opponent was simply 'that robber'. No man played a greater single part in Bonaparte's downfall than Kutuzov, yet history has often either neglected him or misunderstood him. He has been condemned as lazy, incompetent, cowardly, a lecherous imbecile too fat to ride a horse, who sought only fresh virgins and other comforts for his dissipated body. He was intensely disliked by the Russian Emperor who placed him in command of the Russian armies, and the hatred which others felt for him in his lifetime polluted his reputation in death.

Yet Leo Tolstoy provided Kutuzov with a hero's role in *War*

I

and Peace, and, with his blend of a historian's diligence and a novelist's eye, he wrote one of the most accurate and discerning descriptions of this 'Saviour of the Fatherland' which contradicts the customary image. Tolstoy called Kutuzov 'a simple, modest and therefore truly great figure, who could not be cast in the lying mould invented by history'. The military leader is seen as an incarnation of the Russian spirit and of the wisdom needed to guide and rescue the Fatherland in the terrible campaign of 1812.[1]

The life of Kutuzov is the story behind *War and Peace*. It is the story of Russia's fight against Napoleon, but in addition Kutuzov's own life is a reflection of the brilliant and bizarre social history of Russia during his time. In the late eighteenth and early nineteenth centuries all European countries exhibited a startling contrast between rich and poor, justice and injustice, corruption and virtue: in none were the extremes more vivid than in Russia, and Kutuzov witnessed them all.

*   *   *   *   *

Russia represented a gigantic, sharply tapering mountain. Perched on the peak was the Czar or Czarina, and throughout Kutuzov's lifetime the occupiers of this exalted, precarious position would provide grotesque examples of despotism: Elizabeth, who died in 1761 owning 15,000 dresses; Peter, the Emperor buffoon who reigned for six months before being murdered by his wife and successor; Catherine, a royal nymphomaniac who favoured Kutuzov and who employed a special lady-in-waiting as *essayeuse* to sift through the lovers waiting at her bedroom door; 'mad' Czar Paul, murdered only an hour or so after he had entertained Kutuzov to dinner, and whose son Alexander would always be affected by the feeling of patricide – and by dislike of Kutuzov.

Below the Czar stretched the inflated ranks of the nobility, in which Kutuzov and his family were prominent. The aristocracy dwelt in an artificial, honeycombed structure, conforming to rigid social rules, riddled with scandal and intrigue, and members of this hierarchy displayed a peculiar mixture of naïvety, sophistication, Asiatic emotions and European culture. Kutuzov, adept at manoeuvring in this world, would nevertheless fall a victim to it.

2

'Russia is like a girl of twelve,' wrote one Scottish visitor, Katherine Hamilton, in 1806, 'wild and awkward, who has been dressed up in a fashionable Parisian hat. We are living here in the fourteenth or fifteenth century.' She scorned the nobility. 'The open grave yawns at their tottering feet menacing to consign their brocaded existence to earthly oblivion.'[2]

Below lay the serfs. Over half the male population of Russia in Kutuzov's time were tied directly to the serf system, able to be sold, married, transported, flogged by their owners. In 1800 male serfs were generally worth between 200 and 500 roubles in the Moscow market and attractive girls much more. These virtual slaves were distributed unevenly amongst the nobility: in 1800 only 16 per cent of the nobles owned more than 100 serfs each.[3] Kutuzov enjoyed greater serf wealth than this average: as part of his rewards for military success he was given at least 3,667 men and women for his estates.[4]

These vast estates formed the basis of the Russian economy. The largest, owned by Count Nicholas Sheremetev, covered an area equal in size to the combined English counties of Yorkshire, Lancashire, Durham and Westmorland, twice as large as the American state of Connecticut. Roads were almost non-existent apart from the main highways; population centres were extremely sparse, with only St Petersburg, Moscow, Smolensk, Kiev and Kazan reaching the status of cities – in 1777 only three Russians in every hundred lived in a town.[5]

Outside these infrequent urban areas the countryside stretched brooding into the distance. Madame de Staël provided this eloquent description in 1812. 'There is so much space in Russia that everything becomes lost, even the châteaux, even the inhabitants. One would imagine one was crossing a country which had just been abandoned by its people. The lack of birds intensified the silence; herds of cattle are rare, or at least they graze a long way from the road. The spaces make everything disappear except space itself, which haunts one's imagination like certain metaphysical ideas of which the mind cannot rid itself once it has been gripped'.[6]

This was Kutuzov's Russia: like him the Fatherland displayed a mixture of the weird, the extrovert, and a depth of mystery which made everything appear not quite as it seemed, a mixture of artificiality and reality with the one overlapping and confusing the other.

3

Mikhail Illarionovich Golenishchev-Kutuzov was born in St Petersburg during the night of 16 September 1745. His mother, from the noble Beklemishevyi family, died young after giving birth to two other children, a boy Semen and a sister Dar'ya both of whom would outlive their brother. Their father, Illarion Matveevich, had risen to a prominent position in St Petersburg society both through his excellent marriage and through his own career. He had served in the army under Peter the Great, remaining in the Corps of Engineers for thirty years and seeing active service against the Turks. He retired with the rank of Lieutenant-General and transferred to the civil service soon before his first son's birth, and was thereafter engaged in extensive civil engineering works in Russia's new capital. St Petersburg had begun to rise from the marshes and islands at the mouth of the Neva in 1703, one year after Peter the Great's victory over the Swedes at Schlüsselburg provided Russia with a suitable site for an ice-free port at the head of the Baltic. By the time of Kutuzov's birth this 'northern Venice' had taken over from Moscow as administrative capital: buildings had been pushed upwards from the mud and outwards into the forest; Kutuzov's father played his part by designing the Petersburg canal system and a number of other works.[7]

The result brought mixed reaction from foreign visitors. Some appreciated the almost Mediterranean splendour of the palaces and administrative buildings, which contrasted so strongly with the dull northern climate, but according to the English tourist Robert Johnson the city lacked harmony: 'Everything as it were in outline, nothing perfect, nothing to please; everything to astonish; a mixture of splendid barbarism and mighty rudeness.'[8]

Young Kutuzov obtained the benefits of the upper Russian nobility through his father. The elder Kutuzov was appointed to the Senate, and enjoyed the patronage of the Empress Elizabeth, who came to power four years before Kutuzov's birth and who extended the building works begun by her father Peter the Great: her contribution included the 1,500-roomed Winter Palace, unfinished at her death in 1762. As a baby, Kutuzov spent much of his time with his maternal grandmother on the large family estate south of Petersburg. Growing older, he began to alternate between these rural surroundings and his father's house in Petersburg itself. He became accustomed to the company of

4

adults rather than other children, and seemed to prefer this arrangement: his father, renowned for his highly educated mind and known as 'The Wise Book', passed on his intelligence to his eldest son, who was described as having remarkable curiosity as a child, constantly asking difficult questions and being dissatisfied with evasive answers.[9] He mingled with the guests at his father's dinner parties, eavesdropping in the drawing-room as the members of Petersburg society clustered round the sofas; he also went with his father to the court receptions where he met the Empress herself.

Elizabeth's favourite palace was at Czarskoye Selo just outside Petersburg and known as the Catherine Palace after the wife of Peter the Great. Elizabeth herself suffered declining energy by the time Kutuzov met her, and increasingly the Journal of the Court Quartermaster revealed daily entries such as 'Her Imperial Majesty has graciously condescended on this day not to leave her private apartments'. She rarely left her room except on Sundays and holidays, and she often slept while the court met in her sumptuous ante-chamber; instead she remained awake for most of the night drinking with her favourite companions – usually serving-wenches, songsters and grooms. She preferred to have dinner at two o'clock in the morning.[10]

Elizabeth nevertheless remained a dominating personality, and invitations to her palace were eagerly sought. Balls, masquerades and hunts were daily events – a masked ball was held most Tuesdays, when the women were expected to dress as men and vice-versa. Guests entered the palace by the great staircase which was purposely built at one end of the massive building so that visitors had to pass through the succession of brilliant ballrooms. Kutuzov met the leading figures at the court, including the future Empress Catherine, nicknamed Figgy and summoned by Elizabeth from her native Stettin to marry Elizabeth's nephew Peter. Kutuzov's father found favour with Catherine, as he had with Elizabeth and Peter the Great himself, and his son would share this good fortune.

It seemed inevitable that Kutuzov would follow the same career as his father more through preference than through the custom of the time. Peter the Great had passed a law making it obligatory for every young nobleman to serve in the army, first as a private and then as a non-commissioned officer, but many nobles were evading

5

this ruling by the time Elizabeth had come to power. Others enlisted their sons at birth as privates in some regiment, then, by the time the babies had grown into infants the automatic absentee promotion would have taken them up through the ranks; as teenagers they could either serve as full officers or could stay at home having theoretically completed their service.[11]

The Kutuzov family, which revered the name of Peter the Great, refused to join this charade. In 1757 the twelve-year-old Kutuzov was sent to the military engineering school as a cadet-private to work his way up through the ranks. Kutuzov, besides being handsome, strong and an excellent horseman, also proved highly intelligent. He became proficient in mathematics, fortifications, engineering and a number of other subjects, and was also well-informed in theology, philosophy, history, law and social sciences. In addition he was able to speak French, then the court language, German, Polish, Swedish, English, Turkish and a little Latin. In 1759, two years after arriving at the school, Kutuzov was promoted to corporal, and before long to quartermaster-sergeant for special diligence in science and mathematics. Within a few months he became a junior teacher in the first class at the school besides assisting the officers in the tuition of those further up the academic ladder. Kutuzov's special subjects were arithmetic and geometry.[12]

Kutuzov, now aged sixteen, seemed lively and enthusiastic, popular with his fellow-cadets and with the teachers not only through his intelligence in the classrooms but also in affairs outside the curriculum. He obtained a reputation for bravery in the horse races which frequently took place in the school grounds; he proved to be entertaining company, especially through his ability to impersonate senior officers. With his good looks, good connections and natural abilities he seemed highly promising officer material and his future beckoned bright before him: in early 1761 he received his promotion from the ranks to ensign and within two months had left the school to enter full army service.

But drastic changes were being experienced by the Russian army as a whole, which threatened to affect Kutuzov once he left the seclusion of the education establishment. Russia was in conflict with Frederick the Great of Prussia, with Russian soldiers fighting alongside the Austrians and Swedes in the Seven Years' War. By 1761 Frederick the Great could barely assemble 100,000 troops with which to face three times that number of Austrians and Russians in Silesia, and by December 1761 Prussia teetered on the brink of defeat. Kutuzov still hoped that time remained for him to see active service. And then, on Christmas Day 1761 Empress Elizabeth of Russia died and her nephew Peter began his short, disastrous rule.

Peter III, who preferred his native Holstein to Russia and who held an inordinate admiration for Frederick the Great, immediately opened peace negotiations; he even lent Frederick a Russian corps to help the Prussian monarch stave off defeat by the Austrians and Swedes. Kutuzov, posted *aide-de-camp* to Prince Holsteinbeck immediately after leaving military school, had been seeking employment with the armies in the field during the latter months of 1761; now he found his request granted, but war was virtually over by the time he left St Petersburg.

At least Kutuzov's departure from the Russian capital spared him from witnessing the direct affects of Peter's rule. Grossly immature and licentious, the Emperor proceeded to display contempt for everything which the Russians held sacred. He provided an early example of his puerility at Elizabeth's funeral procession: he lagged farther and farther behind the ornate coffin, then suddenly hoisted his robes and sprinted to catch up, causing the elderly chamberlains holding his long black train to fall over themselves as they struggled to keep pace. The 33-year-old Czar danced for joy and repeated the performance.[13] But more important than this infantile behaviour was his high-handed attitude towards the army and towards Russia's foreign policy. From the Treaty of St Petersburg, 15 May 1762, Russia emerged with extremely dishonourable terms: all territory won by Russian troops was to be handed back to Prussia, unconditionally, and instead Peter proposed to embark on war with Denmark to recover the territories of Schleswig-Holstein. Discontent immediately flared among Russian officers and the atmosphere at court became increasingly tense.

Kutuzov, now a captain, was well away from the quarrel. Early in 1762 he rode into the Volga delta and to the town of Astrakan, where he would serve in the Astrakan infantry regiment. In August this regiment came under the command of Colonel Alexander Suvorov. The two men, later to be equally famous among Russia's military leaders, only spent a few weeks together

7

in 1762, but soon they would meet again and Kutuzov would become Suvorov's most fervent admirer and pupil.

Alexander Suvorov, thin, brusque and intensely determined to overcome physical deficiencies, had only been commissioned eight years before, aged twenty-four; he had seen action for the first time the previous year, 1761, leading small Cossack groups against the Prussians. His reputation for daring combined with speed and determination was already rapidly rising; now, during his short stay in Astrakan he displayed another side to his brilliant military character – organizational and training skills on a regimental level.[14]

A Russian infantry regiment numbered just under 2,000 officers and men, comprising two companies of grenadiers and ten of musketeers, an artillery unit with four guns, and a regimental staff of over fifty. Under Peter the Great the Russian regiments had become respected and feared throughout western Europe, especially after the defeat of the Swedes under Charles XII at Poltava in 1709. By 1721 Peter the Great had organized a standing military establishment based on fifty-six infantry regiments, including the famous Semeonovsky Guards and the Preobrazhenski Grenadiers, thirty-three cavalry regiments and one regiment of artillery. Troops were reasonably well armed with flintlocks and bayonets, originally imported from England but later manufactured at Tula.

The Russian army declined steadily after Peter I's death in 1725, although the deterioration was not immediately noticeable to other European powers. Discipline became extremely unsatisfactory with the officers relying on brutality to enforce order, and Russian success in battle depended upon massive firepower rather than through tactical innovations. All too often the soldiers merely acted like a rabble. 'I couldn't give you any idea of all the barbarities that these infamous people commit,' wrote Frederick the Great to his brother Henry during the Seven Years' War. 'My hair stands on end. They strangle women and children; they mutilate the private parts of the unfortunate whom they catch; they pillage, they burn; in fine, these are horrors which a sensitive heart cannot support except with the most cruel bitterness.'[15]

With the absence of firm control from the central military authorities, much of the training, organization and discipline of the individual regiments depended upon the colonel in command.

8

Many of the officers were barely trained, owing their position to aristocratic influence, and the rank and file were recruited by a quota system from the illiterate serfs and peasantry: the proportion of conscripts varied from two men in every 500 in time of peace to one in every twenty in time of crisis. Substitutes could be bought, and landowners usually only sent their most inefficient or unhealthy serfs. Under an incompetent colonel a regiment could be militarily valueless as an individual unit, and even the most energetic and conscientious commanders were faced with a difficult task. Suvorov showed himself a master, and from him Kutuzov learnt lessons on leadership which he would never forget.

Suvorov recognized the basic qualities of the Russian soldier – extreme bravery and matchless endurance. Maximum use should be made of these virtues, rather than suffocating them through finicky parade-ground performances which were so beloved by many senior officers – the ponderous, goose-stepping marching, wheeling and counter-marching, the emphasis on meticulous turnout, the useless ceremonial frills. To compensate for the general lack of literacy and to save energy for the battle, Suvorov believed that orders should be simple, direct and reduced to the minimum. Moreover, the soldier should be led from the front rather than pushed from behind by barbaric discipline: the commander must set the prime example.

Suvorov began to introduce his system of command at Astrakan and displayed a tireless interest in both the welfare and training of his men. Kutuzov gave enthusiastic support; despite his youth – he was still only seventeen – he became one of the twelve company commanders. Like Suvorov he realized the vital importance of creating a close relationship with his men, and throughout his life Kutuzov would benefit from this rapport with those serving under him.

Soon after Kutuzov's arrival at Astrakan the first reports arrived of the latest dramatic change-over in the Russian court. Catherine seized power from her husband in June; Peter signed an instrument of abdication on the 29th, declaring: 'In the short time of my reign as Self-Upholder of All the Russias I have realized only too well the strain and burden of a task to which my powers are not equal. Neither as Self-Upholder nor in any other capacity am I fit to rule. . . .' The document, probably drafted by

Catherine herself, was followed by Peter's incarceration in Ropsha Palace where the ex-Emperor pleaded for his dog, negro and violin – which Catherine granted – and his mistress, which Catherine refused. The army welcomed the new ruler with enthusiasm. A few days later further news reached Astrakan: Peter had been seized with a 'haemorrhoidal colic and fever' and died one week after his imprisonment. Reports were already circulating that the ex-Emperor had been beaten half to death and finally despatched through strangulation, with table-napkins pulled tight around his throat by a gentleman sergeant of the Guards who stood on Peter's chest for greater leverage. Catherine was clearly involved, but now ruled supreme.

Kutuzov and Suvorov moved apart in late 1762, Suvorov to take command of the Suzdal Regiment and Kutuzov travelling northwards again to become *aide-de-camp* to Prince Golshtein-Bekckii, Military-Governor of Revel in Estonia. Amongst Kutuzov's main characteristics was his ability to adapt to his surroundings. He proved equally at home amongst the troops in the field and amongst courtiers: those contemporaries who admired him frequently commented on the brilliant governmental career Kutuzov might have had if he had so chosen.[16] Already, still in his teens, he could display considerable charm and diplomacy, combined with intense shrewdness and the ability to hide his own opinions whilst listening to others. As *aide* to the Military-Governor in Revel he attended the multitude of formal dinners and balls; he enjoyed good food and wine and the glitter of the courtly occasions, and for over a year he seemed content with his posting. But beneath the courtier still lay the soldier. The Empress Catherine visited Revel in early 1764 during a tour of inspection, and talked for a while with the 19-year-old captain whom she remembered from his visits to Elizabeth's palace with his father. On her departure Catherine called Kutuzov to her again and asked if he wished 'to distinguish himself on the field of honour'. He answered: 'With great pleasure.' Within a short time Kutuzov proved his reply had been more than customary courtesy.[17]

During her visit to Estonia Catherine's attention had also been cast further west, to Poland. Anxious to secure Russian domination over the country, she had already planned a virtual takeover with a scheme devised soon after her accession. The Polish King,

Augustus III, had seemed unlikely to live much longer; Catherine therefore informed one of her ex-lovers Stanislaus Poniatowski, who came from the powerful Polish Czartoryski family, that she intended to declare him king upon Augustus's death, and if this declaration failed she would insist upon the head of the Czartoryskis, Prince Adam.

Augustus died in October 1763. After a suitable diplomatic interval, during which Polish affairs fell into disorder, about 8,000 Russian troops were moved close to the border with some detachments marching into Poland itself. In Revel, Kutuzov seized upon this opportunity for active service: he successfully petitioned to join the troops in the field and left Revel in spring 1764 only a few weeks after Catherine's visit. But he was still denied action. In June 1764 Prince Adam proposed his nephew Stanislaus as Polish King; Prussia backed Russia, and in August Catherine's nominee was duly elected. The Russian Empress immediately extended her influence, advising the new monarch over attempted reforms of the Polish constitution, and for three years Stanislaus Poniatowski sat uneasily on his throne while Polish patriots gradually organized against him.

Kutuzov returned to his duties at Revel in 1765 and remained aide to the Military-Governor for three more years. Meanwhile, rebellion began to stir in nearby Poland. The majority of Poles were fervent Catholics; the Protestant and Russian Orthodox minority started to clamour for equal rights, and Catherine, partly to divert attention from peasant unrest within Russia, supported the dissidents. The number of Russian troops within Poland gradually increased, and rebellion against this foreign interference flared in 1767, led by a group of French-supported Polish noblemen who had their headquarters at Bar.

Strong Russian forces invaded in autumn 1768, and with them rode Kutuzov. Also serving in the country was Suvorov and his Suzdal Regiment – although the two men probably did not encounter each other during this campaign. Service in Poland proved miserable; Suvorov soon sought to escape by moving south against the Turks, Russia's latest enemy.

The campaign largely amounted to actions against guerrillas; rarely did a definite target present itself. But for a 23-year-old infantry captain the experience continued to be exciting, and on the occasions when the rebels organized solid defensive positions

Kutuzov displayed courage and decisiveness in the attack. He led his infantry company against enemy trenches on the banks of the river Ovruch and against a rebel stronghold just outside Warsaw, and he undertook energetic pursuits across the rain-swept countryside.[18] Unlike many Russian officers he seemed to like the Polish people; he remained cheerful despite the depressing surroundings and showed a welcome ability in finding the most comfortable bivouacs for himself and his men.

'We lived very merrily,' commented Kutuzov later, summing up this period of his career. 'We fought with the Poles; but I didn't yet understand war.'[19]

Meanwhile the conflict was spreading southwards. Poland pleaded for Turkish assistance against Russia, but the pleas were ignored until Russian troops pursued Poles into Turkish territory during 1768. Turkey declared war against Catherine in October 1768, and in the following year a Russian force under Count Rumyantsev invaded the Turkish provinces in the Balkans, defeating an enemy force on the banks of the Dniester before moving on to seize Jassy and overrun Moldavia and Wallachia. The climax came with the occupation of Bucharest.

Kutuzov, now a major, moved south through Bessarabia in 1770 to join Rumyantsev's army. The mighty Turkish empire had begun to dwindle, and the power of Constantinople to evaporate, yet Turkey still earned her reputation as a formidable foe. Her troops were largely untrained and inadequately supplied, but they more than made up for their lack of tactics and weaponry through their fanaticism; they attacked with terrifying force, driven by a lust to kill all infidels on the sacred Moslem soil. So fearful did these warriors look as they charged screaming upon their enemy that even seasoned Russian troops had been known to turn and run without discharging their muskets; on one occasion Suvorov told his soldiers not to look at the frenzied, distorted faces of the advancing enemy. 'Don't look at their eyes lads,' he shouted, 'look at their chests – that's the target for your bayonets.'[20]

For the moment Rumyantsev maintained his steady advance. Shortly before Kutuzov's arrival a Turkish and Tartar army had been defeated at Karkal, after which the Russian forces systematically captured enemy fortresses along the Danube and Pruth rivers. Each stronghold had to be stormed against heavy opposition; according to one official report after an action in autumn

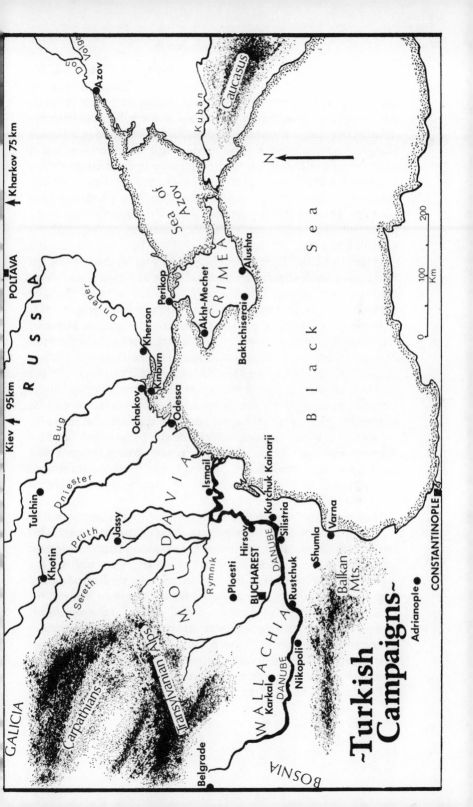

~Turkish Campaigns~

1770 Kutuzov 'showed astonishing courage, standing with his troops for a long time in close formation under the enemy's heavy fire, and he beat them back with continuous cannon fire; when enemy cavalry attacked he rushed upon them himself with his detachment and constantly repulsed them.'[21] Soon afterwards Kutuzov was transferred from service with an infantry regiment to Rumyantsev's staff. He had better opportunity to study his commander and once again the experience proved valuable. Rumyantsev and Suvorov were the two men from whom Kutuzov obtained greatest military tuition. His two teachers were completely unalike, and Kutuzov blended something of both with his own abilities.

Peter Alexander Rumyantsev, aged only 43 at the time of his invasion of Turkish territory and said to be a bastard son of Peter the Great, had distinguished himself in the Seven Years' War; he exploded into fame through his occupation of Bucharest in 1769, with his troops being the earliest Russians to reach the Danube. He showed himself a master of manoeuvre despite the difficulties of supply over the vast campaign area. His methods and attitude resembled warfare at sea rather than the concentration of armies on land; his prime concern was to keep his army in being, believing that as long as his forces remained intact defeat would be impossible. Conversely, the enemy must be annihilated and victory would then be inevitable. Battles should be avoided unless a decisive result could be obtained; rather than fighting a disadvantageous or unprofitable pitched battle, it was better to step back out of reach and wait for a more favourable moment, even if this meant abandoning territory.

'The objective,' declared Rumyantsev, 'is not the occupation of a geographical position but the destruction of enemy forces.' This famous maxim would have immense impact on Kutuzov and on other Russian commanders in later decades, who realized the aptness of Rumyantsev's method in relation to Russia's huge steppe-land stretching like an ocean from horizon to horizon.[22]

Kutuzov enjoyed his duties as a staff officer, and revealed his competence in handling complex situations: his natural intelligence could combine with his courage. The opportunity to display his ability arrived in mid-1771 with the most responsible task so far entrusted to him in his military career.

Rumyantsev had still to venture across the Danube and his

14

headquarters remained at Bucharest. The Turks attempted to seize the advantage, moving against the extended Russian communications with a flanking attack across the Danube and behind Bucharest; reports reached Rumyantsev that this movement had begun. Kutuzov was ordered to take a small detachment out from the main Russian positions and into the hills: he was instructed to return with full details of the enemy strength, composition and direction, together with information on the terrain through which the Turks were advancing and the most suitable site for a Russian counter-offensive.

Kutuzov left Bucharest with a handful of mounted troops and made his way up into the hills. The Russian detachment managed to avoid the Turkish scouting patrols and worked towards the main enemy army which they located southwards from the village of Popeshti: one after another the Turkish units swarmed into view. Kutuzov estimated enemy strength to be almost 40,000 men. He noted the types of troops, the approximate numbers of cannon and cavalry, the direction of the advance, then he reconnoitred the surrounding area and reported back to headquarters. He made the same dangerous journey again to obtain further information on the best Russian attacking positions before joining Rumyantsev's forces for the counter-offensive, in which he participated.[23]

Lieutenant-General Essen, serving under Rumyantsev, wrote the official report on Kutuzov's performance. 'Not only was he sent more than once to different places to observe their positions, and notwithstanding the great dangers brought back the most trustworthy reports to his commanders, but even on the day of the battle took upon himself the most dangerous attack.'[24] Kutuzov's exploit brought him promotion to Lieutenant-Colonel, and he continued to undertake staff duties in exemplary fashion. Then, in 1772, came an abrupt check to his career, brought about for the most irrelevant reason.

Kutuzov, now aged 28, had retained his skill at impersonating fellow-officers which he had first displayed as a young ensign. His mimickry, together with his high spirits, quick wit, and love of good living, made him a wide circle of friends in the army. Inevitably, his boisterousness and irreverence resulted in disapproval from stiffer senior officers.

One night Kutuzov went with his friends to a favourite Bucharest haunt. They wined and dined, with the party becoming steadily more noisy; Kutuzov, an excellent story-teller, began to embellish his tales with impersonations. One story concerned the commanding general. Kutuzov jumped to his feet and began to mimic Rumyantsev's walk – stiff, jerky, rather like a strutting hen. Everyone watching shouted their approval – except one. This unnamed officer reported the incident to his superior, and Rumyantsev reacted with intense irritation, summoning Kutuzov to his quarters.

The commanding general, only 47 years old himself, dealt harshly with the young Lieutenant-Colonel. Kutuzov was thrown out of the Army of the Danube and his name struck from the list of those awaiting the award of decorations for service against the Turks. Only his previous fighting record saved Kutuzov from further disgrace; Rumyantsev permitted him to seek employment with the Russian Second Army, then campaigning further along the coast under Prince Dolgorukov.[25] Kutuzov packed and left Bucharest with his personal servants. His stern treatment has been claimed to have had severe effects on his character: some Russian historians insist that thereafter he always treated others with suspicion and that he became more retiring. One of his friends said: 'People's hearts are open to Kutuzov, but his heart is closed to them.' He reserved his opinions, distrusted the motives of others, and in general became far more self-contained.[26] Kutuzov joined the Second Army in the winter of 1772. Prince Vasily Dolgorukov had invaded the Crimea the previous year, storming the Isthmus of Perikop and striking south into this Turkish territory. By the time Kutuzov reached the Prince's army the occupation of the Crimea had been completed, except for the conquest of isolated Turkish positions and the eradication of roving Tartar horsemen. Kutuzov switched from an infantry to a cavalry role, commanding a mobile force against the marauding Tartars. He became acquainted at first hand with the unique Cossacks, famed throughout Europe and feared as much as their Tartar opponents, and once again the knowledge which Kutuzov gained would be put to excellent use in later campaigns.

The majority of Cossack soldiers came from the lower reaches of the Don or Volga rivers. The men and their mounts seemed completely at variance, with the riders being huge and overpowering, and their horses appearing weakly and slouching in movement. Combined, the Cossack and his animal formed a highly effective partnership, able to travel awesome distances over the harshest terrain, enduring all extremes of weather. Now, in late 1772, Kutuzov donned the traditional blue jacket and full trousers of the Cossack uniform, together with the high black sheepskin hat, and he rode with them across the plains and ridges of the Prichernomorsk around Kherson. Then he moved south with his Cossacks into the Crimea itself. Kutuzov appreciated the value of these deadly and highly mobile fighters, especially working in conjunction with a regular infantry force. Kutuzov and his horsemen probed among the undulating marshy land westwards towards Kinburn on the shores of the Black Sea. They cleared a path through the thin Tartar defensive lines, reconnoitring an advance for Russian infantry and sending back invaluable reports to the advancing troops. Kinburn was successfully assaulted in the early months of 1773, after which Kutuzov and his riders swung back and headed south over the Perikop Isthmus, returning to the Crimea. Only a few weeks later Kutuzov took part in the storming of Alushta on the south-eastern Crimean coast.

For this offensive Kutuzov reverted to a regimental role. The first assault faltered in the face of well-protected Turkish guns, and the Russian troops seemed about to fall back under the barrage. Kutuzov seized the regimental standard and led the troops forward again: his men swept through a breach and into the Turkish trenches; the enemy began to retreat, abandoning guns and colours, and Kutuzov's troops pushed forward in pursuit.

There, amidst the ruins of Alushta, Kutuzov fell seriously wounded. A Turkish bullet had struck him in the head, and when the surgeons cleared away the blood they found that the ball had entered his right temple, fortunately at a slight angle so that it had torn out again just by his right eye. The brain seemed to be undamaged, but expectations for Kutuzov's recovery were slender.[27] He regained consciousness. And slowly his wound started to heal. The bullet had severed muscles behind the right eye, which would thereafter be slightly twisted, but for the moment his sight continued unimpaired. He still suffered acute pain and dizziness, and was clearly unfit for military service until recovery had been completed, which the doctors still maintained might never come about. In 1773 Kutuzov therefore left the Crimea and the army, and many believed he would never return.

II

Suvorov

(1773–1793)

Kutuzov's journey northwards, enclosed in a carriage which bumped and swayed over the rutted tracks, would have been miserable even without his injury: Russia was suffering from two ills, both of which Kutuzov witnessed. First, a rebellion of serfs had broken out, led by the Cossack chieftain Pugachev who claimed to be Czar Peter miraculously escaped from the attempted murder by Catherine's assassins. Pugachev obtained a massive following and the whole country seethed with rumours, with strikes against dissidents, and with restrictions on other serfs to keep them under control. The rebellion would continue until Pugachev's capture, largely brought about by Suvorov's efforts, followed by the rebel's enforced tour of principal towns cooped in a cage and by his execution in Moscow.

Meanwhile the country also suffered another calamity. Plague struck with unprecedented viciousness in 1773. Dead were being burnt in the villages along Kutuzov's route, and when he passed through Moscow on his way to St Petersburg he found that Russia's second capital had been almost decimated. Many of the nobles had fled to the country and the streets stank with the fumes of the funeral pyres. St Petersburg, so far untouched by the plague, seemed a welcome contrast although members of the aristocracy were also escaping to their estates.

Catherine remained in the capital, supervising the campaign against Pugachev and urging intensified operations against the stubborn Turks. Guerrilla war continued in Poland despite the partitioning of the country in 1772. The Empress received Kutuzov on several occasions and seemed delighted with the

18

young colonel's company: his wound had made him a hero. 'We must look after our Kutuzov,' she declared.[1] The Russian ruler, now aged 43, had only recently discovered a new lover and the passion of the affair remained the chief conversational topic in Petersburg. The list of Catherine's lovers was lengthening: first, and very briefly, the chamberlain Sergei Saltykov, perhaps used to obtain a royal heir – the future Czar Paul – following the apparent impotence of Catherine's husband, Peter; then Poniatowski had been favoured, succeeded by Captain of Artillery Gregori Orlov. The latter had been ousted in 1771 by Grigori Alexander Potemkin, the greatest love of Catherine's life. According to court scandal Orlov had made way for Potemkin with excellent humour: the two men crossed on the great staircase of the Winter Palace, and Potemkin, ascending, inquired about the Empress's health. 'Unchanged,' smiled Orlov. 'You're going up, I'm coming down; the Empress stays where she is.'[2]

Court intrigues continued despite the threats of total upheaval from the serf revolt, and the Winter Palace itself epitomized the stark contrast in Russian social life. Pomp and sordidness were inseparable. The Palace building looked magnificent from a distance, with its façades plastered and ornamented in red and yellow, blue and white, and with huge ballrooms which rivalled Versailles. But living conditions within the privileged walls were primitive: ventilation was non-existent and the rooms were stuffy and stank; drains were completely absent. Catherine attempted to live in pomp and luxury, but complained bitterly over the squalor which she had to endure in both St Petersburg and Moscow – conditions with which Kutuzov was extremely familiar despite the noble status of his family.

'Moscow I do not like at all,' wrote Catherine, 'but I have no preference for Petersburg. I must discipline myself to be guided merely by public welfare. . . . Moscow, that city which all so love, where all is sloth and indolence! They (the nobility) would gladly pass all their days there, driving about in a broken-down gilded coach-and-six, concealing from the masses by such shows the true worthlessness of their masters. It is far from unusual to see a richly-dressed lady in an ornate carriage, drawn by six horses with greasy trappings, drive out from a great courtyard piled high with filth and dung; while the house that surrounds the courtyard is a mere barrack of rotting timbers.'[3]

19

The Kutuzov family house in St Petersburg now belonged to Kutuzov himself, his father having died during his absence. Kutuzov preferred to live with his uncle I. N. Golenishev, whom he described as his second father.[4] The wounds on his face still weeped, his headaches continued and the dizziness prevented him from enjoying the court balls. Instead he discussed the current state of Russian affairs with politicians and courtiers, including Potemkin and Catherine herself. The war against Turkey had become a stalemate. Rumyantsev seemed reluctant to attempt a full crossing of the Danube, and an attempted offensive in the Silistria area failed. Only Suvorov, newly-arrived in the region, showed decisive leadership, inflicting heavy defeat on the Turks at Kostliju. Russian forces attempting to take Shumla were beaten back and news of this setback prompted Dolgorukov to retreat northwards from the Crimea, leaving a bloody trail of wreck and pillage. Russia had failed to gain uncontested access to the Black Sea, and peace negotiations began in late 1773.

Kutuzov had left Russia by the time these discussions resulted in the unsatisfactory Treaty of Kuchuk Kainarji on 16 July 1774. He departed from St Petersburg, heading for Prussia on an extended tour of Western Europe to obtain foreign medical treatment. Travelling by easy stages he reached the Prussian capital of Berlin in early 1774, where he was examined by doctors and where Frederick the Great received him with kindness and interest. The Prussian monarch had enjoyed power for thirty-four years, and his nation had emerged from the Seven Years War with vastly increased prestige and influence, which Frederick had employed to bring about the partition of Poland in 1772. Frederick's special interest, the improvement of the Prussian army, appealed to Kutuzov and the two men spent a considerable time discussing tactics and details of weaponry and uniform.

From Berlin, Kutuzov journeyed to Leyden in Holland, then a great centre of learning and science. He spent many weeks resting and undergoing eye-treatment: the doctors apparently considered him something of a medical curiosity.[5] Kutuzov then crossed the Channel to England. In London all talk was concentrated on the troubles with the American Colonists. British authority had begun to collapse, especially around Boston where, following the 'Tea Party' of 26 December 1773, the port had been closed until 'peace and obedience to the laws' was restored. On 5 September 1774 fifty-six colonist delegates met at Philadelphia for the first Continental Congress of America, adopting the Declaration of Rights; and, when the British Parliament met at Westminster in November 1774, King George III declared: 'The New England governments are in a state of rebellion. Blows must decide.'

Kutuzov would continue to study the progress of the American Revolution, especially the way in which the troops under George Washington gradually began to gain the edge over the British in the war of attrition after 1776. And the American experience perhaps reinforced the lesson already taught to Kutuzov by Rumyantsev: victory in battle did not necessarily win a war. Washington was to win only two of the fourteen major military actions between 1774 and 1783, yet emerged successful; the British, despite successes, were unable to subdue the opposing force.

Back in Europe, Kutuzov travelled south to Vienna. There he met leading Austrian military figures, including General Gideon Ernst von Laudon, who had led the Austrian army allied with the Russians in the defeat of Frederick the Great at Kunersdorf, 12 August 1759. Kutuzov finally returned home in 1776 after a short visit to Italy. His two-year tour had been beneficial both from the point of view of health and experience; the only major gap in his itinerary had been France, where successive Ministries were attempting to rebuild the country after the disasters of the Seven Years War and where, for the moment, attention remained focused inwards.

Kutuzov only spent a short time in Petersburg. He paid his respects to Catherine and reported on his tour; he also sought renewed military employment. Potemkin probably helped Kutuzov to find an army posting entirely to his satisfaction: in late 1776 Kutuzov took to the road again, this time travelling south to serve under Suvorov in the Crimea. He could have chosen no better commander.

The Treaty of Kuchuk Kainarji had declared Crimea to be independent, although the Turkish Sultan remained the religious leader of the Tartars as the Moslem Caliph. Tension was still high despite the ending of hostilities: the Crimean area was too weak to act as an effective buffer between Turkey and Russia and both attempted to interfere. The Crimean Tartars had overthrown the unpopular leader Sahib-Girei in 1775, and his successor, Devlet-Girei, was considered by the Russians to be no more than a

Turkish puppet. Catherine therefore insisted upon the selection of Shahin-Girei, educated in St Petersburg, and sent troops to back his candidature. Amongst these Russian forces was the Moscow Division, based 250 kilometres north of the Crimea at Poltava and commanded from November 1776 by Suvorov. It was to this division that Kutuzov now travelled.[6] The Moscow Division marched south in January 1776 as part of a force commanded by Lieutenant-General Alexander Prozorovski, itself part of Rumyantsev's Ukrainian Army. Suvorov soon discovered that Prozorovski was too ill to take effective control and he himself assumed the burden of responsibility. All went well: scattered opposition was brushed aside and in February 1777 Shahin-Girei was safely escorted to the Crimean capital of Bakhchiserai.[7]

Kutuzov spent the next ten years in these wild regions of southern Russia, six of them under Suvorov's direct command. Throughout this decade war with the Turks was expected to erupt at almost any moment, and constant small-scale clashes took place with pro-Turkish Tartars. Service in the area required a combination of military and diplomatic dexterity; Suvorov proved capable of both, and often entrusted Kutuzov with delicate missions. The two men became firm friends, their close similarity of views contrasting sharply with their outward physical differences: Kutuzov, always well-built, was thickening round his waist and the scar around his right eye provided an appearance of false ferocity to his bear-like hulk; Suvorov, always skinny, continued to look undernourished and resembled a poet rather than the hardened soldier.

The divisional headquarters shifted from area to area according to the points of highest tension: sometimes in the Crimea, sometimes near the Turkish–Polish border, occasionally westwards to the Kuban close to the majestic snow-capped mountains of the ancient Circassia. Always, Kutuzov continued to study his commander, learning both strategic and tactical lessons down to the most minute detail. Suvorov had begun to formulate his tactical methods into a wide-ranging document, which would eventually appear as *The Science of Victory*; some of the ideas it contained stemmed from those he had developed when he commanded the Astrakan regiment, in which Kutuzov had served as a Captain. *The Science of Victory* was to be a remarkable document, not only through its sound content but through the fact that it was calculated to be understood by the soldiers themselves rather than just the officers. The language reflected the manner in which Suvorov – and Kutuzov – spoke to their men.

'The soldier must be healthy,' wrote Suvorov, 'brave, resolute, determined, truthful, pious. Pray to God! He gives us victory. Fighters, it's wonderful. God leads us. He is our general!' Suvorov taught that the ordinary soldier must be allowed to use his native intelligence and initiative. 'Every soldier must know his manoeuvre' – an idea greeted with horror by more conservative commanders. Further up the scale, added Suvorov, officers should know instinctively what was required from them by their superiors; he once cited the relationship between Kutuzov and himself as the perfect example of this automatic response. 'Order one, hint to another, but there's no need even to speak to Kutuzov – he understands it all by himself.'[8]

Militarily, the decade therefore proved to be hard yet satisfying for Kutuzov. Largely owing to Suvorov's influence he was promoted to the rank of Brigadier-General in 1782 and soon afterwards received the command of one of Suvorov's famous Corps of Chasseurs into which all the best soldiers in the area were posted. Always, Suvorov insisted upon maximum mobility and the exploitation of rapidly changing circumstances: commanders must be extremely quick-witted, and Suvorov recognized this characteristic in Kutuzov: 'He's crafty, crafty! And shrewd, shrewd! No one will fool him!'

Changes occurred in Kutuzov's private life during this period. On 27 April 1778 he married Ekaterina Il'inichna Bibikova, daughter of Lieutenant-General Bibikova and sister of Alexander Il'ich Bibiko. The latter had proved courageous and skilled in the war against Poland and died during the struggle against Pugachev's serfs. Ekaterina's family, well-placed in the ranks of Russian nobility, was already connected to Kutuzov's through marriage, and Ekaterina herself was considered an excellent choice: pretty, intelligent and sociable. The marriage appeared satisfactory although not especially passionate: Kutuzov's wife tolerated his numerous passing love-affairs and sometimes accompanied him on campaign, but Kutuzov's letters to her during their separations were sparse, and although his words were affectionate they displayed no real depth of feeling. Six children were born to them, five girls and a boy. The son, Nikolai, was accidentally smothered by a nurse in his first year.

Each of the daughters eventually married well: Praskov'ya to M. F. Tolstoy, a distant relation of the author, Anna to Major-General N. Z. Khitrov, Elizaveta to Count F. I. Tizengauzen, Ekaterina to Prince Nikolai Kudashev and Dar'ya to F. P. Opochinin. Kutuzov was closest to Ekaterina, whose husband would be one of the leading Cossack and partisan commanders during the 1812 campaign.

Kutuzov and his wife set up house in Poltava, where the first children were born, spending leaves in St Petersburg, Moscow or on the respective family estates. During these breaks Kutuzov continued to create an excellent impression at the Russian court, remaining in favour with Catherine and Potemkin: the latter, as commander of the Ekaterinoslav Army, became Kutuzov's superior above Suvorov.[9] Inevitable war with Turkey at last crept closer. Respective interests in the area to the north of the Black Sea were too strong to be quietened by diplomacy, and in early summer 1787 the Empress embarked on a tour intended to provide a strong hint that Russia was too powerful to be deterred. Potemkin arranged all the details with Suvorov providing invaluable support on military matters. The tour was to enter Russian history as a magnificent example of the might and authority of the Imperial Court – and of the ludicrous aspects which often accompanied this power.

Potemkin was determined to create the best possible impression on his Imperial lover, both to retain her devotion and to avoid supplying his many critics with grounds for complaints against him. He intended to prove himself a worthy adminstrator on behalf of the Empress, and some of the measures he took to achieve his aim bordered on the farcical. Whole congregations of peasants were arranged along Catherine's route down the Volga, dressed in new bright clothes with herds of picked cattle eating peacefully nearby; each village depicted an idyllic rural scene, with fairs and merry-go-rounds in full swing: then the same laughing peasants, cud-chewing cattle and brilliant fairs were rushed by short cuts to the next village for the performance to be repeated.[10] The charade continued towards Suvorov's command area, with Catherine's huge entourage including kings, princes, and all the highest nobility of the land. Suvorov himself needed no pretence to obtain a favourable impression: his troops were in perfect condition wherever Catherine chose to inspect –

Kremenchung, Kiev, the new city of Kherson, and down to the south coast of the Crimea. Catherine reviewed the new Black Sea fleet then turned northwards again.

Kutuzov and his Chasseurs waited amongst the other forces at Poltava, where they took part in a huge mock battle re-enacting the magnificent victory won in the area by Peter the Great against Charles XII of Sweden. After further manoeuvres Catherine awarded medals: Kutuzov received the Order of Vladimir Second Class. Later, the Empress noticed that he rode a high-spirited horse, and she called him to her. 'Kutuzov,' she declared. 'You must look after yourself. I forbid you to ride on mad horses, and I'll never forgive you if I hear that you've disobeyed my order.'[11] The Empress and the Imperial procession of carriages and coaches swayed northwards again, arriving home in Petersburg in July. The journey, for all the pomp and bombast, failed to frighten the Turks. War erupted on 13 August. Kutuzov and his Corps of Chasseurs were positioned near the border with both Turkey and Poland along the river Bug. Various small-scale incursions by Turkish detachments were beaten back during the summer and autumn of 1787, and Kutuzov undertook extensive patrolling measures, spending long days in the saddle. He received an encouraging letter from Potemkin during the late summer: 'I am convinced that the Turks will not be successful where bravery and skill are combined against them, as I expect from you.'[12]

Meanwhile the main actions took place further south, initially focused on the garrison at Kinburn held by Russian troops under Suvorov, together with the Turkish fortress of Ochakov lying just across the Dnieper and Bug estuary from Suvorov's position. A Turkish offensive across this narrow strip of water was repulsed in early October, but Kinburn remained severely threatened as long as the giant citadel at Ochakov stayed in Turkish hands. Both sides awaited the next campaigning season; Kutuzov continued his patrolling duties on the icy east bank of the Bug. Then, in early spring 1788 fresh orders arrived at his camp: Potemkin instructed him to move south with his Chasseurs, to join the army intended to besiege and capture the Ochakov fortress.

The Russian army swung westwards over the Dnieper led by Potemkin himself, arriving outside the massive walls of Ochakov at the end of June. Quarrels immediately broke out between Suvorov, still suffering from a wound received the previous October and strongly urging a direct storm on the Turkish citadel, and Potemkin who favoured a prolonged siege to save Russian casualties. Potemkin, being the superior and backed by Catherine, ordered the siege to continue despite Suvorov's strident protests, and the Russians lost growing numbers of men through sickness. Potemkin, disappointed by the lack of progress, retired to his tent where he spent most of his days sniffing lavender water in an attempt to smother the smells of the decaying dead. The Turks proved stubborn and aggressive. Constant sudden sorties were made under cover of heavy cannon fire which ripped into the vulnerable Russian positions. And, during one of these attacks, Kutuzov again fell wounded.

His wound was received during a flurry of fighting between his Chasseurs and a strong detachment of Turks which had ridden into the Russian lines. Amidst the screams, flashing sabres and humming musket balls, Kutuzov suddenly jerked violently in his saddle and slid from his horse. A musket ball had entered his right temple, in almost exactly the same place as that fifteen years before, and had torn a similar path to erupt beside his right eye. Kutuzov was dragged unconscious from the fight and carried to the surgeons. The doctors believed it impossible that he could recover from the same wound twice – it had been a miracle that he had survived the first. Prince Charles von Ligne, the Austrian soldier-diplomat then in the Russian camp, wrote a laconic letter to his ruler, Emperor Joseph: 'Yesterday they shot Kutuzov's head again. I suppose that today or tomorrow he'll die.'[13]

Instead, Kutuzov recovered far faster than on the previous occasion. His eye was even more crooked, and his headaches harsher, but he returned to duty by the time Ochakov was finally taken by storm in December. Suvorov's original policy was proved correct, although only after Potemkin's failure cost up to forty Russian soldiers freezing to death each day during the latter stage of the siege.[14]

Kutuzov continued to command his Chasseurs in the renewed campaign opening in the spring of 1789. By now the Austrians had joined the war on the side of the Russians, and a massive allied advance into Moldavia began in the early summer. Potemkin, retiring to Petersburg, had been succeeded by Prince Repnin: the latter's forces formed the left of the allied line, linked to Austrians under Field-Marshal Saxe-Coburg by Suvorov's Third Division. The advance pushed westwards with Kutuzov displaying his usual vigour in actions on the Bug and then the Dniester: he took part in the storming of Hadjibey castle at Odessa, and in the successful attacks on the Turkish strongholds at Bender and Akkerman. The Austrians, now commanded by Laudon whom Kutuzov had met in Vienna in 1775, repulsed a Turkish invasion of Bosnia, then besieged and took Belgrade. By the end of the year the Turks had been forced back to the Danube.[15]

Still the war continued. One decisive defeat had yet to be inflicted on the Turks, and the obvious target for such an attempt was the great castle of Ismail, key to the Danube. Siege began in May 1790 and lasted throughout the summer. Winter weather again set in, and the surrounding Russian forces suffered a repetition of the miseries endured outside Ochakov two years before. The Austrians quit the struggle; Catherine urged greater efforts, and Suvorov was at last given responsibility. The small, grey-haired general, newly created a count, immediately began preparations and amongst his first moves was the appointment of Kutuzov to command his strongest column.

Suvorov summoned a War Council on the morning of 9 December. According to regulations formulated by Peter the Great, Suvorov's thirteen subordinate commanders were officially obliged to give approval to plans proposed by the senior officer; Suvorov told the Council: 'I am determined to capture this fort or die in the attempt,' and he asked for opinions as to how the capture should be effected. One by one the officers replied. Brigadier Matvei Ivanovich Platov of the Cossacks was first to speak; he simply said: 'Storm.' The others agreed in turn. Kutuzov made no answer because there seemed no need – Suvorov would know his opinion.[16]

Ismail fort lay on the steep northern bank of the Danube, constructed with the advice of the most skilled French and German military engineers and surrounded by high walls with bastions, together with a deep moat. Upper and lower rows of artillery covered all approaches, especially the main four gates. The 35,000-man garrison, commanded by Aydos Mehmet Pasha, had been warned that if the fort fell the Turkish survivors would be decapitated by the Sultan, Selim. Suvorov planned a six-prong

27

attack from the west, north and east, combined with an assault across the river in the south. The Turkish commander rejected a final Russian ultimatum, replying that 'the Danube will stop still in its course, the heavens will fall into the earth before Ismail surrenders', and on the morning of 10 December the Russian guns opened fire.

Bombardment continued throughout the day. Kutuzov deployed his column in the low hills to the south-east of Kilia Gate, his primary objective. He walked amongst his nervous troops during the evening, encouraging them and supervising the sharpening of bayonets, sabres and lances. Just after midnight he read Suvorov's Order of the Day to his men: 'Brave warriors! Remember, this day, all the victories you have won in the past prove that nothing can withstand the power of Russian arms. . . . We must either conquer or die a glorious death.'[17] The waiting Russians could hear a low hum from inside the Turkish fortress as the defenders prepared for the expected attack. By three o'clock in the morning of the 11th all Kutuzov's men were in their places, and at that moment a single rocket arched slowly over the city.

Kutuzov immediately ordered his men into the advance. At first they moved silently, shuffling into lines, then they picked up speed; ahead the burning fires from inside Ismail outlined the fortress against the early morning sky. The first line in Kutuzov's column reached the moat, to be met by a devastating barrage of close-range artillery and musket fire. Kutuzov's troops came to a halt, hunching together and offering a still greater target. Kutuzov ran amongst his men, shouting them on, and some managed to scramble across the moat to the wall, but terrible grapeshot riddled amongst them; ladders thrown against the wall were hurled back; the tumult steadily increased. The din spread all the way round the walls of Ismail: to the north, attacks by Major-Generals Meknob and Bezborodko towards Bender Gate had been blocked, but further to the west footholds were secured by soldiers under Generals Lvov and Lascy, commanding the first and second columns. The battle swung in the balance as the sky lightened over the city.

Kutuzov's men began to fall back under the devastating fire. He rallied them and led the way onwards but his casualties mounted rapidly and the troops once more withdrew. Kutuzov shouted them forward and again took them over the bodies heaped along the edge of the moat. Ladders were thrown against the walls, only to topple back, and Kutuzov's column started to give ground. Lvov's and Lascy's troops were in a highly dangerous situation on the opposite side of the city. Clinging to the top of the wall, they were being subjected to concentrated fire from the defenders: Suvorov realized that only added pressure from the east, Kutuzov's sector, could save them. The commander is believed to have sent Kutuzov an outrageous message, revealing both Suvorov's characteristic audacity and his knowledge of Kutuzov: the message contained highly premature congratulations to Kutuzov on his appointment as commandant of Ismail, and informed him that a courier was already on his way to Petersburg with the news for Catherine that the citadel had been taken.[18]

Kutuzov, blackened by smoke and his men wavering and terror-struck, reacted with astonishment. Then he crossed himself despairingly, muttered 'God help us!' and ordered his troops into the attack again. He himself led leading sections of the Kherson Grenadier Regiment and the Bug Corps of Chasseurs against the battered walls, and despite ghastly casualties they managed to claw their way to the bastion. They fell on the Turks and bayoneted a path into the citadel; others swarmed in behind and gradually Kutuzov's column pushed into the streets of the city. By mid-morning the Russians were moving house-by-house towards the centre from east and west. The Turks continued to fight with fanatical determination, but were being steadily swamped by the Russians pouring over the walls; guns in the bastions were dragged round to face the garrison; Bezborodko's troops, now led by Platov after his commander had fallen wounded, forced southwards from the Bender Gate, and behind them surged cavalry squadrons which clattered over the cobbles hacking down all resistance.

By early afternoon the last organized opposition had been overcome with the majority of Turks fighting to the death. The enemy commander died in the rubble. Over 2,500 Turks perished in the battle, and one out of every three Russians was either killed or wounded.[19] Kutuzov emerged unscathed. He met his commanding general and commented on the premature message; Suvorov replied in his customary terse style: 'I know Kutuzov, and Kutuzov knows me. I knew Kutuzov would take Ismail, and if

Ismail had not been taken Suvorov would have died under its walls, and Kutuzov with him.'[20]

'We've not seen such a business for a long time,' wrote Kutuzov to his wife. 'It made my hair stand on end. This fearful town is in our hands!'[21] Suvorov dictated his official report on the battle, in which he heaped praise on Kutuzov's actions. 'Showing himself as an example of bravery and intrepidity, he overcame all difficulties which met him under heavy fire. He leapt over the pallisades, forestalled the efforts of the Turks, seized the rampart, bastion and many batteries, and, when the enemy reinforced in superior numbers and compelled him to stop, he shouted: "God is with us!" With these words he manfully and bravely fell on the enemy, repulsed their attack, held his place against further stubborn resistance and gained a foothold in the fortress. He continued to inflict blows and to spread his attack into the very heart of the city, everywhere gaining victory, superiority and domination.' Suvorov added a paragraph in his own writing: 'General Kutuzov showed new examples of military skill and personal bravery. He was on my left wing but he was my right hand.'[22]

The commanding general left Ismail almost immediately, heading north to Jassy and then to Petersburg where, despite his victory, he received insufficient recognition through fear of overshadowing Potemkin. The latter received a field-marshal's baton; Suvorov was hurried off to Finland to inspect the frontier. Meanwhile, Kutuzov assumed his duties as Commandant of Ismail, together with the command of Russian forces between the Dniester and the Pruth. His task proved unpleasant. Ismail itself presented a horrible spectacle, littered with corpses and with whole streets ruined both through the battle and the subsequent ravaging by the Russian troops. Wounded had been mutilated, women raped, and many Russian regiments had degenerated into an undisciplined rabble. Kutuzov gradually managed to restore order and by spring 1791 was ready to move out from Ismail against Turkish troops in the surrounding area. Newly promoted Lieutenant-General and awarded the Order of St George Third Class, he was faced with a difficult campaigning season. Turkish garrisons still existed in towns such as Machin, Babadag and Isakchk, and other detachments lurked in the mountainous terrain. Kutuzov steadily extended his area of control, displaying a high degree of manoeuvring skill to strike against the enemy's flanks and rear. Repnin, commander-in-chief of the Moldavian Army, wrote to Catherine: 'General Kutuzov's efficiency and quick-wittedness are beyond praise.'[23]

Peace negotiations opened at last, with Russia anxious to end hostilities in view of renewed tension in Poland, caused by attempted reforms within this troubled country. Talks led to the Treaty of Jassy, 9 January 1792, under which Russia returned Moldavia and Bessarabia to Turkey but retained all conquered territory east of the Dniester including Ochakov. Ismail was once more a Turkish possession and Kutuzov departed with his troops.

Russian forces were already moving into Poland; the Prussians also invaded, anxious to prevent their Russian rival from gaining a dominating position, and together these armies advanced against the heavily-outnumbered Polish units. Kutuzov played his part by advancing north from Ismail along the Galician frontier to enter Poland from the south on the flank of the Polish army. By 23 July 1792 the Polish Government had yielded to a Russian demand that all reforms should be annulled and the old constitution restored, and on 23 January 1793 Russia and Prussia agreed to a further dismemberment of the country.

Kutuzov received further awards for his campaign in Poland, including the Order of St George Second Class and a rich estate to the south of Moscow complete with 2,667 serfs.[24] He returned to St Petersburg preceded by a reputation as a fierce, energetic and intelligent commander with every hope of early advancement to the most senior ranks of the victorious Russian army. Instead came prolonged years of peace, during which Kutuzov would be obliged to assume entirely new, non-military roles. He would find himself involved in court intrigues and scandals which blighted not only the remainder of his military career but his reputation in history.

III

'Mad' Paul

(1793–1801)

Kutuzov, reaching St Petersburg with his wife and young family in early 1793, found the capital and the court considerably changed. Potemkin had died in October 1791, and Catherine had been inconsolable in her grief – perhaps partly through guilt since she had taken a new lover only a few weeks before. The latest favourite was Count Platon Zubov, young and good-looking, and now resident in a specially-built suite of rooms at Catherine's favourite palace.

Potemkin's death resulted in upheaval both in major military and political affairs and also in the domestic life of the Russian court. Hitherto Catherine had remained reasonably faithful to the lover of the particular time; now, in her sixty-fourth year and after thirty-four years as Empress, she became a virtual nymphomaniac. Zubov remained in favour, continuing 'to give every satisfaction', and even procured suitable bed-fellows for her – as Potemkin had used to do. But instead of relying on the choice of others Catherine struck out on her own, selecting anyone who seemed proficient regardless of rank or social status. Kutuzov, despite his growing stoutness, was still an attractive figure. His sagging right eye added an air of lechery which appealed to those with sufficient passion, especially as this appearance of ferocity was combined with extreme charm and a ready wit. Already he had become renowned for his skill with women. Now, in St Petersburg during the spring months of 1793 Catherine referred to him as 'my own general'.[1] Moreover Kutuzov was on excellent terms with Zubov, considering himself to be one of the Count's 'most humble servants'. How far his intimacy with Catherine progressed is

32

impossible to determine, but probably his friendship remained restricted to that of confidant. Catherine undoubtedly enjoyed his smooth humour, his stock of stories and his combination of toughened soldier and polished courtier, but both of them preferred to partner younger members of the opposite sex, and Kutuzov was shrewd enough to be able to manoeuvre from any embarrassing Imperial invitation.

Those aspects of his character which appealed to Catherine in Petersburg – his wit, urbanity, discretion and charm – also led the Empress in the selection of Kutuzov's next appointment. Her choice seemed at first sight to be astonishing, but on closer examination revealed a perception on the part of the Empress resulting from detailed knowledge of Kutuzov's personality. He would now leave the army, to be ambassador to Turkey, so recently an enemy of Russia and in whose capital Kutuzov was known as one of the most belligerent fighters in the Russian forces, a worthy disciple of Suvorov.[2]

Selim III still ruled Turkey: young and energetic, he had roused the nation to new levels of determination in the struggle against Russia. Now this fervent nationalist was being asked to welcome one of the victorious Russian generals into his capital. The relationship between the ambassador and the Sultan promised to be tense. Yet from the start Kutuzov displayed exactly the right amount of firmness and diplomacy: he planned to stress the power and authority of Russia, using his own reputation to underline the message, and at the same time to soften the impression through his charm and inborn diplomacy.

Kutuzov's entry into Constantinople in the early summer of 1793 represented the first of these aims. The new ambassador carefully arranged his procession within sight of the white minarets, golden balls, mosque domes and rich cedar trees of the Sultan's capital, and then began to move forward in stately fashion. Behind Kutuzov stretched an entourage of army officers, counsellors, equerries, musicians and pages, plus an escort of cavalry and infantry, all dressed in magnificent uniforms. The effect was excellent.

'You might think,' wrote an eye-witness to the Empress of Russia, 'that you were reading the Thousand and One Nights when you learn all the details.'[3] The Sultan and his court stood to meet Kutuzov, who smiled with satisfaction at the florid Oriental

33

speeches of welcome and then delivered an exquisite reply which contrasted effectively with his rough reputation from the battle-field.

Kutuzov stayed in Constantinople for about twelve months. His diplomatic dexterity did much to restore satisfactory relations between Turkey and Russia, drawing his host country closer into the Russian sphere of influence and securing Russian naval passage through Turkish waters. He also thoroughly enjoyed himself: later he recalled his time in Constantinople as being the happiest in his life.[4] He astonished the Turks by the splendour of his receptions and ceremonies, and invitations to his dinner-table were eagerly sought. The Turks responded to his charm and wit: after one dinner the Constantinople society delighted in the report that a very ancient *effendi*, whom nobody could remember ever having smiled, had burst out with merriment in Kutuzov's company.[5]

The city fascinated him. He toured the bazaars, the walls of the Seraglio, the celebrated subterranean cistern of Constantine the Great with its 436 massive pillars, the hippodrome and the various monuments to Turkish glory. One day Kutuzov visited another sight, strictly barred from curious eyes; in Russia the story became famous of how the ambassador had invaded the Sultan's harem. Kutuzov, sightseeing one day on horseback, suddenly turned towards the Sultan's private garden in which the harem walked. A Turkish officer ran to warn him that anyone who stepped through the entrance would be put to death.

'I know, I know,' smiled Kutuzov, and heeled his horse forward again towards the gate. The head of the Sultan's bodyguard rushed forward, pike lowered, and demanded to know the identity of the trespasser. Kutuzov answered in best Oriental fashion. 'The representative of a monarch before whom nothing withers and everything flowers – Catherine the Great, Empress of All the Russias, who now grants eternal peace to thee.' The guard commander fell to his knees with his head on the sand, the rest of his men moved respectfully to one side, and Kutuzov rode calmly into the forbidden garden. He saw all that he wished, bowed to the girls, and returned to the Embassy.[6]

Trouble rose again in Poland. In early 1794 Polish nationalists revolted against Russian and Prussian domination, and after Russian forces suffered humiliating defeat at Raclawice on 3 April 1794, after which the garrison at Warsaw was obliged to withdraw, further Russian regiments were hurried into the country. Among them were soldiers under Suvorov who re-took Warsaw after a forty-four-day campaign, entering the Polish capital on 29 October. Suvorov's involvement meant that a successor had to be found at his previous posting in Finland. The choice fell on Kutuzov, who left Constantinople amongst magnificent ceremonies in the autumn of 1794, arriving in Viborg soon in the New Year.

The latest appointment marked a considerable change from the warmth of the Black Sea to the damp, cold and marshy surrounding of the north, from diplomatic receptions to arduous inspections of scattered units. Russia had obtained Finnish territory from the Swedes in 1742. Swedish troops invaded Russian Finland in 1788, despatched by Gustavus III, to offset possible moves against his country by either Russia or Prussia, but the status quo had been restored at the Treaty of Wereloe on 15 August 1790. Suvorov, as commander of Russian forces, had spent much of his time constructing defensive works along the border with Sweden to guard against another invasion, and Kutuzov continued this activity.[7] Kutuzov was also made director of the Sukhoputnii Cadet School for sons of nobility, a duty which provided him with great pleasure. He reorganized the system of discipline, emphasising mutual trust, and paid special attention to the most promising pupils whom he often invited to dine with him. Sometimes he taught the cadets himself, specializing in military history and literature; the school obtained greater prestige under his direction and he himself proved an excellent instructor.[8]

Kutuzov remained in Finland while a dramatic upheaval shook Russia. On 22 September 1796 the Empress Catherine suffered a slight stroke; she seemed to recover, but nevertheless informed her grandson Alexander that in the event of her death she wished him to succeed to power, rather than her illegitimate son Paul, whom she hated. Alexander responded in typically evasive fashion. On the morning of 15 November the Empress suffered a second stroke, whilst seated on her commode, and this time lost consciousness. Alexander reached his grandmother's sickbed; messengers were rushed the 50 kilometres to Gatchina, Paul's residence where he spent his days playing at being a soldier with specially selected troops. Catherine died on the evening of 17 November, and despite her wishes her 41-year-old son became Emperor, with disastrous results.[9]

Paul, probably the issue of Catherine's heir-producing episode with the chamberlain Sergei Saltykov, had waited thirty-four years for his place on the throne, a right which he believed should have been his on the death of Peter III. He revered Peter, his official father, and he showed himself even less fitted to rule. Paul has been described as mad. Probably this is an exaggeration, but certainly he exhibited extreme unpredictability. One moment he could shower favours on someone at his court, and the next moment the recipient would find himself banished to Siberia. His unfortunate appearance did nothing to improve his image: dwarfed, with a back which showed a slight hump, receding brow, half-closed shifty eyes, slack mouth. He could be monstrously cruel and for the five years of his rule he treated his subjects to all the misery which this haughty, delusioned megalomaniac could devise.

Paul's behaviour with regard to the army presented the greatest threat to Kutuzov's career, and many senior officers were adversely affected. He had a passion for parades and for useless ceremonials. Soldiers must be made beautiful, he declared, regardless of military efficiency. New uniforms were designed which were so tight that the wearers were scarcely able to breathe, let alone fight. Soldiers staggered under the weight of wigs which had thick, stinking grease plastered over them, and which had iron rods inserted into the queues to make them fall straight. Men were obliged to wear a type of strait-jacket in order to train them to stand erect, and steel plates were strapped round their knees to prevent legs bending when marching on parades. Hours had to be spent polishing weapons, buttons and buckles, pipe-claying belts and powdering the greasy wigs. Musket-butts were hollowed out and filled with loose shot to make them rattle nicely as the men went through the various exercises. Discipline was intensified so that the troops would behave in puppet fashion.[10] 'The guard-parade became for him the most important institution and focal point of government,' wrote Frederic Masson, tutor to Alexander. 'Every day, no matter how cold it might be, he dedicated the same time to it, spending each morning in plain deep green uniform, great boots and a large hat exercising his guards. . . . Surrounded by his sons and aides-de-camp he would stamp his heels on the stones to keep himself warm, his bald head bare, his nose in the air, one hand behind his back, the other raising, and falling, a baton as he beat time, crying out *'One, two – one, two.'*[11]

Inevitably Paul's meddling extended from the parade-ground. Officers skilled at ceremonials were placed in prominent positions and worthy men removed; those who dared to grumble were finished. Yet many disagreed openly with the new Emperor, and chief among them was Suvorov whose ideas directly contradicted those of Paul. First, Suvorov sought a twelve-month leave of absence; this was refused. Then he applied to be retired, in March 1797, but three days later he received a curt note from Paul. 'Field-Marshal Suvorov, having declared to His Imperial Highness that since there is no war he has nothing to do, is hereby to remain without service for making such a remark.' Suvorov's dismissal was accompanied by an order forbidding him the right to wear uniform; he left the army and retired to the remote village of Konchanskoye in the Novgorod province.[12]

Kutuzov was spared such treatment, even though he shared so many of Suvorov's views. But he was removed from the post of Director of the Cadet School, possibly to prevent his influence on future officers, and at the same time was retransferred into diplomatic service. In 1797 he left Russia to become ambassador in Berlin.[13] His escape was merciful, removing him for a while from the atmosphere of suspicion and intrigue within Russia which intensified with Paul's growing fears of plots against him.

Prussia had been heavily involved in Western European affairs whilst Russia concerned herself with largely domestic matters. The War of the First Coalition had broken out in 1792, with Prussia and Austria joining to fight against the newly-fledged forces of the French Revolution. The struggle swung backwards and forwards along the Rhine from 1792 to 1795; in Italy a new French commander suddenly sprang to fame in 1796 – the young Napoleon Bonaparte. Prussia had already quit the struggle with the Treaties of Basel in spring 1795; Napoleon proceeded to shatter the Austrian forces at Lodi, Castiglione, Bassano, Arcola and Rivoli, crossing the border into Austria in March 1797 and forcing the enemy to agree to the preliminary peace of Loeben in April. Prussia, recovering from her wounds, joined Russia in adopting an inward-looking policy. When Kutuzov reached the capital the country was also preoccupied by another domestic affair: a new monarch had succeeded to the Prussian throne, 27-year-old Frederick William III, following the death of his father Frederick William II. The latter had expired, according to his critics, 'as a dreadful sacrifice to his own excesses'.[14] The new king seemed good-natured and mild, and determined to steer his country away from the whirlpool caused by the French Republic.

Others in Berlin urged increased Prussian participation; Kutuzov discussed the situation with these more energetic figures at Frederick William's court. Some enlightened officers had studied the tactics of the French Revolutionary soldiers, trained and organized by War Minister Lazare Carnot, and it soon seemed that the changes might have severe effects on the pattern of battle. The French exhibited a new degree of flexibility, especially through the use of the *tirailleur* skirmishers which contrasted so sharply with the traditional rigid infantry lines relying on massive volleys. Moreover, the *levée en masse* conscription introduced by the French Committee of Public Safety in August 1793 ensured a plentiful supply of men imbued with a new spirit of patriotic fervour. Napoleon Bonaparte displayed a new degree of manoeuvring skill and opportunism. All these factors demanded close examination by other European armies. Instead, Frederick William preferred to remain aloof and his army continued to be based on the now outdated lines laid down by Frederick the Great.

In Russia, Paul continued to train his troops for parades, not war. Yet conflict approached. Russia had stood apart during the War of the First Coalition, although in the last days of her reign Catherine had made inconclusive plans to send a small force to assist the Austrians. In the summer of 1798 Paul involved himself in European affairs, prompted by a typically nonsensical grievance. In June the Emperor accepted an invitation by the head of the priory of the Maltese Knights of St John to be Grand Master of the Order, even though Paul himself was Orthodox in religion and the Order was Catholic-based. The Russian Emperor then demanded that the French should withdraw from Malta, and when the French refused he began to organize a Second Coalition. On 24 December 1798 Paul allied Russia with Britain. Suvorov was brought back to St Petersburg and given command of a Russo–Austrian army intended to drive the French from Italy.

Kutuzov also returned to the Russian capital, but only to leave again shortly afterwards, appointed Governor-General at Vilna. To ease his disappointment he also received the Order of John of Jerusalem in 1799 and another estate with 1,000 serfs.[15] Suvorov departed for Italy on 17 February 1799 to begin a brilliant campaign which by August would eradicate almost all Bonaparte's 1796–97 gains, and which brought about a fresh bout of senseless behaviour from Paul. Envy and suspicion led the Emperor to despatch interfering directives and insufficient supplies. Ill, exhausted and without adequate men or equipment, Suvorov was ordered north into Switzerland; his Austrian allies were defeated at Zurich in September, and Suvorov barely managed to escape with his battered forces. Paul recalled Suvorov and the army to Russia, where he refused to allow a planned triumphant reception on the grounds that Suvorov had permitted the soldiers to cut off their wig pigtails. Suvorov, weary and demoralized, was informed that he would not be welcome at Court. He died on the morning of 6 May 1800, with his last word reported to be 'Forward'.[16]

At about the same time as his hero's death, Kutuzov returned to Petersburg from his eventless period as Governor-General at Vilna. He felt great affection for Vilna, but otherwise his duties had been dreary, and chances of fighting slipped away again; Paul had withdrawn from the Second Coalition, leaving the British and especially the Austrians to the struggle against the French. Kutuzov now became acting Governor-General in Petersburg. The appointment would have been welcome under Catherine, offering plentiful opportunities to enjoy the social life in the capital. But the atmosphere had altered drastically since Paul's accession; nor, with so many distinguished officers disliking the Emperor, did the appointment hold the same honour. Those connected with the despised Russian ruler inevitably became tainted, and they lived an uncertain existence fearing Paul's favours might be summarily removed. The court was impregnated with suspicion, both through Paul's constant – and justified – fears of plots against him, and through the feeling among courtiers that any one of them could be a spy for the Emperor. The whole situation provided a fertile breeding ground for jealousies, feuds and factions. The atmosphere deteriorated still further when Paul's foreign policy underwent a characteristic shift in 1800: Napoleon, First Consul of France since 24 December 1799, was now deemed by Paul to be a man whom he could respect. The Russian Emperor began to make approaches to the French ruler, suggesting a meeting at which they could plan a joint campaign against India; Britain, previously an ally, was now to be distrusted. This abrupt change brought fresh disgust from those Russian officers who had fought against the French in Italy: it seemed a slur on Russian honour and upon the memory of Suvorov.

Kutuzov was in a difficult position. As acting Governor-General of Petersburg he was responsible for law and order: the police came under his jurisdiction. He attempted to fulfil his duties impartially, nor had he ever been a member of any particular court clique. Yet in the tense atmosphere of 1800 and 1801 a neutral stance was virtually impossible. Moreover, Paul seemed to trust and confide in Kutuzov: he invited him to his private rooms on frequent occasions, most of which were spent discussing security arrangements – Kutuzov was closely concerned with the safety measures to protect the Emperor's life. Plots festered with the feelings of greater hatred against the Emperor following his shameful treatment of Suvorov. Many senior officers wished to be rid of Paul if only to revenge their hero's humiliation, and Kutuzov, among Suvorov's most fervent admirers, was even more involved. To many of those in the anti-Paul faction, he appeared a traitor.

The governor-general tried to manoeuvre a way through this tangled, unhealthy mess. Never before had his skill at diplomacy been more needed, and he used to the full his ability to avoid presenting his own opinion; he listened, appeared to be sympathetic, yet remained uncommitted. In all likelihood Kutuzov merely attempted to undertake his duties in the most effective way possible without becoming too tied to the fortunes of the Emperor: there is no evidence that his activities resulted in any acquaintances being denounced; but the conspirators believed that if Kutuzov refused to support them, then he must be against them, and the distrust generated during these months would remain for the rest of his life.

Paul became increasingly paranoic as 1801 opened, suspecting everyone, including his wife and his son Alexander. On 13 February he took up residence in the newly-built Mikhailovsky

Palace, believing himself to be safer behind its thick grey-stoned walls, moat and five stout drawbridges.[17] The plotters were undeterred: the castle, rather than being impregnable, could be turned into a trap from which Paul would have no escape. These conspirators were headed by Count Peter von Pahlen, Military Governor of St Petersburg and a close acquaintance of Kutuzov. Amongst the other plotters was General Levin Bennigsen, a Hanoverian-born professional soldier who had spent many years in Russian service and who was dedicated to her army: Bennigsen, later to be amongst Kutuzov's bitterest enemies, believed Paul must be removed for the honour of the Fatherland and for the future safety of his adopted nation.

At the beginning of March Paul ordered his sons Alexander and Constantine to move into the castle, so that he could keep closer watch over them. Only a few days later the Emperor received an accurate report of the conspiracy from his own agents, implicating Pahlen. He confronted Pahlen who insisted that he already knew about the plot and had pretended to give his support in order to discover the details. Paul appeared to believe the smooth-talking Count, but the plotters decided they must now act quickly.[18]

Early in the evening on Monday 23 March Kutuzov's carriage rumbled over the main drawbridge of Mikhailovsky Palace and into the courtyard. The general answered the salutes of the men on guard duty, who were dressed in the dark blue and white uniform of the famous Semeonovsky Guards. The night was bitterly cold, with a strong wind driving slurries of sleet from the Gulf of Finland. Kutuzov and his wife were escorted into the main reception room of the Palace, where they joined the sixteen other dinner guests invited by the Emperor. Most of those present were officers of the Petersburg garrison, of whom Kutuzov was the most senior. The officers wore full uniform and decorations – Kutuzov's Order of St George Second Class hung from his neck – and the wives were dressed in the latest fashions imported from France, with flimsy chiffon, low necklines and high waists. The assembled company was joined by Paul, by his sons Alexander and Constantine, and by his 14-year-old daughter Marie. They sat down to dinner beneath the glittering chandeliers which flickered in the draughts. The stoves around the room smoked badly, and the heat brought out the damp from the walls. But the dinner seemed successful: Paul appeared to be in a sociable mood, chatting with Kutuzov who commented politely on the Emperor's new porcelain dinner service.

Only Alexander seemed quiet. Paul suggested to his son that if he felt unwell he should consult the Emperor's doctor. Then, at the close of the meal, an *aide* brought the usual nightly report for the Emperor: Paul reacted with anger and perahps fear when he learnt that his regular guard at the Palace had been replaced by men from the Semeonovsky whom he distrusted, and he condemned Pahlen in public for this presumptuous alteration. The dinner party broke up early, with Alexander retiring to his rooms complaining of indigestion, and with Paul disappearing to his own suite on the first floor. Kutuzov talked for a while with other officers and then left with his wife to drive home through the empty streets of St Petersburg.

Just before midnight Pahlen, Bennigsen and other conspirators collected in the Palace courtyard, readily admitted by the officers of the guard. Men of the Semeonovsky were singing in the guard-room, after having been plied with extra wine; some of the conspirators were also drunk. Pahlen ran up the staircase and turned left towards Alexander's apartments facing the Summer Garden. He waited in Alexander's outer reception room, making no attempt to enter the bedchamber. Meanwhile Benningsen led the main party of assassins to Paul's suite. They burst open the door. The Emperor had apparently been disturbed by the noise of the carousing guards: a single candle in the room revealed his bed was empty. Then Bennigsen saw a shadow moving in the corner, half-hidden by a cupboard door and draped flags, and there he discovered the cringing Russian ruler. Bennigsen informed Paul that he was under arrest, on the orders of 'Emperor Alexander'. At first Paul made no answer, too frightened to speak. Then his desperate words began to flow as he pleaded for his wretched life; Bennigsen interupted, shouting at his comrades: 'If you hesitate, I'll butcher you all!' Nicholas Zubov, brother of Catherine's lover, apparently struck the first blow, using a snuffbox. The Emperor sagged to the floor, and the other officers fell upon him with their swords, fists and boots; one man wrapped a silk scarf round the Emperor's neck and tried to strangle him; another pounded a paper-weight against Paul's windpipe. They stood back. The body appeared to twitch, whereupon one of the murderers jumped on Paul's stomach with both feet 'to drive out his soul'.[19]

A messenger informed Pahlen that 'the deed was done'. Pahlen in turn told Alexander, whose fear of the new life before him almost equalled his father's terror at imminent death. In the early hours of Tuesday, 24 March 1801, with the wind still howling through the Petersburg streets, Kutuzov was informed that Paul had died from apoplexy; like most Russians in the capital, he knew that the cause of the Emperor's death was far more unnatural. Now Russia had a new ruler to lead the country in the approaching struggle with Napoleon, and one who would soon show suspicions of Kutuzov which developed into virtual hatred.

IV

Alexander and Exile

(1801–August 1805)

Alexander, grandson of Empress Catherine, was in his twenty-fourth year. His childhood had been strongly influenced by the Great Catherine, who had insisted upon her close supervision of his upbringing – hay instead of flock for his cot mattress, nursery window wide open in winter, spartan foods. Catherine had placed the baby in the wing of the Winter Palace beside the Admiralty so that he should hear the constant booming of ceremonial guns – perhaps one reason for early signs of deafness in the child's left ear. Added to this physical defect was a slight short-sightedness and a limp caused by an early fall from a horse. But Alexander's looks more than compensated for these imperfections. He grew to be tall and dignified, retaining a youthful appeal.

'Despite the regularity and delicacy of his features and the bright freshness of his complexion,' wrote Countess Tiesenhausen, 'his physical beauty was at first sight less impressive than the air of kind benevolence which won all hearts and instantly inspired confidence. . . . The rounded contours of his face resembled those of his august mother, as also did his profile. His forehead was slightly bald, giving to his whole countenance an open and serene expression, and his hair – which was golden blond in colour – was carefully groomed as on the heads of classical cameos or medallions.'[1]

'Were he a woman,' enthused Napoleon later, 'I think I should fall passionately in love with him.'[2]

Alexander's character had been moulded by three main factors: the domination of his grandmother Catherine, the awesome unpredictability of his father Paul, and the continuing domination of Elizabeth Feodorovna whom he had married in 1793 in his six-

44

teenth year, and who desired power more than himself. This combination of two strong women and a mentally unstable male had immense effect on the impressionable youngster. From his father he acquired the appearance of having military attributes which he did not in fact possess; from the forceful women resulted his difficulty in reaching firm decisions – he had been too used to having others make them for him.

Now, in the dark hours before dawn on 24 March 1801, Alexander sobbed in his room.[3] Alexander's nerves were shattered by his father's murder even though he had been fully aware of Pahlen's plot. Perhaps he sincerely believed that his father's removal could be affected without resorting to violence; certainly he supplied no express permission for assassination. But as Pahlen commented: 'You can't make an omlette without smashing eggs.'[4]

News of the fearful murder and of his own responsibilities plunged Alexander into despair, and throughout his life he would reveal feelings of guilt: the shadow of patricide hung over his throne. Alexander became even more emotional and uncertain; moreover, he proved incapable of handling his relations both with those who had helped place him in power and with those who had withheld active support. Pahlen was obliged to resign soon after Alexander's succession and most other conspirators disappeared from the capital. Bennigsen departed to be Governor-General at Vilna, Kutuzov's old post, but he would retain the Emperor's trust; Alexander seemed to believe that the general had acted from idealistic motives rather than from personal advancement, and he would always consider Bennigsen a worthy servant of the state.

The Emperor could never be sure that Kutuzov, in his position as acting Governor-General and a confidant of Paul, had been ignorant of Alexander's participation. Kutuzov had been present at that last dinner; he may have suspected Alexander of playing a part not only in Paul's downfall but also in his death. Kutuzov, so skilled at hiding his own feelings when he so wished, gave no indication of his thoughts. And from March 1801 Alexander therefore distrusted him. Yet the Emperor lacked evidence and Kutuzov remained polite, courteous and inscrutable. For a while the general received reasonable treatment: he was appointed full Governor-General of Petersburg, rather than acting in temporary fashion as previously, and Alexander even presented him with a snuffbox upon which was depicted the new Emperor's portrait. On the surface all seemed well.[5]

Kutuzov witnessed the delighted reaction which swept through the capital at the ending of Paul's tyrannical rule. 'Under my reign,' declared Alexander, 'everything will be as it was during Grandmother's rule,' and the people welcomed this return to the conditions of Catherine's time.[6] St Petersburg seemed to flourish, and the effect was most noticeable in the high society circle through which Kutuzov moved. Amongst Paul's quirks had been his attempts to interfere with society life, even details of fashion – men had been forbidden to wear waistcoats and obliged to have hats of a certain size and shape. Police permission had been often required before dances and receptions could be held and a virtual curfew existed. Conversations at the *soirées* and dinners had become stilted, and St Petersburg aristocrats had looked back with nostalgia at former days. Now it appeared that those times might return. The whole capital seemed to shine.

'It is difficult to describe the beauty of this spot,' wrote one visitor, Countess von Voss. 'The Isaac Square with the statue of Peter the Great is superb, and the whole city as far as we could see wonderfully fine. The palaces are far more handsome and imposing than those in Berlin. . . . The houses all look like palaces, they are so handsome and stately, and so evenly built, and they are as clean as if they were only just finished. The quays, the walks, everything is covered with deep, deep snow, and shines dazzling white in the sun.'[7]

Another tourist, Baroness de Bode, described the Emperor's palace. 'It is indeed filled up with so much luxury that it strikes with the idea of a castle belonging to some fairy or giant. They say that without the furniture and fittings it cost seven million roubles. Many of the rooms are hung with velvet and gold, and stuffs richly embroidered with gold. The chimney-pieces of lapis-lazuli, agates, cornelians, and Siberian pebbles – magnificent.'[8]

Kutuzov moved with ease in the artificial atmosphere of social ranks and rigid etiquette which could be extremely daunting to those not born to it. 'There is very little real politeness in these ladies,' commented Katherine Hamilton. 'Their education is entirely superficial, and there is not a trace here of the charming lightness of French society. When Moscow ladies have eyed you from head to foot and kissed you five or six times (though twice, one would think, would be ample), have assured you of their undying devotion, told you to your face that you are absolutely bewitching, asked you the price of everything you are wearing, and babbled about the coming ball at the Assembly of the Nobility, their repertoire is at an end.'[9] As with Kutuzov himself, a strong, coarse streak lay scarcely hidden by the social veneer. Sir John Carr described his 'horrible fascination' with the contradiction in Russian cultural life. 'The nobility . . . live in the voluptuous magnificence of eastern satraps: after dinner they frequently retire to a vast rotunda, and sip their coffee, during a battle of dogs, wild bears, and wolves; from whence they go to their private theatres, where great dramatic skill is frequently displayed by their slaves. . . The aristocracy enjoyed Molière and Racine in these private theatres, yet the best households would also keep dwarfs and cretins on their staff for knockabout amusements.'

Alexander left St Petersburg on 11 September to journey south for his coronation in Moscow, the spiritual heart of Russia and the traditional home of the Czars before Peter the Great had created his new capital. Ceremonies began in Moscow on 20 September, leading to the coronation itself on the 27th, after which the Emperor and Empress remained in Moscow for a further month. In the first week of October Russia and France signed a treaty in Paris formally establishing peace between the two countries, and during the long winter months it became apparent that with his coronation behind him Alexander had obtained greater self-confidence. He began to reject the advice of the council, known as the Secret Committee, which he had established in the uncertain days immediately following Paul's murder. The Emperor started to consider a policy of alliances. The Treaty of Amiens between France and England on 27 March 1802 brought general peace to Europe for the first time in a decade; the way appeared open to obtain valuable results for Russia through diplomacy, and Alexander responded favourably to suggestions from Frederick William III of Prussia that the two monarchs should meet and discuss the state of international affairs.

The meeting took place at Memel on 10 June, with Alexander's visit to this Prussian city lasting seven days. He discussed matters of international importance with Frederick William, especially regarding the future of the Germanic states, and he took an earnest interest in his host's proposal. He took equal interest in

47

Frederick William's young wife Louise, once renowned for her limpid beauty and still attractive despite her tendency to stoutness.[10] Other aspects of his Memel visit attracted Alexander, notably the precision performance of the Prussian guard of honour. His admiration was obvious to all, noted by some in his entourage with alarm: to Count Victor Kochubey, nominally in charge of Russian foreign affairs, it almost seemed as if Paul's personality was reappearing in his son: Alexander fussed over trivial details of uniforms and decorations, became short-tempered with his staff, and proved uncontrollable.[11] This behaviour continued after his return to Petersburg; he acted in high-handed manner at court, apparently bolstered by the belief that the Russian people adored him and would support him with a loyalty that his father had not been able to command.

Kutuzov became a target. Despite the outward expressions of satisfaction with the Governor-General, Alexander's distrust had continued. Before, he had felt unable to act; now, with his new self-confidence, the situation changed. The Emperor frequently summoned Kutuzov to his palace, and, after having kept him waiting in the ante-chamber, subjected him to long interviews in which he criticized the general's administration: the Petersburg police were mismanaged, inefficient and in an unsatisfactory condition. The charges of 'irregularities in the police service' were made repeatedly regardless of any defence offered. Kutuzov's presence reminded the Emperor of that fearful night in March the previous year: he must go.[12]

Kutuzov obliged in August. Alexander announced that the Governor-General was 'dismissed at his own request'. The general departed from St Petersburg soon afterwards, leaving his wife in the capital, and journeyed south-west via Moscow to the village of Goroshki in Volinsk province. Kutuzov had virtually been exiled, suffering the same fate as Suvorov under Paul. It seemed Kutuzov's career was finished. Russia remained at peace; Napoleon's power was consolidated with his proclamation as Consul for life, issued in the same month that Kutuzov left Petersburg; Kutuzov, in his fifty-seventh year, was no longer required.[13]

* * * * *

48

Exile in Goroshki lasted three years. For most of this time Kutuzov's wife remained in St Petersburg and the general stayed isolated from society affairs. He became almost a recluse, devoting himself to farming. His estate spread over thousands of acres, worked by 2,600 serfs. The latter lived in turf huts concentrated round the village; each family 'owned' a small strip of land which technically still belonged to Kutuzov, in return for which they worked a certain number of days in his fields – probably three full days each week. Kutuzov took a close interest in agricultural matters and spent many hours each day in the fields and plantations with his overseer. He was known as a fair landowner although strict; he concerned himself with the family affairs of those who worked for him, inquiring into their wellbeing and welcoming requests for advice. His serfs seemed content, responding to the ease with which he talked to them – Kutuzov's manner was similar to that displayed to his troops and met with equal success.

Major problems nevertheless confronted Kutuzov. He was short of money, with the estate barely managing to pay its way and with the necessity of having to maintain his family in Petersburg. His house at Goroshki was unpretentious and simply furnished, exceptionally so for someone as fond of comfort as Kutuzov; his hospitality to guests was still as liberal as always, but this itself caused a further drain on his finances. His health presented another source of anxiety. He tried to keep as active as he could, both through the daily work on the estate and through his love of hunting. But his legs, which were already slightly bent through long periods spent in the saddle, began to bow even further through rheumatism; his body grew heavier.

Most of all Kutuzov suffered from his eye. On waking every morning Kutuzov noticed that familiar articles round his bed were becoming dimmer, and his right eye reacted more and more painfully to light. His doctor tried a variety of treatments, none with appreciable success. Increasingly desperate, the doctor attempted another cure which not only caused Kutuzov great pain but which proved to do more harm than good, and the doctor told Kutuzov to stop the treatment immediately. The patient disobeyed. Kutuzov sat for hours with his eye covered by a handkerchief, frequently rigid with pain; periodically he would pull aside the cloth and look about him: the objects in his room

49

were fading further into blackness. He would apply more medicine, replace the handkerchief, and sit patiently again in his chair. At last his right eye was dead. The doctor asked him in amazement why he had continued the treatment with the damaging medicine.

'It is better that way, my friend,' replied Kutuzov. 'Since I have no means of saving the eye, of what use was it to me, an old man? Now it will cause me no more hurt.'[14]

Financial worries still remained. Kutuzov wanted to buy more land to make his estate a more viable economic unit, but he lacked capital; the only other way he might have obtained further possessions would have been through service to his country, now barred to him. 'I am sending you a thousand roubles, my dear,' wrote Kutuzov to his wife in 1804, 'and will send you more, as much as I can.' He added: 'It is a dull business trying to put the estate on its feet when everything is in such ruin. Upon my word, sometimes I feel like throwing up everything in despair and resigning myself to the will of God. Seeing myself at my present age and in my present state of health unable to acquire a new estate, I am haunted by the fear of spending my old age in penury and want, and of having laboured, faced danger and suffered wounds in vain. And this sad thought distracts me from everything and makes me incapable. . . . I am totally without company here, and the evenings are very dull.'[15]

Kutuzov's last words in this letter were not entirely correct. Visitors still came to see him and received an eager welcome. Some were military, others civilian; especially welcome were churchmen. Kutuzov had always had a deep interest in religion, and now this steadily increased. The deep mystery of religion appealed to him, and he enjoyed talking for hours about theological subjects, history, or the social sciences, often surprising his listeners by the extent of his knowledge.[16]

He also managed to keep himself reasonably informed about the state of affairs in Russia and in Europe generally. And within a few months of his arrival at Goroshki it had already become increasingly clear that peace might soon end. Rivalry between the Powers remained as strong as ever; diplomatic methods of obtaining national desires looked insufficient. The Peace of Amiens had ended in May 1803. Rumours increased that Bonaparte intended to invade England and was assembling a huge army for this purpose. Then, in spring 1804, further evidence of Bonaparte's belligerence reached Kutuzov. The French leader had ordered the arrest of the young Duke of Enghein, *émigré* prince of the French royal Bourbon-Condé line living in German Baden. Enghein was dragged to Vincennes and executed as a British agent. His death was seen by Alexander as regicide; moreover, the family of Empress Elizabeth originated from Baden, thus adding further insult.

Alexander summoned a meeting of the Council of State in mid-April, which decided to break diplomatic relations with France. The Russian court went into official mourning over Enghein, a note of protest was despatched to Paris, and Alexander attempted to persuade Frederick William of Prussia to adopt a similar stern stance – without noticeable success. Discussions took place between Russian envoys and British Ministers in London, but the talks failed to bring substantial agreement and for the moment the two countries lacked mutual understanding. As 1805 opened a working relationship had still to be established amongst France's enemies; by contrast, Napoleon stood at the peak of authority. 'Power is my mistress,' he declared. 'I have worked too hard at her conquest to allow anyone to take her from me.' But then Napoleon threatened to overreach himself. Already, the previous year, he had offered to guarantee the integrity of Turkey against her traditional enemy, Russia; now, on 30 January 1805, he despatched an arrogant letter to the Turkish Emperor, Selim.

'Have you, a descendant of the great Ottomans, emperor of one of the greatest empires in the world, ceased to reign? How is it that you allow the Russians to dictate to you?'[17] Similar efforts were made by Napoleon to bring Persia closer into his anti-Russian and anti-English arrangements, rumours of which reached Petersburg. In May the French leader declared himself 'King of All Italy'; on 6 June he annexed Genoa and the Ligurian coast. Faced by this flagrant disregard for peace, Russia signed a treaty of alliance with Britain on 28 July; the Austrians added their signature on 9 August, so creating the Third Coalition. Hurried allied discussions resulted in a preliminary plan of operations: first the French army in Italy, 50,000 men under André Masséna, would be destroyed; then an overwhelming allied force would strike westwards on the northern side of the

Alps towards the Rhine and France. It was hoped that Napoleon would be caught off-balance with the bulk of his main army still assembled near Boulogne for the proposed invasion of England.

A messenger reached Goroshki in late August with a summons to Kutuzov from Alexander. Orders awaited Kutuzov in St Petersburg for him to assume command of the Russian army. He hurried north as fast as he could. His body still ached from rheumatism; his eye still pained him though it was no longer alive; within a month he would celebrate his sixtieth birthday. And, by the time Kutuzov reached St Petersburg and received his instructions, the gigantic campaign leading to Austerlitz had already begun.

V

Duel Along the Danube

(August–November 1805)

Despite his personal feelings towards Kutuzov, Alexander realized that no other choice existed for commander of the Russian forces. Kutuzov's reputation was unrivalled; he was known as an aggressive, resourceful and intelligent military leader, well-trained by the great Suvorov, who had never been involved in a major setback. Now Kutuzov would lead a vanguard of 38,000 Russians, with more following, to act in conjunction with the Austrians thrusting into southern Germany; other Austrians would deal with Masséna in Italy; the British agreed to send 26,000 men to link with the allies in Hanover. The French would be destroyed by a massive pincer movement.

But allied hopes that Napoleon would be caught unprepared were preposterously inflated. Napoleon moved first. 'The more I reflect on the European situation,' he wrote to his Foreign Minister Talleyrand from Boulogne on 23 August, 'the more I see the urgency of taking decisive action. I am off at full speed. I am striking camp, and replacing my fighting battalions with reserves, which in any case give me a formidable enough army at Boulogne . . . I march on Vienna . . . I don't return to Paris till I have reached my goal.'[1]

Napoleon wrote this letter at about the same time that Kutuzov received his first message from Alexander; the Russian commander had still to receive full orders. Even before this date Napoleon had already made detailed plans which revealed a close appreciation of his enemy's intentions: this assessment, dictated by Napoleon on 13 August, was centred on the likely allied aim of striking against south Germany and Italy. The map showed that the route to be taken by a combined Russo–Austrian

53

army would probably be down the Danube valley, the primary route from Vienna towards Strasbourg – and ultimately perhaps to Paris. This valley, therefore, threatened both south Germany and the flank of France herself, besides offering links with Austrians in Italy.

The Danube became the key to the whole campaign. Moreover, the river provided the earliest point of union for the Austrians and for Russians approaching from Galicia. Napoleon's plans were based on the fact that the French must prevent such a junction: speed was indeed therefore the first essential – the Austrians must be dealt with before the Russians arrived.

By the last day of August the French Grand Army was on the move from the Boulogne area, striking south-east. Regiments marched one after the other with excellent efficiency. 'A roll of the drums,' exclaimed Hugues Maret, Napoleon's Secretary of State,

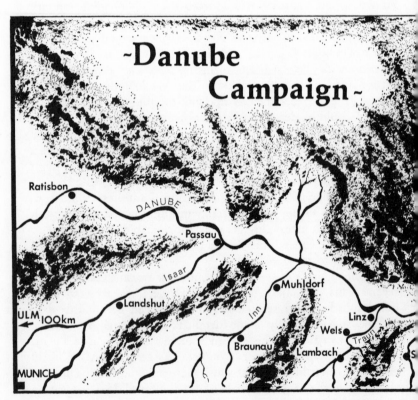

'and ten thousand men are astir!'[2] In fact the Grand Army would number nearly 200,000 men. By contrast the allies lacked both efficiency and correct timing. Napoleon had caught them off-balance rather than the reverse, and the allies would never be allowed to recover.

Kutuzov has been condemned for disastrous delay which led directly to the subsequent allied tragedy. His critics charge him with loitering on the march to join the Austrians, with a lack of energy, and even with adopting a deliberate policy of deserting the allies. According to a recent historian on Austerlitz: 'The old Prince, surly and prudent, owing his position to the favour of St Petersburg, where he had known how to foster his reputation as the owner of a lucky star, had a horror of fighting, or rather, since his physical courage was not in doubt, a horror of sending his soldiers into battle.'[3]

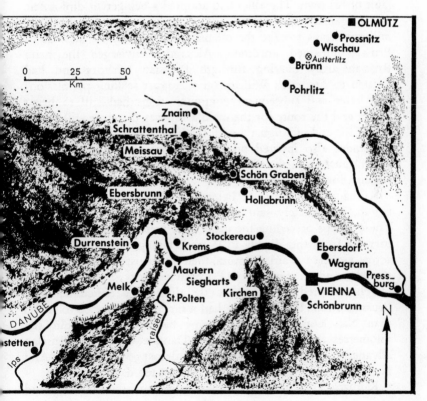

Apart from the fact that Kutuzov had not yet been created a prince, the statement is inaccurate for a number of reasons. Contrary to the view which later became commonplace, Kutuzov had already urged the Emperor to adopt an offensive policy – to attack as soon as possible because delay might be disastrous. 'Move the whole army to the pre-designated point and take the offensive,' he had written to Alexander. 'Every delay and indecision causes ruin and even more so now when the whole of Europe does not know what Napoleon may do to it. We must attack and not be on the defensive.' Kutuzov's letter added: 'During the present storm nothing could be more frightening for Bonaparte than to have the strong levies threatening him from Russia. He, I think, will use all means and intrigues to stop the rapid advance of our armies.'[4]

Kutuzov's aggressive policy was not put into effect, through no fault of his own. The allies had adopted a belligerent diplomatic stance against Napoleon without preparing in sufficient detail the military means to take the offensive. Above all, the attitude of Prussia remained uncertain. Alexander envisaged the main Russian army moving through Prussian territory and had written to Frederick William on 7 August seeking permission: this letter and subsequent communications had still to bring result, and the route for the main army was therefore still uncertain at the end of August – with the French already on the move. Alexander also insisted on modifications to the Russian plan which caused a further delay in the concentration of the principal Russian forces.[5]

Kutuzov, arriving in St Petersburg after the war had already begun, immediately sent on advance orders to his regiments. These troops preceding the main army were instructed to march forward from the Vistula in Poland, taking a route south-west across Galicia towards Olmütz, then into Austria. This direction would avoid trespassing on Prussian territory. But this line of march, adopted to overcome the diplomatic difficulties with Prussia, meant that Kutuzov had a far longer distance to travel than Napoleon. The latter's army had to march about 500 kilometres from Boulogne to the Danube valley; the Russian advance guard was obliged to cover almost 900 kilometres. And Napoleon had snatched a start of at least ten days.

Kutuzov knew nothing of the departure of the French Grand

Army from Boulogne yet nevertheless suspected the enemy might have begun such a movement. He assessed Napoleon's plan correctly – to strike at the Austrians before the Russians could arrive – and in a letter to Alexander he stressed the danger of a premature Austrian move. 'The Austrian army must without fail wait for us until such time that our army gets to Prague. Then it must cross the river Inn and go straight across Munich in one or two columns, holding towards Ulm.' The allies must act in unison, with the Austrians informed of every detail of the Russian advance towards them 'so that the Austrians and Prussians could not justify themselves by pleading ignorance of our advance, and so that they would not either act before or after us, but would be together with us in fortune and misfortune.'[6]

The Austrian High Command lacked Kutuzov's perception and acted directly contrary to his thinking. Emperor Francis declared war on 3 September, and his forces under General Mack von Lieberich began moving almost immediately, marching into Bavaria in a number of separated groups. The Austrian plan envisaged Mack's First Austrian Army, about 51,000 men, heading to the Danube valley to secure Ulm when junction could be made with the Russians, after which a thrust would be made into the French flank; meanwhile Archduke Charles, with 100,000 Austrians, would cover the Venetian provinces and would attack Masséna. But Mack moved far too early. His forces crossed the Inn, 150 kilometres south of Ulm, on about 8 September – at least three days before the Russian vanguard began its 900-kilometre advance: yet Kutuzov had warned that the Inn should not be passed until his troops reached Prague. Within three days Napoleon received reports of the Austrian move: the French commander, now at St Cloud, issued orders on 17 September for his forces to start crossing the Rhine towards Ulm on the 25th.[7]

French and Austrian armies were fast converging. But the Russian vanguard was impossibly far behind, despite maximum speed being maintained on the march. Russian troops covered an average of over thirty-five kilometres each day, and only bivouacked four times between 13 September and 8 October totalling one week of rest; Kutuzov ordered that the men should carry the minimum necessary, with their heavy knapsacks loaded on carts, and the troops should take turn in riding on waggons. Mobile field kitchens were sent ahead so that meals would be ready when the men arrived for their brief night's rest. Contrary to the common belief, the Russian troops under Kutuzov in fact moved faster than the French. Napoleon's famous march from Boulogne to the Rhine took twenty-five days – 31 August to 25 September; Kutuzov's regiments took twenty-four to march from the Vistula to Braunau: the distance covered by the French for this major portion of their advance was 350 kilometres, compared with over 600 for the Russians. But the latter could never have arrived in time to support the Austrians no matter how hard Kutuzov urged them on.

Moreover Kutuzov was denied accurate information concerning enemy, Austrian or the Russian main army movements. At least he was spared from interference by Alexander at this stage, although this situation would later change dramatically. In an effort to avoid the Emperor's involvement in the direction of the campaign Kutuzov had already urged him 'not under any circumstances [to] go further than the frontier, but have your main headquarters at Brest[-Litovsk] and all the allied Ministers with you.'[8] Alexander left Petersburg on 21 September; he reached Brest-Litovsk on the 27th, where he received news that Frederick William still clung to a Prussian position of neutrality. Alexander continued his journey to Pulawy, 100 kilometres from Warsaw, where he would stay at the country estate of his Deputy Foreign Minister Adam Czartoryski and would await the result of fresh appeals to Frederick William in Berlin.[9]

The Russian vanguard reached the Austrian frontier in Galicia on 22 September. Two days later Napoleon travelled eastwards to join his army; within twenty-four hours his forces had already begun to cross the Rhine between Mannheim and Strasbourg: the French were within 150 kilometres of Ulm whereas the Russians had still about 370 to go – the difference had been narrowed but remained too great. By 2 October the French were moving on a 120 kilometre front between Stuttgart and Würzburg. Mack's Austrian forces, totalling about half the French strength, were still scattered.

Mack acted in uncertain and confused fashion, noted by Napoleon who wrote: 'The enemy is marching and countermarching and appears to be embarrassed.' The Austrian commander, deceived by the movement of French cavalry in the

Black Forest to his front, believed that the enemy was approaching from this westerly direction; instead, the French were curving round his northern flank. Reports of such a move at last reached Mack on 4 October, and he began marching towards Ulm the following day to prevent the flanking attempt. Napoleon responded on the 5th and 6th: his corps were in an excellent position to concentrate at short notice, and the net began to close.

Mack now appeared to be full of confidence. He believed that his early arrival at Ulm would provide the allies with the key point in the campaign; he accordingly sent a despatch to Kutuzov, claiming that his manoeuvring had already obtained a victory over Napoleon and requesting Kutuzov to approach Ulm to help strike the final blow. The Russian commander, who reached Braunau on about 8 October and whose presence at the town was reported by the French on the 11th, refused to oblige. [10] Braunau lay about 200 kilometres east of the Austrian army. The weather, hitherto fine, had now turned foul and the tracks were covered with mud. Kutuzov's troops were exhausted, many of them barefooted after their long slog, and so far only about 8,000 had reached Braunau itself; by comparison the Austrian forces were relatively fresh. To Kutuzov it seemed far more advisable that the Austrians should slip away from Ulm and join him further along the Danube valley, rather than the Russians entering the trap which Napoleon was preparing. The Russian vanguard must be kept intact for the decisive battle. [11]

By 11 October Ulm was virtually invested, with Napoleon ordering Joachim Murat to move in with his cavalry at maximum speed. 'The Russians are approaching rapidly; advance on the enemy, then, wherever he may be.' [12] For the next week Mack blundered one way then the other in an attempt to break the circle around him; instead the threads grew steadily tighter. Kutuzov remained in the vicinity of Braunau, aware that strong enemy forces lay across his path towards Ulm should he have tried to reach Mack. He collected his troops together as they arrived at the grubby, rain-swilled town, attempting to provide them with fresh equipment prior to a clash with the French. [13]

Mack's position became hopeless. Negotiations between the French and Austrian commanders opened on 15 October; next day Mack agreed to surrender on the 25th if not relieved. But by the 19th the Austrian Marshal realized the uselessness of waiting longer; he rode over to Napoleon's camp and uttered the famous sentence of surrender: 'Sire, behold the unfortunate Mack.'

'I am more tired, my dear Josephine,' wrote Napoleon to his Empress that night, 'than I ought to have been. After being wet through every day for a week, and my feet frozen with cold, I'm not feeling particularly well. I am going to advance on the Russians. It's all up with them. . . .'[14]

Next day, as the regiments of the Austrian army in Ulm filed past Napoleon, orders were issued for the concentration of the French army eastwards on the Isaar, halfway to the Russian position at Braunau. The First and Second Corps, under Jean Baptiste Bernadotte and Auguste Marmont, were to occupy Munich; Louis Davout's Third Corps was to take up position at Freising, north of Munich, while the remainder of the Grand Army stayed further to the west.[15] The Austrian capital of Vienna, 230 kilometres behind Kutuzov's outnumbered forces, became Napoleon's most important target: defeat the Russians and the city would be wide open. Conversely, Kutuzov's first reports of the disaster at Ulm, received on 22 October, were accompanied by strident calls for the defence of the capital. But Kutuzov now began to display the stubbornness which would reappear in the 1812 campaign. He strongly disagreed with the supposed value of defending any city; far more important, he believed, was the continued existence of his force and the need to effect a junction with the main Russian army.

'Having made now, so to speak, a single defence of Vienna,' reported Kutuzov to Alexander on the 22nd, 'if I go out forward I could be cut off by the enemy which is three times stronger than I am. Remaining here I must equally expect that I will be attacked, and it is very probable that I will be forced to retreat to Vienna itself.'[16] Not even Suvorov could have defended Vienna with such disparity in strength. Kutuzov could only hope to lure the enemy away from the capital; yet his logical thinking, so clearly based on lessons learnt from Rumyantsev, was completely rejected by the Austrian and Russian Emperors, and his operations merely seemed to support those who accused him of over-caution and even cowardice.

Alexander had been dallying at Pulawy since 3 October, still hoping for permission from Frederick William for Russian troops to march through his country. This permission finally arrived after French troops under Bernadotte violated Prussian neutrality by advancing into Ansbach on 6 October. Yet Alexander still delayed moving forward to Kutuzov; instead he left Pulawy on 21 October for a social visit to Frederick William in Berlin.[17] Kutuzov, who certainly did not want Alexander with him, was nevertheless bombarded with instructions from the Emperor based on inaccurate information and incompetent assessments. 'Advance, and attack the enemy,' wrote Alexander, 'and do not wait for him in the [defensive] position. I can only be content when I know that you have taken upon yourself the supreme responsibility of defending Vienna.'[18]

To add to the confusion Kutuzov was even denied information of the whereabouts of the Russian main army, supposedly moving to his support under General Frederick William Buxhöwden and numbering over 40,000 men. 'Up to this time,' wrote Kutuzov from Braunau, 'I have no knowledge of the army of Count Buxhöwden which must have moved fairly far if it hasn't been delayed by the diplomatic considerations. The position in which I find myself now especially demands that I know whether the army is behind me or not, so that I can make my decisions accordingly.'[19]

On 21 October the French Emperor issued a triumphant message to his troops. 'Soldiers of the Grand Army. In a fortnight we have carried out a campaign; what we set ourselves to do has been done. . . . But we shall not stop at that. You are impatient to begin a second campaign. This Russian army, that the gold of England has transported to the ends of the earth, we shall cause to meet with the same fate. . . .'[20]

Next day, 22 October, Mack passed through Braunau on his miserable route to Vienna, following Napoleon's permission for him to depart; he informed the Russian commander that he could expect no support unless Archduke John managed to reach him from the Tyrol, where he commanded 20,000 Austrians.[21] Kutuzov studied his maps. He still had no knowledge of the position of Buxhöwden's forces; Archduke John was likely to be blocked; Archduke Charles, with the strongest Austrian force, remained in the Adige and would be fully involved with Masséna. The only remaining Austrian army, about 15,000 men under Archduke Ferdinand, lay in Bohemia to the north. Kutuzov therefore reached his decision. He would withdraw down the

Danube: initially he would cover the 100 kilometres to the line of the Enns, almost half-way to Vienna, and then would seek to establish contact with the main Russian army somewhere to the north-west. He would avoid a set battle and would instead extend the French lines of communication. Kutuzov summoned his senior officers. 'The Austrians have given way,' he declared. 'They are defeated. Many are fleeing towards us. The cowards have laid down their arms at the enemy's feet. Inform your comrades.'[22] Orders were given for the withdrawal, and on 24 October the Russian forces struck camp. The war of manoeuvre opened.

Dominating the campaign area was the Danube river itself, curving gently south from Ratisbon (Regensburg) above Munich to Vienna. From the main river ran a succession of tributaries: the Isaar upon which the French now stood, the Inn, Traun, Enns, Ips and Traisen. Kutuzov planned to use each as rearguard positions: blown bridges would delay the French. The valley down which Kutuzov intended to march gradually narrowed, from about 100 kilometres wide at Braunau, thirty-seven at the Enns, to an even more constricted width at Vienna with the mountain spurs pressing close to the Austrian capital. Communications therefore became concentrated, rendering a French flanking movement more difficult. Moreover, Napoleon would presumably have to guard against a strike from the north by the main Russian army, by the Austrians under Ferdinand and even by Prussian troops should Frederick William enter the war. Kutuzov enjoyed a further advantage. The speed and need for secrecy of the Grand Army's march from Boulogne had prevented the formation of a full supply system back into France: troops had been obliged to live off the country. To continue to rely on such a method would be highly dangerous, with Napoleon following in the wake of the Russians, and the French commander therefore had to establish a magazine at Augsburg to feed his further advance; even this might not be sufficient.

All these factors influenced Kutuzov in his subsequent actions, and all were militarily sound. But other elements existed. Utter chaos had broken out in Vienna, where the Russian Ambassador reported: 'The consternation and confusion are so great that we lack even an account of the operations which preceded the capitulation [at Ulm], or of what prompted it.'[23] Emperor Francis of Austria appealed to Kutuzov to save his capital: 'I depend on you and you may rely upon my eternal gratitude.' Kutuzov replied in typically noncommittal fashion: 'The setback Your Majesty's Army has sustained at Ulm is extremely grave, but not so grave that it cannot be rectified by fortitude and courage.'[24] Kutuzov also received Imperial instructions to hold firm on the line of the Inn, which he ignored apart from placing a small rearguard on the eastern bank; instead he ordered the bridges over the river to be destroyed and headed towards Wels, sixty kilometres back on the Traun.

Alexander entered Berlin on 25 October amidst massive pomp while his troops trudged along the muddy tracks beside the Danube. The Prussian monarch welcomed the Russian Emperor with fireworks, regimental reviews and magnificent banquets. Alexander distributed diamond earrings and pearl necklaces to the ladies, and in the meantime failed in his effort to obtain a firm military alliance with Frederick William.[25]

Napoleon entered Munich on the same day Alexander reached Berlin. He also received plentiful acclamations, but military news continued to occupy his time. His forward troops, regiments of the Fourth Corps under Nicholas Soult and closely followed by Murat's cavalry, were heading towards Mühldorf on the west bank of the Inn. This objective was reached on the 27th, with the Russian rearguard falling back; on the same day Kutuzov reached Wels. By now Napoleon realized that the Russians were withdrawing to avoid being trapped; he ordered the Grand Army to march as rapidly as possible for Vienna, and he himself left Munich on the 28th.[26]

Within twenty-four hours Napoleon rode into Braunau where he occupied Kutuzov's former headquarters. He remained at the town directing his forces forward; now, with Russian detachments starting to launch sudden strikes against his leading units, the French Emperor appreciated that his advance should proceed cautiously. 'The Russians are not yet broken,' he wrote to Murat on the 30th. 'They know how to attack.'[27] The terrain favoured the Russians; nor had Napoleon been allowed sufficient opportunity to assess the opposing commander.

Kutuzov, heading for Strenberg on the Enns, ordered a delaying action by the Russian rearguard on the 31st. His troops obeyed at Lambach on the right bank of the Traun, where they burnt the bridge and fended off French assaults by Davout's soldiers. Musket fire continued until darkness, then the rearguard slipped away threatened by an outflanking movement. The first day of November dawned cold and dry; rain clouds which had hung low over the valley almost since 8 October drifted northwards beyond the mountains. The edge of the rivers began to freeze with the sudden drop in temperature and ice formed over the puddles in the rutted roads. Many Russian soldiers had still to be supplied with fresh equipment following the harsh march from the Vistula; Kutuzov's staff officers anxiously awaited the arrival of winter clothing and boots for the troops, and the number of sick steadily rose.

'We are marching at night, livid with cold,' wrote General Dmitri Sergeivich Dokhturov, one of Kutuzov's most valuable corps commanders. 'Officers and men are barefoot and have no bread. What a misfortune it is to be the allies of such scoundrels; but it cannot be helped!'[28]

Those 'scoundrels' the Austrians were increasing their demands that the Russians must make a stand and protect Vienna. Kutuzov refused to listen. He reached Strenberg on 1 November and immediately ordered further withdrawal to the next river, the Ips. Vienna lay less than ninety kilometres away. Within twenty-four hours Kutuzov was on the move again, withdrawing towards Melk. But he stopped at Amstetten on the 3rd, deploying his troops to cover the single road winding among the low hills beside the Danube, and it seemed for a while that he intended to fight a battle; hopes rose in Vienna.[29]

Also on 3 November the Russian and Prussian rulers completed a draft treaty in Berlin. Even if Kutuzov had known the content it would have provided him with no encouragement: Frederick William agreed to go to war if France refused to accept proposals based on agreements reached between the Russians, Austrians and British. Prussian support was therefore still tenuous and likely to be delayed.[30] Alexander, apparently well satisfied with his week's stay in Berlin, prepared to depart for the fighting front. First he indulged in a melodramatic performance with Frederick William, embracing his fellow-monarch over the candle-lit tomb of Frederick the Great with tears streaming down his face. While Alexander's carriage creaked south over the icy roads, Kutuzov's men were desperately fighting off French advance assaults. Kutuzov, still starved of knowledge concerning any support, moved even nearer Vienna at the end of the first week in November, but the French were pressing close behind.

In command of the valiant Russian rearguard was Prince Peter Ivanovich Bagration, twenty years younger than Kutuzov but also a disciple of Suvorov, under whom he had fought in Italy and Switzerland in 1799. Suvorov called Bagration 'Peter Prince' and said he possessed 'a spirited presence, skill, courage and good fortune'. Bagration, tall and thin with a hawk-like nose and slanting, piercing eyes, was an excellent tactical commander with a magnetic effect on his troops – who called him 'God of the Army'. But he could also be over-ambitious and reckless, and he lacked Kutuzov's almost supernatural calm in the face of adversity.[31]

Now, on 4 and 5 November, Bagration's rearguard fought fanatically to hold off Murat's units outside Amstetten. The French cavalry made excellent use of the hard ground, moving rapidly through the woods and over the fields in an attempt to encircle the Russian positions. Men of the Pavlograd Hussars repeatedly drove them back, bursting from the pines and thundering down the slopes against the French; throughout the day the sound of crackling musket fire and the occasional thud of cannon echoed in the mountains, Bagration rode backwards and forwards amongst his men, urging them to stand fast, and Kutuzov sent back troops under General Mikhail Miloradovich as reinforcements. 'Act as befits Russians,' he told them as they marched towards the firing.[32] But by 6 November Bagration was having to fall back under intense pressure from infantry commanded by Jean Lannes and Soult.

Murat, exhausted from the constant activity, received criticism from Napoleon for neglecting to send information; the Emperor, now at Linz, ordered his cavalry commander to write two or three times a day.[33] But Napoleon remained out of touch almost sixty kilometres to the rear; Kutuzov was in excellent control of the situation. And now the Russian commander proceeded to reveal both his cunning and his manoeuvring skill; the revelation came as a shock to the French Emperor.

The Russian rearguard and the advancing French troops lost about 1,000 dead at Amstetten. Many of the fallen lay locked in hand-to-hand combat, their corpses covered by the shifting snow which had begun to fall. But the sacrifice of valuable men in

Bagration's regiments was considered worth while by Kutuzov: their defence had allowed him to put fresh plans into operation. When the French advance guard finally moved cautiously forward on 6 November they found that the opposition had disappeared. Woods and fields were silent. The eerie absence of any Russian enemy continued on the 7th, apart from the occasional single musket shot. Murat spurred on his exhausted cavalry; Lannes lashed his infantry forward, in a foul temper as usual; and, in their haste to regain contact with the Russians, these two French commanders dangerously stretched the line of the advance, causing Napoleon to be in even less control of the situation at the front. Meanwhile Kutuzov had pulled back through the town of Melk, where the magnificent wine cellars in the abbey were left intact for the approaching French, and during the night of 6 November he reached St Polten on the Traisen. The latter ran into the Danube only thirty kilometres from Vienna, and the river marked the last natural obstacle before the Austrian capital. Kutuzov immediately threw out an imposing line of Russian troops bolstered with Austrian detachments. The Russian commander, who acted as his own chief of staff during the operations along the Danube, supervised the deployment himself.

Insistent demands from the Austrian capital for a battle were now expected to be met, despite the noncommittal replies which Kutuzov had made; Napoleon also took for granted that this defence would be attempted. When advance troops under Lannes and Murat suddenly established contact with the Russian line on 8 November, they therefore assumed that the enemy was making the crucial stand. Lannes and Murat, their units extended by the rapid move forward over the last forty-eight hours, awaited reinforcements; in the meantime they enjoyed the wines of the Abbey of Melk, with troops drinking in groups of six or eight, dipping their straws into the massive earthenware containers.[34]

Emperor Francis of Austria attempted to gain time by proposing an armistice. His envoy, General Count Gyulai, reached the French headquarters at Linz on 8 November but received a frigid welcome; he left soon afterwards with an arrogant letter from Napoleon. 'It is not for me to decide what Your Majesty ought to do in your present situation; but I see with some regret that you agree with the Emperor of Russia: for he has not the same interest in our quarrels as we have, nor do the safety and welfare of his subjects depend upon what is happening at the moment. For Russia this war is mere make-believe. . . . I do not intend any reflection on the personal character of the Emperor Alexander. . . . He is still young; he will gather experience. . . .'[35]

Napoleon believed the end to be firmly in sight: the Russians were about to be annihilated. But Kutuzov was already putting his plans into effect. Early on 9 November the Russian line at St Polten suddenly disappeared.

Murat and Lannes discovered to their astonishment that the force before them at St Polten had only amounted to a thin screen; the main Russian regiments had continued to withdraw. And, instead of pulling back in the direction of Vienna, Kutuzov had suddenly switched northwards to cross to the far bank of the Danube. On 9 November, as the French realized they had been deceived, Kutuzov was already at Krems with the bridges over the Danube blown behind him. He intended to strike north, using the vital hours he had gained through his deception, then tempting Napoleon deeper into the mountains and opening the possibility of inflicting defeat on the French after junction with Buxhöwden – whom Kutuzov could reach far quicker now that he had avoided the detour through Vienna.[36] Kutuzov displayed a high degree of military dexterity; now he attempted diplomatic deception in his explanation of the abandonment of Vienna.

'I foresaw that the enemy would not let slip the opportunity to fall on my communications behind Krems, to occupy the bridge over the Danube and to squeeze me between him and his main army if I did not forestall him. These considerations led me to the decision, in spite of all entreaties, to leave the position at St Polten within two days and to march to Krems.'[37] Kutuzov therefore still refused to admit finally that no defence would be attempted before Vienna: his move to the far bank of the Danube was claimed to have been made to cover an attempted move forward by French forces on that bank in the direction of Krems. At that stage Kutuzov inferred that a battle might yet be attempted. In fact he had no intention of fighting such a useless engagement: instead he hoped that the French would be tempted to take Vienna, thus allowing the Russians more time to manoeuvre into the mountains.

This plan worked. Murat was unable to resist veering away from the Russians towards the capital. He led his cavalry blindly

67

The Fox of the North

onwards during 10 and 11 November, urging Lannes and Soult to accompany him and only coming to an abrupt halt in the mountain pass of Kahlenberg, ten kilometres from the city, where he received a vicious message from Napoleon: the French commander appreciated the thinking which lay behind the Russian plan.

'You are behaving like a lunatic,' exclaimed Napoleon to Murat, 'and you are taking no account of the orders I've sent you. The Russians, instead of covering Vienna, have recrossed the Danube at Krems. This circumstance should have made you understand that you should not act without new instructions. Without knowing the enemy's plans, or my wishes, you continue to rush my army to Vienna. Yet you were ordered to chase the Russians with your sword in their ribs. It is a curious way of pursuing them to move away from them by forced marches. You have considered nothing but the petty triumph of entering Vienna.'[38]

The French were in disarray. On 11 November Murat's cavalrymen were still scattered in the vicinity of Sieghartskirchen, over thirty kilometres from the Russians at Krems and on the opposite side of the river; Lannes lay between Murat and St Polten; Soult's troops were spread along the Traisen, although with some detachments at Mautern facing Krems. Bernadotte's corps was deployed further back at Amstetten, with Davout's to the south. North of the Danube, on the same bank as the Russians, marched isolated French troops, under Adolphe Mortier, which had crossed the river at Linz on 6 November. The latter were in an extremely exposed position with the leading division, under General Gazan, advancing far ahead of the second division, under General Pierre Dupont. And, on the morning of the 11th, Kutuzov suddenly switched from his withdrawal policy to throw his men into the attack against these nearby French.

Russian strength had to be limited to two divisions led by Miloradovich and Dokhturov, leaving the rest to guard against a French assualt across the Danube, but the enemy were nevertheless outnumbered by almost three to one. Gazan's artillery officer Colonel Fabvier frantically organized a battery of ten guns as the Russians started to swarm down the slopes; the cannon opened fire at almost point-blank range, and massive explosions ruptured the Russian ranks. But still the Russians pushed forward; one by

68

one the guns were swamped. Kutuzov ordered a flank operation, pinning Gazan's division against the Danube, and throughout the day the carnage continued. Dokhturov's division encircled the French from the south-west and seized the village of Durrenstein, forcing the French out into the open. Mortier himself, trapped in the Russian grip with the rest of Gazan's troops, was urged to escape across the Danube by boat but refused to leave.

Then, as fighting continued in the darkness and the flames from Durrenstein reflected red on the low black clouds, Dupont's division managed to force a way through from the west. The Russians began to disengage, slipping back into the hills north of Krems. Gazan's division had been decimated but Kutuzov could ill-afford to become further entangled with Dupont: he had shown that the Russians could still strike; manoeuvring must continue.[39]

Between the two armies stretched the Danube, over which all bridges had been blown – except one, at Vienna itself. The French Emperor therefore sent urgent orders to Murat: he must dash to the city – not to occupy the capital but to seize the great Tabor bridge spanning the river beyond the suburbs. If successful, Murat must then pass the Danube with part of his cavalry and Lannes's division, to be followed by Soult, and should thrust north towards Hollabrünn to cut off the Russians.

Murat's mission should never have been successful. The Tabor bridge had already been prepared for demolition with mines stuffed beneath the arches; Austrian troops holding either end could easily have held off the French for the few seconds required for the fuses to burn. Instead Murat and Lannes presented themselves before the Austrian commander, resplendent in plumes and magnificent uniforms, and insisted an armistice was about to be signed between France and Austria. The Austrians hesitated; French troops rushed forward and seized the bridge intact. Murat's cavalry trotted over, heading north.[40] This incompetence on the part of his ally played directly into Kutuzov's hands: he could no longer defend Vienna, even if he had so wished.

'The taking by the enemy of the bridge under Vienna,' wrote Kutuzov, 'an event which it would have been impossible to predict, and his march across Stockereau to Hollabrünn, forced me to change my whole plan. Instead of defending the crossing of the Danube and patiently waiting for our reinforcements, I was forced to quicken my march in order to escape an unequal battle against a

69

force incomparably superior, and to follow the original plan of union with the army of General Buxhöwden.'[41]

Now Kutuzov had to extricate himself from the French encirclement. Murat reached Stockereau during the evening of the 13th; Kutuzov's headquarters were hurriedly established in Ebersbrünn to the north-west. Next day Napoleon entered Vienna and received the keys of the city from its citizens; eye-witnesses said that he rode through the streets in a calm and dignified manner. Some of his troops were able to sample the delights of the city: 'Dear cousin, My God, these people know how to drink!' wrote one inhabitant. 'I believe your cow drinks less water a day than a Frenchman does wine.'[42] But the majority of the French regiments were thrusting north, and it seemed increasingly likely that Kutuzov and his army, down to about 37,000 men, would be trapped. Kutuzov reached Meissau on the 14th; Murat's route, towards Hollabrünn, would block the Russians from Buxhöwden's army, believed to be in the vicinity of Brünn seventy kilometres through the mountains.

Kutuzov evaded the disaster through speed and deception. He urged his troops on throughout the wild night of 14–15 November over the mountains to Schrattenthal, riding backwards and forwards along the line encouraging his 'children' and repeating his favourite exhortation: 'Behave like Russians!' The troops stumbled onwards to by-pass the French but Kutuzov knew this stolen march would be insufficient to prevent Murat's cavalry catching up and carving into his weary forces. The Russian soldiers were suffering from lack of sleep, constant marching, continued tension; some of them were wounded from previous engagements, staggering onwards with the help of comrades with their injuries untreated through lack of opportunity; the men were bewildered, relying only on their blind faith in their commander. Once again, Kutuzov called upon Bagration's help to gain more time: the rearguard was ordered to march as rapidly as possible across country to Hollabrünn to hold off the French.[43]

'Our people are very exhausted,' wrote Kutuzov in a despatch to Alexander. 'I have strengthened the sixth column and ordered it . . . to hold on long enough for me to pass on the other road in order not to be cut off.' Kutuzov wept as Bagration and his 7,000 men began their march; he wrote later: 'Although I saw the certainty of destruction facing Bagration's corps I would have nevertheless considered it satisfactory to sacrifice one corps for the sake of the army.'[44]

Kutuzov employed one more means to save his force. He intended to trick Murat with the same ruse that the French marshal had employed against the Austrians at Tabor bridge. Kutuzov told Alexander: 'I sent Adjutant-Generals Wintzingerode and Prince Dolgorukov to the French to have talks so that after a few days of truce we may gain even a little time. I instructed them to make conditions, if possible, not binding us to anything, relying upon their discretion entirely because it is impossible to waste a moment.'[45]

Bagration's corps reached the village of Schön Graben, just north of Hollabrünn, on the morning of the 15th after an appalling night march through the dense forests and along the winding mountain road. The Russian rearguard had marched almost without break hour after hour towards the French, the men cursing in the darkness as they stumbled along the rocky path or trudging in silence against the background noise of scraping hooves and screeching gun-carriage wheels. Almost one-third of Bagration's force had dropped out during the night, too exhausted to proceed further: the Russian rearguard barely amounted to 4,000 men by dawn on the 15th, ill-shod, badly equipped and utterly exhausted. In front of them lay Murat's cavalry and Lannes's infantry. The Russians formed into line for battle amongst the woods and foothills, cold and famished and apparently without hope.

But Murat, hearing from his scouts that enemy forces had approached, rode forward himself and believed that Kutuzov's main army must be deploying. Then, across the field between the two lines of troops, approached a Russian delegation under flag of truce. Acting as Kutuzov's spokesman was Wintzingerode, a charming and intelligent Prussian in service with Russia, whose politeness cloaked an intense hatred of the French. He addressed himself to Murat, far more impressionable than the cynical Lannes.

'General Kutuzov sends me to inform you, My Lord, of the arrival at Schönbrunn of negotiators who are to sign peace. In consequence, he proposes to you an armistice whose main condition is to halt our troops forthwith in the positions they mutually occupy. In the event of operations being resumed, the one to break the truce would give notice six hours in advance.'[46]

Murat fell into the trap. Still believing that he faced the main

71

Russian regiments, he planned to use the truce to bring up reinforcements. He therefore declared he would accept the armistice under certain conditions and subject to the approval of the French Emperor, to whom he would despatch an *aide*. The Russian rearguard and the French vanguard watched one another over the wood-fringed field – while Kutuzov's main force continued to hurry northwards. Russian and French soldiers talked together in this temporary, unofficial truce; men dragged birchwood and fences to make fires and used the opportunity to dry their clothes, sodden for a week or more. Bagration walked forward to meet Lannes, and the two men, both hardened professionals, discussed the situation over glasses of mulled wine. 'If I'd been alone,' said Lannes, 'we should now be fighting each other instead of exchanging civilities.'[47]

A messenger reached Kutuzov with the conditions proposed by Murat; Kutuzov reported to Alexander: 'I held back an answer more than twenty hours, not thinking of accepting it at all, and meanwhile I continued the retreat of the army and I managed to get away from the French by two marches.'[48]

But the truce ended with the arrival of an incensed message from Napoleon to Murat, received by the cavalry commander at noon on the 16th. 'It is impossible for me to find words in which to express my displeasure with you. . . . You are causing me to lose the fruits of a campaign. Break the armistice immediately and attack the enemy. . . . It is only a ruse. March! Destroy the Russian army. You are in a position to take his baggage and his artillery. The Emperor of Russia's *aide-de-camp* is a jackass. The Austrians let themselves be duped over the passage of the Vienna bridges – you have let yourself be duped by an *aide-de-camp* of the Czar!'[49]

Murat hastened to prepare his cavalry for the attack. Yet the offensive was delayed a short while longer, this time by Lannes who insisted upon fulfilling his word as a gentleman: he notified Bagration formally that it would be necessary to fight.

The French opened fire during the early evening. The Russian commander had made use of the ceasefire to order earthworks to be constructed above the hamlet of Grün behind Schöngraben itself; now, under the impact of the French assault, the Russians pulled back to this defensive position. The regiments streamed up the hill in apparent disorder, French volleys still blazing and cannon balls thudding into the earth around them, but once in the prepared defences the Russians turned to throw back the advancing enemy. Bagration's guns were positioned to cover the road from Hollabrünn, while his cavalry waited in the woods on either flank. French infantry swept up the slope again, drums throbbing, yet the Russians stood to meet them and the murderous volleys and counter-volleys lacerated the opposing lines. The French fell in scores, but more pressed on; the Russians pulled back to another prepared position, giving ground slowly and continuing to inflict heavy casualties.

Murat, furious from his humiliation and desperate to redeem himself, hurled his men against the Russian centre. Soult's infantry tried to outflank Bagration's line but were repulsed by the Chernigov Dragoons, the Kiev Grenadiers and the Chasseur Regiment. Lannes thrust round the other flank and managed to trap the Podolski, Azoz and Pavlograd regiments yet most of these men battered a way through again.

Night fell but the battle of Schöngraben still raged. Bagration refused to reply to an invitation from the French to surrender, and his men fought their way steadily back towards the village of Gutensdorf. Finally, just before midnight, Bagration realized he could do no more. Over half his men were dead and wounded; the remainder were beginning to panic; the French were pressing round behind in the dark. Bagration issued the order for withdrawal and his survivors staggered away into the night dragging wounded men with them. The remnants of this rearguard joined with the rest of Kutuzov's force at Pohrlitz late next day, 17 November. Kutuzov and Bagration embraced with tears wet upon their faces and those who fought in the battle of Schöngraben were later awarded medals with the proud inscription 'Five against Thirty'.[50]

On the same day Napoleon reached his forward regiments and the Grand Army hurried on in pursuit. Kutuzov still received demands from the Austrian Emperor, now at Olmütz 100 kilometres to the north, that he should fight a battle – despite the Russian effective strength being only about 30,000 men plus the Austrian garrison from Vienna, against three times as many French. The sarcastic sentences in Kutuzov's reply scarcely concealed his contempt.

'My devotion to Your Majesty would be sufficient to prompt me to fulfil your command to the letter even if my sacred duty to

73

submit to Your Majesty did not oblige me to do so. I dare not, however, conceal from Your Majesty that much as the opportunity has occurred to stake the fortune of war on a single battle, I dare not do so, for my troops though imbued with zeal and an ardent desire to distinguish themselves, lack the strength.

'Wearied by forced marches and ceaseless bivouacs, they can scarcely drag themselves along, having gone without food sometimes for whole days, because no sooner do they begin to cook their meal than the enemy swoops down upon them, and they must throw the food out of the cauldrons. I deem it necessary to retreat until I join Count Buxhöwden and the various Austrian units. Reinforced by these troops, we shall compel the enemy to keep at a respectful distance and give us a few days' rest, after which we may be able to attack.'[51]

But on 18 November the Austrian Emperor received powerful support from the presence of Alexander. The Czar at last reached Olmütz after being delayed *en route* from Berlin by bad weather; he had also spent a pleasant interlude visiting his sister Marie Pavlovna, wife of the Crown Prince of Saxe-Weimar, who insisted on introducing him to the great literary figures of Weimar including Goethe and Herder.[52] Now Alexander arrived to hear violent accusations from Emperor Francis that Kutuzov had failed to defend the Austrian capital and had scuttled like a coward from Napoleon's advance.

Within twenty-four hours Kutuzov at last joined forces with the advance regiments of Buxhöwden's army. Junction took place at Brünn amidst pouring rain, swirling clouds and buffeting winds. Kutuzov sat on his horse on the outskirts of Brünn as his battered regiments marched in; he wore his customary plain grey tunic covered by a green greatcoat which was so old that it looked mildewed; on his white hair was a flat round cap, like a sailor's hat, which had no other decoration than a single red ribbon round the brim. The lack of showiness, contrasting so strongly with the ornate tunics and plumed cocked hats normally worn by Russian generals, made him all the more distinctive. The 'Hurrahs' of his troops as they greeted him mingled with the thunder from the nearby mountains.[53]

The French were still close behind. On 20 November Kutuzov withdrew to Prossnitz, where he wrote: 'All the enemy's forces are now opposite me. Bonaparte's headquarters is five kilometres away.'[54] His assessment was inaccurate – Murat, leading the French advance, had positioned himself about fifteen kilometres from the Russians – but the French were nevertheless still imposing an acute threat. Napoleon established his headquarters at Brünn during the 20th, arriving in the old walled town at ten o'clock in the morning, and there he began to plan the next step.

To Kutuzov, the allies had only one sensible choice. Withdrawal must continue. 'The further we lure Napoleon,' he told Alexander, 'the weaker he will be and the farther from his reserves, and there in the depths of the Galicias I will bury the bones of the French.'[55] Time and space were on the side of the allies, he argued: Napoleon was unlikely to launch an all-out attack at the moment, since his troops must be as weary as the Russians; he should therefore be tempted deeper into the mountains.

Kutuzov's judgement of the state of the Grand Army later proved to be accurate. Already, at Znaim, Napoleon had been obliged to allow his troops a day's rest, and reports reaching him at Brünn indicated that the sick lists were lengthening at alarming speed. Supplies, dragged over the harsh mountain roads, were arriving too late and in insufficient quantities. The Grand Army urgently needed rest and reorganization, during which the Russian and Austrian regiments could slip away.

But Kutuzov could no longer act as he thought best. His command had been eroded. Only twenty kilometres separated his temporary headquarters at Prossnitz from the Austrian and Russian Emperors at Olmütz. And both Francis and Alexander were determined to fight a glorious battle: Austerlitz lay only ten days ahead.

VI

Austerlitz

(November–December 1805)

Napoleon sought time in which to organize his forces. On 21 November Murat's cavalry pushed back the forward Russian posts and established advance positions at Wischau, after which fighting dwindled. French regiments were regrouped and resupplied as fast as possible; guns were hauled over the roads from Vienna; Napoleon gathered his corps around him and the previously peaceful town of Brünn bustled with activity.

At Olmütz the allies suffered increasing dissension. And all Alexander's dislike and distrust of Kutuzov grew stronger than ever before; Kutuzov found himself virtually removed from command, outvoiced in conference, even though he retained the title of Commander-in-Chief. Alexander preferred to listen to the Austrian Emperor and to those who accused Kutuzov of seeking only to avoid battle.

'The young men around the Emperor,' wrote General Count Louis Langeron, 'referred to him [Kutuzov] as General Dawdler and he was left without authority and without influence.'[1] These young staff officers, resplendent in their feathers and froggings and with as little experience of war as Alexander himself, urged the Emperor to restore Russian honour through victory: further retreat would be utterly ignoble. Many of Alexander's senior advisers felt the same, including his military tutor Alexei Arakcheev who, like the Emperor, was seeing active service for the first time. Bagration was eager for action, as always; Wintzingerode's hatred of the French smothered all caution; Dolgorukov was also impatient to hit back at the French. Other generals owed their positions to the Emperor's favour, including

76

Buxhöwden, Quartermaster-General Sukhtelen and even Langeron, the sophisticated French soldier who now served as a Russian corps commander.

The Austrians unanimously urged a battle; Vienna must be recovered, the disgrace of Ulm must be wiped away – even if the bulk of those fighting the French would be Russians. Chief among these Austrian advisers clustering round Alexander was General Weirother, chief of staff to the Austrian Emperor Francis, to whom the Czar listened with eager attention. In 1804 Weirother had conducted manoeuvres in this district of Moravia and claimed to know the terrain in detail: he assured the two Emperors that the plan of battle which he would present must surely bring magnificent victory.

Some Russian officers doubted the value of Weirother's advice even though they disagreed with Kutuzov. There were those who remembered that this same pompous Austrian, then a colonel, had served in the Swiss Alps in 1799 and had nearly directed Suvorov's forces into disaster by presenting a highly inaccurate map to the Russian commander. Bagration and Miloradovich had narrowly escaped on that occasion; now they had no faith in his words. And the story quickly circulated around the headquarters at Olmütz that Weirother had in fact lost his way during the manoeuvres in the Austerlitz area in 1804.[2]

Weirother nevertheless worked busily on his plan and Kutuzov remained isolated. He spent most days with his men, discussing with them the events of the last hectic weeks and listening to their problems. The regard of the rank and file soldiers for the old commander contrasted with the apparent apathy which they felt for Alexander's presence, further aggravating the Emperor's relations with the commander. Moreover, the troops resented the interference of men like Arakcheev, who insisted on spit-and-polish and useless parades: Kutuzov followed Suvorov's belief that the men should be as comfortable as possible in order to recover from past ordeals and prepare for the next.

Among the factors which influenced those who urged battle was the numerical superiority enjoyed by the allies over the French. Weirother believed the Grand Army to total about 40,000 men – in fact Napoleon had about 75,000 within easy reach of Brünn.[3] Others had been left at Vienna or were deployed elsewhere. This total still gave the allies greater manpower: the

77

combined forces of Kutuzov, Buxhöwden and the Austrians in the vicinity totalled about 80,000, increased to some 90,000 on 25 November when the Imperial Guard arrived under Constantine, Alexander's brother. Archduke Ferdinand's force, about 18,000 men, lay at Prague to the north-west but could not arrive in time; Archdukes Charles and John, with 80,000, were blocked by Ney and Marmont from crossing the Alps following a defeat inflicted by Masséna at Caldiero on 30 October.

Napoleon planned to allow the allies to come against him. His forces would be concentrated while those of the allies, on the march, would be extended. This difference would compensate for Napoleon's lack of numbers, and he would be able to use his cavalry and cannon – both of which were far below Russian and Austrian strength – to greater effect.

To Weirother, this lack of movement by Napoleon seemed to indicate timidity: the allies were being permitted to seize the initiative. His greatest fear was that the French would attempt to escape before the allies advanced. Napoleon's greatest fear was that the Russians and Austrians would withdraw – as Kutuzov urged. The French Emperor therefore began tempting his enemy into resuming the offensive by feeding the belief that he, Napoleon, might be seeking peace. On 25 November he sent an emissary to the Russian Emperor bearing a suitably obscure message: this assured Alexander of Napoleon's good wishes and expressed the hope that occasion might soon arise of providing proof of his goodwill. Chosen as messenger was General Savary, Napoleon's *aide-de-camp*, who had played a leading part in the seizure of the Duke of Enghein in 1803: his selection now either indicated gross arrogance or a desire to forget past quarrels.

The Russians received Savary courteously. Alexander had ridden forward to the small town of Wischau the previous day, from which the French had just withdrawn, and there he granted the emissary an interview. He wrote a reply to the French Emperor, although he declined to grace Napoleon's name with its proper rank and instead addressed the letter childishly to 'The Head of the French Government'. This reply expressed Alexander's 'desire to see the peace of Europe re-established with fairness and on a just basis'. The message suited Napoleon well, containing just the right amount of belligerence to indicate that the Russian Emperor seemed determined to fight.

Austerlitz

The allies began to shift cautiously forward; Napoleon ordered outlying French troops to withdraw after only minimum resistance and at the same time sent orders summoning Bernadotte from Znaim and Davout's corps from the south-east. The French Emperor also tempted the allies further by despatching Savary late on the 28th with more supposed evidence that the French were frightened and would rather agree to peace than to fight: this time Savary was instructed to present Alexander with an invitation for the two Emperors to meet. Savary made his way to the forward Russian lines, where he was detained by Bagration until the following morning, 29 November. Alexander, when he finally interviewed the emissary, decided to send Dolgorukov back with Savary to sound out the situation.

But by this time Napoleon considered the pretence could be ended. The French commander, described by Dolgorukov as 'a little figure, extremely dirty and ill-dressed', subjected the emissary to a violent tirade and sent him back with the words: 'Your master wants us to fight. I wash my hands of it!' Dolgorukov nevertheless returned to the Russian lines boasting that he had displayed similar aggression and that 'Bonaparte had completely lost his head'.[4]

The basic allied plan envisaged isolating the French from Vienna by outflanking Brünn to the south-west – exactly the operation which Napoleon hoped the enemy would attempt. The area itself stretched featureless, a wide and undulating district intersected by small marshy streams and with only the occasional rise. The highest ground, named the Pratzen Plateau, lay between Brünn and the chateau of Austerlitz which would give the battle its name. To the west of the Pratzen plateau trickled a stream known by local inhabitants as the Goldbach, never more than a man's stride wide and fringed with reeds and ice-covered ponds. The fields lay desolate beneath the grey autumnal sky, gloomy and dank, a fitting place for slaughter.

The allies moved slowly forward in five columns on the 29th and 30th, the right on the Olmütz–Brünn road, the left to the south of the road heading towards Austerlitz itself. Gradually the columns began to incline southwards to start the turning movement around Brünn, and Napoleon made his plans accordingly. These were based on his strongest forces being massed behind the Goldbach, ready to spring forward at the right moment to pierce

79

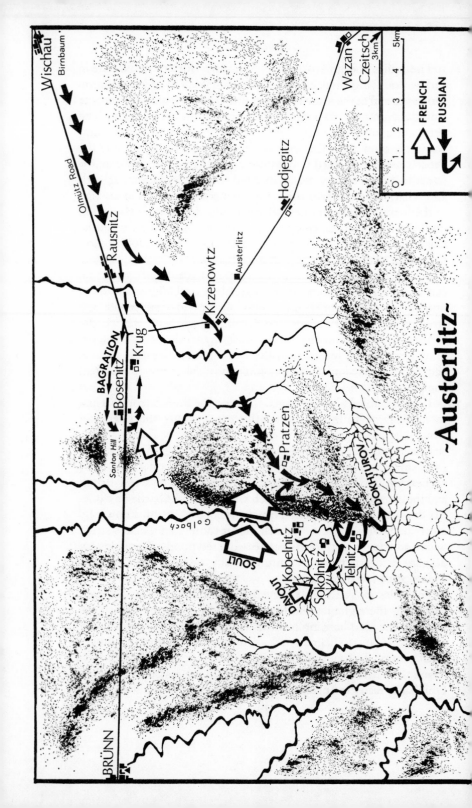

~Austerlitz~

FRENCH
RUSSIAN

0 1 2 3 4 5km

Wischau
Birnbaum
Olmütz Road
Rausnitz
BAGRATION
Bosenitz
Krug
Santon Hill
Krzenowtz
Austerlitz
Wazan
Czeitsch
3km
Hodjegitz
Pratzen
DOKHTUROV
Golbach
SOULT
Kobelnitz
Sokolnitz
Telnitz
DAVOUT
BRÜNN

the allied centre, after which the wings would be destroyed in turn.[5] Both armies shuffled cautiously into position during 30 November and 1 December. Kutuzov directed the mechanics of the allied movement from his headquarters in the hamlet of Birnbaum, one kilometre from Wischau where Alexander and his staff were quartered. The weather remained misty throughout the short hours of daylight, obscuring visibility and muffling the sounds of cavalry harness and gun-carriages. Alexander, Francis and Weirother believed everything to be proceeding satisfactorily.

Kutuzov would position himself with the allied centre commanded by Generals Kollowrath and Miloradovich and comprising about 22,400 Russian and Austrian troops. He remained in close touch with the situation during the last days of November. Yet rarely had a commander-in-chief wielded so little command. Kutuzov had voiced his opinions at the allied war councils, notably on the 24th and 27th, and had failed to convince the Emperors and their supporters of the need for withdrawal; and after the decision had been confirmed on the 24th, that the allies would attack under a plan to be presented by Weirother, Kutuzov's influence could only be limited.

Kutuzov had two choices. Either he could issue the strongest possible protest and resign, or he could accept the inevitable and stay knowing the decision for battle was likely to be disastrous. Most commanders in his situation would have quit the army in disgust, and even Kutuzov's supporters have criticized him for not taking this action: by resigning he would have saved his reputation. His decision to stay has been interpreted by his critics as meaning he yielded to the Austrians, or that he sought only to preserve his military career – once he resigned, Alexander would never have allowed him back into Russian service.[6]

Consideration of his future probably indeed influenced Kutuzov's decision to stay. But a more important reason existed. Both critics and supporters of Kutuzov agreed that he enjoyed a close relationship with his men in true Suvorov tradition. His only hope at Austerlitz was the matchless courage of the Russian soldiers, whom he had led through the terrible days of manoeuvring in the last six weeks. Like the Prussian general Blücher, a similar great leader of men, he called his troops 'children', and it would have been entirely out of character for Kutuzov to desert them now. Moreover, Kutuzov's departure from the army at any stage after 24 November would have been catastrophic: morale amongst the Russian soldiers would have collapsed, opening the way for even greater slaughter.

So Kutuzov remained powerless while the final moves were made for battle. Critics condemn him for not making a more vigorous effort to change the actual tactical plans for the battle – but these were not presented by Weirother to the allied generals until the evening of 1 December. Kutuzov could do nothing at that stage, even though his lack of activity would later be stressed as another example of his laziness and dissipation.

'There he was,' wrote one modern historian, 'lying rather than sitting in a huge portable armchair. . . . To his left, despatches were piled on a great oak table, where he tolerated only one candlestick with three candles. He did not want it to be seen that he was asleep. He was drunk. He usually overcame his annoyance with some girls: he had three in his baggage-train and would undoubtedly have sent for them all together, in accordance with the habits attributed to him for many years on great occasions, if his wagons had not remained near Olmütz.'[7] This description, so typical, is a parody of the truth. Kutuzov, for all his fondness for women, never allowed his passions to interfere with his military campaigns; there is no evidence that women ever accompanied him apart from his wife on some occasions in Turkey.[8] Kutuzov could indeed be lazy, but only when it seemed pointless to waste energy; often he appeared to be asleep, yet in reality sat wide-awake listening intently. It seems clear that he encouraged the false image of himself as being idle, half-asleep, indecisive, so that he could act in opposite fashion and so surprise his enemies. Kutuzov fell victim to his own propaganda.

His attitude was revealed most clearly at the allied commanders' conference held on the evening of 1 December. By then the Russian and Austrian columns were ready for battle: Bagration, with 13,000 men, had halted in front of Rausnitz on the Olmütz road about fifteen kilometres from Brünn, and south of him stretched Dokhturov's 9,000 men, Langeron's 12,000 on the eastern edge of the Pratzen Plateau, General Prszbyzewski close by with about 14,000, and behind him Kollowrath and Miloradovich with about 23,000 in the vicinity of Krzenowtz. The main allied cavalry, 6,000 strong under Lichtenstein, was positioned at the foot of the Pratzen Plateau adjoining Langeron's corps.[9] Russian and Austrian senior officers rode from their headquarters at these positions during the evening and collected at Kutuzov's staff offices established in a country house near Birnbaum. The generals helped themselves to the plates of venison and chicken spread on the sideboard, then stood awaiting the arrival of Weirother with his final plans. Bagration apparently felt it not worth his while to attend. Weirother appeared soon after nine o'clock. Kutuzov immediately turned away from the table in the centre of the room and slumped in a deep armchair by the fire, ignoring the Austrian who in return took no notice of the commander-in-chief.

Weirother was exhausted, having been in the saddle for much of the day; his clothes were splattered with mud and began to steam from the heat of the room. His face was eager and excited. The other officers clustered round him as he unrolled his maps on the table; Kutuzov remained in his chair, staring into the fire.

The Austrian chief-of-staff began to speak, revealing his precious plan upon which all hopes depended. Immediately, his words were almost nonsensical for many of those present. '*Da der Feind mit seinem linken Flügel an die mit Wald bedeckten Berge. . . .*' 'In that the enemy rests his left wing on the wooded hills and extends his right wing along Kebelnitz and Sokonitz to the rear of some marshes that are to be located there, while we on the other hand with our left wing far outflank his right, it will be to our advantage to attack this last-named wing. . . .'

The words rolled on describing extremely complex dispositions in pompous and circumlocutory phrases. The complicated German sentences meant that Weirother's exposition was unintelligible for some of the Russians present; his phrases became so entangled in translation that they remained incomprehensible despite the patient efforts of Colonel Karl von Toll, who acted as interpreter. Dokhturov, small and fussy, persistently asked Weirother to repeat difficult passages.

Kutuzov understood but made no comment. Langeron also grasped the meaning, and his subsequent account revealed the contempt he felt at the time. 'He read his dispositions to us in an elevated tone and with an air of boastfulness that proclaimed his intimate conviction of his merit and our incapacity. He resembled a form-master in a high-school reading a lesson to the young pupils. We were perhaps indeed pupils; but he was far from being a good teacher.'

Weirother finished after about sixty minutes. The officers remained silent; Miloradovich sat staring vacantly in front of him; Buxhöwden stared at a candle as if hypnotized by the flame; Kutuzov appeared to be asleep. Langeron turned away and broke the pause. 'A geography lesson!' he muttered. Someone said to Weirother: 'Don't make the same mistake that you made at the manoeuvres – don't lose your way!'

Desultory discussion took place. Kutuzov slipped deeper into his chair, his good eye closed. The plans were useless, but the time for changes had gone. The allies would attack at daybreak: Bagration was to assault Santon Hill on the French left, supported by the cavalry, while Dokhturov swung southwards in the opposite direction, heading towards the village of Telnitz below the Pratzen Plateau. Langeron and Prszbyzewski would follow to join with Dokhturov under Buxhöwden's overall command, in order to roll up the French against Bagration's corps near the Olmütz road. Kutuzov would direct the columns under Miloradovich and Kollowrath which would push behind Buxhöwden's advance to provide added impetus for this outflanking attempt. The allied centre would therefore be extremely vulnerable, weakened by the movement south towards Telnitz which opened a gap between Bagration and the rest of the allied army. This gap would be especially noticeable in the vicinity of Pratzen Plateau, from which the southern columns would march.

Langeron politely sought information on one vital point. 'All this is extremely fine. But if the enemy forestalls us and attacks us near Pratzen, what would we do?'

'That', replied Weirother, 'is not anticipated.' He insisted that Napoleon was only intent on withdrawing and would attempt all means possible to avoid a battle.

At last Kutuzov stirred; the assembled generals expected a profound pronouncement. 'Gentlemen,' he declared, 'the dispositions for tomorrow, or rather for today since midnight has gone, cannot be altered. You have heard them read out. We shall do our duty. But before a battle, there is nothing more important than to sleep well. Gentlemen, let us take some rest.'

The generals filed from the room, leaving Kutuzov alone with his staff. An *aide* asked the commander for his opinion of the imminent battle; Kutuzov replied: 'I think the battle will surely be lost.' Kutuzov had already revealed further evidence of pessimism

84

or simply his natural prudence: before Weirother's arrival he had advised the corps commanders and the Czar's *aides* that if the plan of attack should fail, then the Russians would fall back on the river Morava; the first rallying point would be the village of Hodjegitz three kilometres east of Austerlitz.[10]

Napoleon issued his final orders at 8.30 this same evening. In effect these were based on a deliberate weakening of the French right in order to mass maximum strength in the centre along the Goldbach, facing the Pratzen Plateau. This heavy emphasis on the centre would be cloaked from the enemy by the terrain and by diversionary movements. Napoleon would await a suitable opportunity to strike: it seemed to him extremely likely that gaps would appear in the allied line as the Russians and Austrians attempted to swing south of the Olmütz road; Napoleon would seize upon this over-extension of the allied advance. In a proclamation to his troops he declared: 'We occupy a formidable position and while the enemy are marching to turn my right they will present their flank to me.'[11]

Sudden alarm spread through the forward Russian posts as the commanders rode back from the conference. Lights began to flare from the French lines, one after another, spreading across the slopes; the tensed Russian and Austrian troops could hear shouting from the enemy, and with nerves already raw they believed for a moment that the French were about to launch a surprise attack. Some units in Prszbyzewski's column were called to arms and the soldiers blundered into one another in the dark as they ran to form lines. There they stood, facing the French. But the lights died down and the shouting subsided. Russian and Austrian troops continued their wait for dawn.

Napoleon had been visiting his positions. The Emperor tripped in the dark and a nearby grenadier lit a torch so that he could see; others did the same, much to Napoleon's initial annoyance – the lights could provide a target for the enemy. But the torches continued to flare and seemed to illuminate the scene in a triumphant, glorious explosion of flickering fire. Napoleon's anger disappeared, and the soldiers cheered him on his way. He returned to his headquarters and exclaimed: 'This is the finest evening of my life.'[12]

At 4 o'clock in the morning, 2 December, Kutuzov climbed from his couch. As usual on campaign he had slept in his uniform, and he took only minimum time to prepare himself: his simple tunic and hat needed no special care. He left his headquarters and rode slowly forwards to General Kollowrath's position.

By six o'clock the Russian and Austrian columns were on the move. The noise of the thousands of boots thudded in monotonous rhythm on the frosty ground, and above this dull hammering sounded the usual shrill shriek of the artillery caissons. Breath from the soldiers rose in a cloud to mingle with the thick dawn mist. Staff officers constantly galloped up to Kutuzov as he rode forward with Kollowrath; he barely listened to the reports they brought him. The conduct of the battle was beyond his control. The bulk of the allied army moved slowly and ponderously along the Pratzen Plateau towards the French left at Telnitz and Sokolnitz, operating under Weirother's plan. Emperor Alexander rode with his staff of glittering officers at the rear of the army and Kutuzov, still with Kollowrath, kept well away from the Imperial presence. To the north, Bagration's corps on the allied right prepared to assault along the Olmütz road. Snapping musketshots cracked through the mist at about seven o'clock as skirmishers clashed with one another along the Goldbach; then the single shots suddenly broke into the thunder of volleys. Battle had begun.

The first clash erupted on the far left of the fifteen-kilometre allied line as Dokhturov's column attempted to drive the French from Telnitz. Moments afterwards the firing spread to nearby Sokolnitz. The mist began to swirl away from the higher ground, revealing to Napoleon the movement of four allied columns down from the Pratzen Plateau towards the French right. The mist clinging to the marshy ground by the Goldbach still cloaked the French centre, hindering allied assessments of enemy strength in this vital sector. Neither the allied movement nor the weather could have better suited Napoleon's plan.

Yet for the moment the allies seemed to enjoy the advantage. Dokhturov's column, spearheaded by an Austrian vanguard led by General Kienmayer, thrashed through the scraggy vineyards outside the rough huts of Telnitz and gradually forced back the outnumbered defenders. The French right was the weakest part of Napoleon's line – deliberately made so – and the French units in Telnitz fell back, stumbling through the bogs and icy puddles, and behind them the Russian and Austrian troops shouted their

'Hurrahs' from the smoking buildings. Just to the north the Russian drums beat the advance outside the village of Sokolnitz, and Langeron's troops drove forward; once again the French reeled back.

The sun broke through, watery yet welcome, and to the captors of the two villages at the end of the French line the light seemed to herald further victories to come: now the sweep north could begin, backed by Prszbyzewski's column already in the vicinity and by the other two columns pressing down from Pratzen Plateau.

Napoleon also welcomed the sun. It highlighted the movement of the remaining columns from Pratzen Plateau, with the light glinting on weapons and harnesses; the gap yawned wide in the allied centre and French regiments under Soult were poised to strike. Soult was about to order his 20,000 men forward but Napoleon told him to be patient, asking: 'How long do you need to climb the Pratzen?' Accounts vary of the time Soult specified in his reply – some say ten minutes, others twenty. But then Napoleon added: 'Wait another quarter of an hour. And then it will be time.'

Kollowrath's column moved last in the Russian line across the Pratzen; in a few moments these regiments would start the descent down which Miloradovich's troops were already marching. And even before the mist began to lift to reveal the waiting French Kutuzov knew the danger to which the Russian army was being exposed. He had no control over the army as a whole, but he sought at least to direct Kollowrath's corps in the best fashion: he delayed the descent of these troops from the high ground, using the confusion being created by Miloradovich's column as an excuse. Even this effort to bridge the gap between the allied left and right wings came to nothing. A staff officer in the Emperor's suite saw Kollowrath's regiments apparently dawdling on the plateau and Alexander himself galloped up to Kutuzov: an exchange then took place between the young Emperor, attending his first battle, and the veteran general which was both ridiculously tragic and which epitomized the stark differences between them.

'Mikhail Illarionovich!' exclaimed Alexander. 'Why are you not proceeding further?'

'I am waiting, Sire, until the columns are ready.'

87

'Come now, Mikhail Illarionovich – we aren't on the parade ground where a march past does not begin until all the troops are assembled.'

'Precisely, Sire. It is because we are not on parade that I am waiting. But if you order me to go forward. . . .'

Alexander ordered. Kutuzov bowed in his saddle and the movement to the south continued, and the mist drew back to reveal the assembled French regiments massed in the centre. Soult shouted the command to advance. Two hundred drums suddenly began to beat and the 20,000 French troops started to sway forward, slowly at first because they were so crammed together; before them stretched the empty slope to the Pratzen plateau. At the same time Davout's corps thrust against the allies attempting to move from Telnitz and Sokolnitz on the French left, and far to the north Bagration was battering without success against Lannes's division.

The French streamed up the Pratzen in the centre. Kutuzov, Kollowrath and Miloradovich frantically attempted to turn the columns and regain the heights which had been so uselessly thrown away. But the effort was far too late. Charge after charge up the slopes only left fresh waves of Russian and Austrian dead and wounded. Kutuzov himself narrowly escaped: a bullet scoured across his cheek, ripping open the skin almost to the bone, and he dabbed at the blood with a silk handkerchief while he roared his commands for the continued assault. Moments later his son-in-law Count Tizengauzen toppled dead from his saddle.

Confusion spread rapidly amidst the allied army. Regiments blundered into one another totally bewildered; Russian and Austrian troops opened fire at one another by mistake; each nationality blamed its ally for the disaster now settling over the army. The soldiers began to mill in panic, exposed to the concentrated fire of the French guns, and one by one the confused and frightened regiments began to retreat.

'There was an outcry for the Czar's safety,' wrote Foreign Minister Czartoryski. 'The horses were turned and we galloped off. . . . A large battery of Russian guns, with its commander totally distraught, was being led in the opposite direction from the field of battle. I forced him to turn back and assist the columns hard-pressed in front of us.' Czartoryski remembered seeing 'the wretched Weirother wandering from place to place bravely risking his life in an effort to redeem the disaster of which he was one of the chief causes'.

At least the counter-offensive against Soult's corps on the plateau delayed a full French breakthrough in the centre of the allied line; troops from Kollowrath's and Miloradovich's column continued to launch fanatical charges through the swirling black smoke. Mikhail Miloradovich confirmed his existing reputation of being 'unsurpassed in bravery' whose 'calm indifference to danger was immense and so astounding that one hesitated to believe one's eyes and ears'; he fought in a frenzy as he led his men onwards, his face blackened by powder, a succession of horses shot from beneath him, his voice hoarse from yelling above the sound of the guns.

Kutuzov struggled to reorganize the battered allied regiments and to withdraw part of the army in good order. He sent messengers galloping through the smoke towards Bagration, ordering him to pull the allied right wing back so that contact could be regained with the centre. Bagration acted with his usual efficient courage, and his men responded to his leadership; back they went in squares, step by step, fending off the French until they reached the village of Bosenitz. There they made a temporary stand amidst the ruined houses before retiring again, this time towards the next hamlet of Krüg.

Contact had also to be established with the allied left, flung forward under Weirother's plan for the sweep behind the French and now badly mauled by Davout's counter-attack. Just before noon Kutuzov despatched orders to Buxhöwden, overall commander in this sector, instructing him to retire across the Goldbach. But either the messengers failed to fight a way through the French, or Buxhöwden refused to obey, and his wing became further isolated.

Constantine, Alexander's brother, launched an allied strike at about 12.30 in an attempt to reach Buxhöwden's trapped regiments. Neither Alexander nor Kutuzov had ordered such a hopeless attempt, but Constantine rode forward with supreme self-confidence: he once said: 'You've only got to wave your hat at the French and they flee.' He led the Russian reserve into the open and swept onwards before he could be stopped; his attack was among the bravest and most futile of the whole disastrous day. The French cut down the advancing troops, and although forced back by the impetus of the reserve cavalry, within an hour the position had been restored and over 500 dead marked the path of Constantine's charge.

'There are many fine ladies who will weep in Petersburg,' commented Napoleon. By now snow had started to fall; the winter's afternoon darkened, and the deteriorating weather and approaching night reduced still further the allied chances of organized retreat. The regiments in the centre and on the right were forced steadily back; Kutuzov could do nothing to save the allied left, bogged in the marshes beside the Goldbach. Buxhöwden's regiments were cut in two by the French under Dominique Vandamme; some, with Buxhöwden, managed to break through towards Austerlitz chateau but the rest, under Dokhturov, were trapped beneath concentrated artillery fire. Many soldiers drowned when cannon balls scorched into the ice on the ponds which they were attempting to cross. Only a shattered remnant managed to crawl into the hills to the south-east.

By 4.30 the battle was over. Daylight had gone, wiping away the scenes of slaughter. Sleet whipped the wounded and the retreating survivors; a cold wind shook the icy reeds by the Goldbach, carrying with it the screams of the dying and the cheers of the French as they clustered round their Emperor.

'I have defeated the Russian and Austrian army commanded by the two Emperors,' wrote Napoleon to Josephine. 'I am a little tired. I have been camping for eight days in the open air by fairly cool nights. I shall rest tomorrow at the [Austerlitz] chateau. . . . The Russian army is not only beaten, but destroyed.'

Kutuzov reached the hamlet of Wazan during the early evening, south-east of Austerlitz. The Russians and Austrians camped near by in appalling conditions, and survivors continued to stagger to the miserable smoking fires during the night. Surgeons worked as best they could in the sleet slurries, preparing the wounded for the retreat. The most fortunate soldiers managed to obtain kasha gruel and vodka, their first food of the day, but most had to go without and lay with their dripping greatcoats drawn over their heads. Alexander reached the village of Hodjegitz, six kilometres away, at about five o'clock, but French patrols combined with bad weather and the strange terrain prevented messages from Kutuzov or Alexander reaching the other; the Emperor, with only a small escort, left again during the evening in an attempt to reach the Emperor Francis at Czeitsch, twelve kilometres to the south. He was unable to make the full journey and had to spend the remainder of the night in a village on the way, shivering violently with the cold, a fierce pain in his stomach, and his body constantly convulsed with sobs.

Kutuzov moved out early next morning, 3 December, leading the regiments towards the Morava. He rode into Czeitsch before noon, where he met Francis and Alexander. The latter still seemed determined to fight, but Francis considered the position hopeless and Austrian emissaries were sent to Napoleon's camp. Next day, 4 December, hostilities ended between Austria and France and it was agreed that the armistice conditions should apply to the Russians whilst they marched for the frontier. The campaign was over.[13] The allies lost up to 30,000 men killed, wounded or captured at Austerlitz, out of a total of about 95,000; French casualties totalled between seven and ten thousand. Napoleon's victory represented a superb tactical achievement, displaying acute perception and timing.

Yet the situation might have been far different if Kutuzov's policy had been adopted. Napoleon would have been faced with an extremely dangerous dilemma. To follow the allies would have led him further from his bases, along a route which the Russians and Austrians had already exhausted of supplies; allied strength was likely to grow while Napoleon's dwindled. Yet if Napoleon himself had chosen to match an allied withdrawal by one of his own, his position would still have been precarious. So confident was he of victorious battle that he had not provided for any line of retreat except south towards Vienna or Znaim, a direction open to an allied flanking movement.

'Napoleon staked all for all,' wrote the French military historian Colonel Colin. His audacity succeeded, but only because Kutuzov was ignored.[14] 'I was young and inexperienced,' said Alexander later. 'He should have advised me.' Kutuzov tried but his Emperor refused to listen, and Alexander's knowledge of his own inadequacy would make him hate Kutuzov for the rest of his life.

VII

Into the Shadows

(December 1805–24 June 1812)

News of Austerlitz shook Europe. In London the Ministers and newspapers reacted with disbelief. 'Until the Hamburg Mails arrive,' declared *The Times* later in December, 'it would be idle to observe upon the French account of the battle of the 2nd. If the extent of their successes have equalled their official representations, the war is finished. . . . But we cannot believe that they have obtained so easy a triumph over the hardy Russians.'[1] Details of the battle only reached St Petersburg on 18 December; the citizens of Alexander's capital believed that Austerlitz must have been lost through 'the infamous conduct of the Austrians'.[2] Alexander attempted to slip quietly into the city on 21 December, unable to face the humiliation of his return, but he found himself awaited and apparently forgiven. Crowds packed the square before the Winter Palace and lined the route to the Cathedral when the weeping Emperor went to worship. 'They prostrated themselves,' wrote one eye-witness, 'seeking to kiss his feet and hands, even his uniform; and they were delirious with joy.'[3]

This reception persuaded Alexander for a while that he, after all, should not be burdened with blame for Austerlitz: others must be held responsible and chief among them should be the army commander. Kutuzov accompanied the army back over the border into Russian territory, his troops dragging their way along the winter roads. Sick and wounded were trundled in the wooden carts, many of them dying before they reached the Fatherland. Kutuzov's esteem among the troops themselves remained high: they too blamed the Austrians although the more perceptive among them began to criticize the Czar. Once over the frontier,

92

with the regiments placed in winter camps, Kutuzov headed north for St Petersburg; he remained the commander of the Russian forces and awaited fresh orders: the armistice with France ended with the evacuation of the Russian army from Austrian soil, and the two nations were therefore once more at war.

But for the moment Russia would only have Britain as an ally. On 15 December envoys from Berlin signed a treaty with the French at Schönbrunn, and the Treaty of Pressburg between France and Austria on the 26th resulted in the complete withdrawal of Austria from the war. Emperor Francis surrendered territory in Germany and Italy; Napoleon gained virtual domination over western and southern Germany.

The atmosphere at court had begun to sour by the time Kutuzov reached St Petersburg. Kutuzov, invited to numerous dinners and receptions, refused to enter into argument; he kept his counsel as always, replying with courteous evasiveness when asked for his opinion. Yet even the wound on his cheek, still livid from the frosty winds during the retreat, seemed evidence of his bravery and even his silence seemed to condemn the Emperor.[4] Alexander acted cautiously. Unsure of his position he avoided any attempts at naming scapegoats. His conduct of affairs continued weak and fumbling in 1806, with drawn-out inconclusive meetings.

'We are afraid of everything,' complained Czartoryski. 'We can no longer take vigorous steps. It is not even possible to advise him because he will not take advice. The Emperor still prefers to keep us in order to avoid the embarrassment of making a change, but he would like to act only according to his own fancy. . . . Such accumulation of weakness, uncertainty, fear, injustice and extravagant gestures fills one only with gloom and despair.'[5]

Kutuzov remained untouched by Alexander, for the moment, but the Emperor declined to offer him worth-while employment. Instead Kutuzov was expected to attend parades and ceremonies, as befitted his position, all of which he disliked. The Emperor wanted merely to put him on show. The atmosphere at court became increasingly unpleasant, especially after the appointment of Arakcheev as War Minister during 1806. Alexander's former tutor proceeded to bully his way into further power, compensating for his lack of military knowledge through his brash, no-nonsense manner; he became widely feared, with his bellowing voice, scowling brows and ugly close-cropped head. Kutuzov sought active duties but his requests were ignored, and instead he spent most of his time at such places as the English Club gossiping with colleagues. Friends urged him to resign but he refused, saying he could still perform valuable service for Russia.[6]

Meanwhile Napoleon proceeded to make use of the power and prestige gained through Austerlitz and the Treaty of Pressburg. He treated Frederick William of Prussia with contempt, sending increasingly excessive demands to Berlin; Prussia was obliged to acquiesce to the Treaty of Paris, 15 February. Napoleon then established the Confederation of the Rhine, and the number of troops close to the Prussian border gradually increased. At last Frederick William summoned sufficient courage to order full Prussian mobilization and to demand that French troops should be withdrawn from the frontiers. Napoleon scorned the ultimatum and war between the two countries began on 14 September 1806. Alexander of Russia had so far refused to become directly involved. Yet the prospect of renewed fighting between Russian and French troops loomed larger and in late summer 1806 the Emperor began to make plans for the assembly of a 60,000-man army in Lithuania. Chief among his problems was the choice of commander.

Kutuzov, waiting for such an opportunity and with unrivalled experience, would normally have been the obvious choice. Alexander refused to consider him. Bagration, a friend of Kutuzov and closely involved in the events of Austerlitz, was also passed over. Instead Alexander selected the aged Marshal Kamensky, riddled with ailments and now in virtual retirement; under him would serve Count Levin Bennigsen, the Hanoverian soldier of fortune who had led the group of assassins in the murder of Alexander's father. Kutuzov was shuffled out of the way: in early October Alexander ordered him to leave Petersburg and to take up appointment as Military-Governor of Kiev. The post was considered respectable, but it nevertheless amounted to renewed exile.[7]

Napoleon launched the most spectacular campaign of his career. After one month spent outmanoeuvring the Prussians he inflicted devastating defeat on the main Prussian armies: Napoleon himself led his forces against the enemy at Jena, while Davout attacked the Second Prussian army at Auerstedt on the same day, 14 October. By nightfall Frederick William's shattered forces were streaming northwards; the French seized Berlin ten days later.

Marshal Kamensky failed to summon sufficient energy to leave St Petersburg until 22 November, forty-eight hours before the last sizeable Prussian force under Blücher was obliged to surrender near Lübeck. At the same time French troops thrust into Poland, entering Warsaw on 27 November, after which Napoleon moved east with 80,000 men to the line of the Vistula. Facing him at Pultusk were about 90,000 Russian troops and Prussian fragments under Bennigsen. Kamensky arrived at the army headquarters, but left after one week and retired ill to Petersburg leaving Bennigsen in command.

Kutuzov, isolated at Kiev, anxiously sought all possible news. Meanwhile he attempted to fulfil his duties in this pleasant southern city, once ruled by the Moslem Tartars but holding a special religious reverence to many Russians and known as 'the Jerusalem of Russia'. Kutuzov, always religious, became more so during his short stay at Kiev, sharing the view of many Russians that there existed a spiritual power more permanent than the temporal authority which ruled their daily lives.[8] The Military-Governor created an excellent impression in other respects: he attempted to introduce a better police system, established fire-parties, and interested himself generally in the city's welfare.[9] But all the time Kutuzov awaited news of the struggle far to the north.

First reports seemed excellent. Bennigsen escaped a French assault on his advance posts at Pultusk on 26 December and informed St Petersburg that he had defeated 60,000 troops under Napoleon himself. In fact Napoleon was about sixty kilometres away at the time, and the French force involved totalled no more than 20,000 men, outnumbered by the Russians about three to one. Moreover, despite his 'success' Bennigsen felt obliged to abandon Pultusk and retreat northwards. Bennigsen attempted an offensive in mid-January 1807 but soon revealed he lacked Kutuzov's manoeuvring skill. The weather was deplorable; both armies fumbled for one another across the marshy, desolate countryside around Preussich-Eylau. French and Russian troops clashed on 8 February amidst a swirling snowstorm; Napoleon had less than 50,000 men against nearly 70,000 Russians. The latter staved off an initial French assault, but then Davout's corps arrived to support Napoleon and the enemy thrust forward again. In turn the Russians were bolstered by the arrival of a Prussian corps, 10,000 men, and neither side could gain a decisive advantage. Casualties were heavy – Russian and Prussian losses totalled 25,000 and the French 18,000 – and the battle provided an example of senseless slaughter. Bennigsen would never have been able to reap rewards of victory at that time of the year, and now his army had been severely weakened. The butchery even appalled Napoleon, who declared after visiting the battlefield: 'Such a sight as this should inspire rulers with love of peace and hatred of war.'[10] The battle underlined the basic difference between Bennigsen and Kutuzov which would emerge amidst so much hostility in 1812. Moreover, Eylau was technically a French victory since Napoleon was left in possession of the field of battle and Bennigsen was obliged to withdraw to winter quarters at Königsberg.

Kutuzov received a new appointment in early spring. Thirty-one years earlier he had served for a short while under Alexander Prozorovski, then commander of Russian forces moving south to the Crimea under the overall charge of Rumyantsev; Prozorovski had soon fallen ill and Suvorov had assumed virtual control. Now, in 1807, Prince Prozorovski was commander of the Danube Army with the rank of Marshal. He had been considered as a possible leader of the Russian forces in Poland, but Kamensky had been chosen since Prozorovski was even older and more infirm: his eyes were so bad that on one occasion he failed to recognize the Czar when he stood in front of him.

The Prince remembered Kutuzov's service under him in 1776, and now sought Alexander's approval for the general to come to his headquarters as his assistant: 'He is almost my pupil and he knows my method.' The Marshal also wrote to the War Minister: 'I can testify to my complete satisfaction that he knows the duties of a general and I find in him only one defect: he is not always very firm in his character and especially in connection with court affairs. Moreover he is by nature lazy about putting pen to paper. But as far as military affairs are concerned I am entirely satisfied with him and he would really be a great help to me. I consider him to be one of the best generals of the Emperor.'[11]

Alexander approved and Kutuzov started his new service. Immediately after Austerlitz the Turks had displayed renewed belligerence and war had been declared on 6 November 1806. Desultory land operations began in spring 1807, likely to mushroom into larger conflict at any moment. Russia had therefore to face enemies on two fronts. In Poland Napoleon laid seige to

Danzig on 15 March 1807 and the city fell on 27 April; also in April Alexander arrived in Memel as guest of Frederick William of Prussia and his Queen. The Emperor soon believed with renewed fervour that Russian and Prussian fortunes were intertwined; all possible Russian strength must be deployed on the Polish front against the French, at the expense of forces in the Danube for the war against the Turks.

Conversely, Napoleon attempted to provide all assistance to Russia's southern enemy; in the meantime he prepared to deal with the Russians closer at hand. Bennigsen resumed the offensive on 5 June. Five days later Napoleon repulsed the Russians and Prussians at Heilsburg, and Bennigsen retreated north. On 14 June the two armies met at Friedland and by eight o'clock in the evening the Russians and Prussians were in full retreat after the left flank had been driven in, leaving 25,000 dead and wounded. Napoleon occupied Tilsit on 19 June. Alexander sent a peace emissary, and a temporary armistice was concluded on 21 June. This was followed by the theatrical meeting between the two Emperors on a raft in the middle of the Niemen river, beginning 25 June. Napoleon and Alexander walked and talked with one another during the next seven days, with Frederick William hovering nearby, and the conversations seemed to be a spectacular success.

'In one hour,' exclaimed Napoleon to Alexander, 'we shall achieve more than our spokesmen in several days.' 'Why didn't I meet him before?' cried Alexander to a French diplomat, adding: 'The veil is rent and the time of error is past.' Frederick William continued to receive repeated snubs, with the Russian Emperor completely forgetting the close relationship which he had so recently enjoyed. 'A nasty king, a nasty nation, a nasty army,' confided Napoleon to Alexander.

Alexander committed his country to Napoleon's Continental System, halting all trade with England; Russia would wage war against the Swedes, if necessary, to enforce the System on that country. He concurred in the establishment of the Grand Duchy of Warsaw, comprising the Polish area previously ruled by Prussia. 'God has saved us,' he wrote to his sister Catherine. 'Instead of having to make sacrifices, we have emerged almost gloriously from the struggle. But what do you think of all these events? Just imagine my spending days with Bonaparte, talking for hours

97

quite alone with him! I ask you, does not all this seem like a dream?'[12]

A dream it was. Awakening would soon follow, but meanwhile Alexander drove back to Petersburg, exuberant, and with the scarlet ribbon of the Legion of Honour dangling like a noose from his neck. One result of the Franco-Russian friendship was immediately noticeable to Kutuzov: French assistance to the Turks ended, and an armistice began in August. Kutuzov and his aged commander moved to a peacetime garrison role, spending their time travelling from one base to another – Khotin, Tulchin and Kutuzov's old place of residence at Poltava. Kutuzov's wife moved down to join him.

The routine became extremely boring. Moreover, relations between Prozorovski and his second-in-command deteriorated; the Prince was increasingly senile, unpredictable and completely unfit for army responsibility. Kutuzov found himself having to carry a heavier burden; in turn Prozorovski grumbled that his subordinate was trying to usurp authority.[13] This unsatisfactory situation continued for almost two years. Meanwhile Napoleon attempted to obtain the benefits of his new friendship with Alexander. The latter responded enthusiastically to the French Emperor's suggestion of a joint operation into Asia, threatening the British in India; in March 1808 Alexander sent 24,000 troops under Buxhöwden into Sweden to fulfil another part of his Tilsit agreement, and fighting in this area continued until May. Yet by now the Russo–Franco friendship had begun to cool. The war against the Swedes had never been fully supported by the Russians as a whole; merchants complained about the disruption of trade – and these businessmen were already suffering strongly from the Continental System.

Alexander, aware of the growing feelings against France, therefore adopted a different attitude when he met Napoleon at Erfurt for eighteen days of talks beginning 27 September. Nothing was decided on Napoleon's proposed joint invasion of the Ottoman Empire, and the French Emperor told Talleyrand: 'I can make no headway with him.' For his part Alexander confided to his sister Catherine: 'Napoleon thinks I am no better than a fool, but he who laughs last laughs longest.'[14]

Once again the Napoleon–Alexander situation affected Kutuzov, still with the Danube Army. Hostilities with the Turks intensified almost immediately, although restricted to comparatively small clashes. Renewed activity aggravated the unsatisfactory relationship between Kutuzov and his decrepit commander: decisions had to be taken, and when Kutuzov acted on his own initiative he was condemned by Prozorovski as attempting to seize the army command. The old man became mentally unstable. He burst into hysterical tears after a setback to Russian troops in November, falling on his knees and tearing out tufts of his hair; Kutuzov tried to console him by saying: 'I lost the battle of Austerlitz which decided the fate of Europe, but I didn't cry.'[15] Prozorovski refused to be comforted and during the winter of 1808–09 he began to pester Petersburg with demands that Kutuzov should be dismissed. His allegations against his second-in-command grew increasingly nonsensical.

Alexander, with no desire to bring Kutuzov closer to home, responded on 16 June 1809 with a suggestion that Prozorovski's 'assistant' should be appointed commander of the reserve corps in the Danube Army. Prozorovski immediately protested that if Kutuzov were allowed to control the reserves he would have 'a wide field for all his intrigues against me. . . . More than this, since he is sly and knows the service, he could allow the enemy to burn the [Russian] magazines and in some way he could give the Turks means for this but lay the blame on the general who was at the post, who would suffer for it, but he himself would always be right.' Even Alexander found it impossible to believe such rambling, fantastic charges against Kutuzov. Nevertheless Prozorovski remained in command and Kutuzov received orders to depart from the Danube Army: he would still be prevented from serving near home, and instead was instructed to travel to Vilna in Lithuania to act as Military-Governor of this Russian Poland province. Kutuzov therefore returned to virtually the same post which he had held in 1799, ten years before; his military career had stagnated.[16]

Kutuzov arrived with his wife in Vilna on 15 July 1809. Despite his frustration he enjoyed his return to this Polish centre. Vilna formed an attractive change from the arid towns in which he had spent the last two years, with its tall, sturdy houses, elegant town hall overlooking the central square, the castle with the university buildings jostling in the old quarter immediately opposite. The countryside offered good hunting, and the social life promised good food, wine and stimulating conversation – all of which Kutuzov remembered from his previous service in the town and which he had missed during his incarceration with Prozorovski. Kutuzov had retained his liking for the Poles and for their country.

'The Lithuanians,' wrote one traveller, 'are robust, of medium height, brave, have a fairly military turn of mind, are great eaters and drinkers. . . .'[17] Vilna was far better informed about news from elsewhere, both in Russia and in Europe as a whole. Russian society had become split into pro- and anti-French parties; the former, grouped around the French Ambassador Armand de Caulaincourt, included a number of old generals and also Count Nikolai Rumyantsev, son of the soldier, and now the Foreign Minister. But Alexander himself veered further away from the French Alliance. Already, in January, the Emperor had indicated that he intended to cultivate his old friendship with Frederick William. The Prussian monarch and his Queen visited Petersburg, and Caulaincourt found himself shunned after he had sneered at a reception: 'There is no mystery about the visit – the Prussian Queen has come to fornicate with Czar Alexander.'[18] At the same time the Austrians once more turned towards conflict, encouraged by French preoccupation in the Peninsula. Archduke Charles invaded Bavaria on 9 April, marching on Ratisbon, and Archduke John crossed the Julian Alps to invade Italy. News of the final stages of this momentous campaign reached Kutuzov soon after his arrival at Vilna – Napoleon was forced to withdraw from the battle of Aspern-Essling on 22 April, but inflicted defeat at Wagram on 5–6 June. The Austrians signed the treaty of Schönbrunn in October which reaffirmed Napoleon's pre-eminence in Western Europe.

Far to the south, British troops under Sir Arthur Wellesley had fought a drawn battle with the French at Talavera in July, after which they had withdrawn into Portugal. Only Russia seemed a significant continental rival to France, and Napoleon began to fix his attention in her direction. At first it seemed a new Franco–Russian alliance might be brought about, this time through wedlock. The dinner parties and receptions at Vilna were provided with a new topic of conversation: the rumour of marriage between Napoleon and the 14-year-old Anna Pavlovna, Alexander's youngest sister. The Russian Emperor first received this suggestion via Caulaincourt on 28 December, but Alexander prevaricated; Napoleon's divorce was already completed, and he turned elsewhere, offering his hand to Marie-Louise, 17-year-old daughter of the Emperor of Austria.[19]

Added to personal reasons for a rapidly cooling relationship were international affairs on a wider level, some of which threatened to involve Kutuzov at Vilna. Alexander remained determined that an independent Poland should never be revived – hence his agreement at Tilsit to the name of the Grand Duchy of Warsaw for the small surviving Polish state. But reports reached Kutuzov that Polish patriots were increasingly looking to Napoleon to restore their independence – and Napoleon apparently received their petitions with favour. The Grand Duchy was enlarged at the Peace of Schönbrunn, taking in former Austrian territory in eastern Galicia, and the French began publicly to refer to the Grand Duchy of Warsaw as 'the Duchy of Poland'. Patriots in this territory became self-confident, and Alexander's fears arose that this might affect the situation in the eight Polish provinces still within the Russian Empire, of which Lithuania was the most important.[20]

Another major source of disagreement existed, the most important of all as far as Napoleon was concerned. Alexander had found that his support of the Continental System was intensely unpopular with Russian merchants who depended on English trade. Russia experienced a drain of capital abroad to pay for imported goods, because Russia herself was barred by Napoleon's system from exporting her own products. Increasing numbers of neutral ships therefore slipped into Alexander's Baltic ports to continue the clandestine trade with France's enemy. Napoleon, who declared 'the Continental System is an absurdity without Russia', issued vociferous protests. Alexander responded with a defiant decree on the last day of 1810: this imposed heavy duties on goods coming into Russia by overland routes, referring especially to luxury French items such as wines and silks, and allowed almost complete freedom to Russian exports. In effect sea trade was resumed between Russia and England.

Collision with France was further precipitated over the Duchy of Oldenburg. This territory covered about 2,000 square miles on the western edge of the Weser Estuary; strong family connections had long existed between the rulers of the Duchy and the Russian court, and in 1809 Alexander's sister Catherine had married her second cousin George, one of the Holstein-Oldenburg princes. In late 1810 rumours reached Petersburg that Napoleon had merged all the North German coast into France and was proposing to annex Oldenburg. Napoleon took this audacious step in January 1811, and his offer of the much smaller principality of Erfurt to Duke Peter of Oldenburg seemed almost an insult.[21]

By early spring 1811 Alexander was seriously considering an invasion into Germany. Forces in western Russia were steadily increased, and Kutuzov would be ideally placed in the centre of this activity. Less than 80 kilometres west from Vilna ran the river Niemen, border between Russian territory and Prussia; on frequent occasions during January and February 1811 Kutuzov reviewed regiments as they passed through the narrow Vilna streets, marching to take up position near the frontier. Many of the regiments had been summoned north from the Danube Army, lately commanded by General Kamensky after Prozorovski's long-delayed retirement, and the officers were well known to Kutuzov from his service in that area; he dined them at his house and listened to their eager anticipation of war against Napoleon; many expressed fervent hopes that soon Kutuzov would lead them.

Disappointment arrived in March. A messenger from Petersburg brought Kutuzov fresh orders from the Czar: he must proceed south and assume command of the depleted Danube Army against the Turks; he left Vilna on 24 March, once more pushed into the shadows.[22] His instructions specified that the protracted war against the Turks should be brought to an early conclusion: Russia must free herself from this commitment in order to concentrate against France. Kutuzov acknowledged his order in a message to Barclay de Tolly, now War Minister. 'The trust of the Emperor in such an important appointment includes in it everything that would flatter the proudest of men . . . and I hope my spirit will be sufficiently matched by my bodily strength.'[23]

Kutuzov was in his sixty-sixth year. His rheumatism had increased and his head wound still troubled him. For the past two years his life had been isolated from the activities of an army in the field. The war against Turkey had been simmering for over four years and successive Russian commanders had proved unable to bring the conflict to a decisive end, despite Kamensky's capture of the fortress of Silistria in spring 1810, and despite the eventual employment of nearly 90,000 troops. Kutuzov would only have 46,000 widely dispersed soldiers at his disposal – Prozorovski had insisted that at least 150,000 would be required for a conclusive victory – and in April the enemy strength totalled over 60,000 concentrated around Shumla. Yet Kutuzov succeeded in his task within a year, in a campaign which underlined all his cunning, his manoeuvring ability and his perception in being able to judge exactly when and when not to fight a battle. In many ways the Turkish campaign in 1811 provided a foretaste of Kutuzov's methods against the French the following year.

The Russian forces lay stretched along the Danube south of Bucharest. Immediately after his arrival Kutuzov drew in these isolated garrisons, even if this meant abandoning important fortifications such as Silistria and Nikopoli. He concentrated his outnumbered army in the centre, on the Danube at Rustchuk about seventy kilometres due south of Bucharest, and waited for the enemy to move against him.

'Perhaps I shall succeed in drawing the enemy into battle on the plains,' wrote Kutuzov to Alexander. The Turks responded in August, when the enemy commander, Grand Vizier Ahmet Bey, marched confidently north from Shumla and approached the Danube in full strength. Battle began almost immediately. The Russian regiments stood firm with their backs to the river, repulsing repeated infantry and cavalry charges; Kutuzov ordered the counter-attack and the Turks began to give ground. The Russian commander maintained maximum pressure until the Grand Vizier's forces had been pushed into the hills south of Rustchuk, where the Turks threw themselves into defensive positions. Many commanders would have reorganized their victorious regiments and then attempted another assault: Kutuzov acted in opposite fashion. His strategy was based on his knowledge of the Russian troops, and especially their discipline in close formation when facing terrible enemy attacks: this superior training would, believed Kutuzov, counter-balance inferiority of numbers. But the advantage would only be effective on ground which the Russians themselves had chosen, preferably out in the open where the regiments could form to best effect: a dispersed assault against enemy forces entrenched in the hills would allow the Turks to overwhelm the separated Russian columns. Kutuzov therefore withdrew, back over the Danube.

News of this unexpected retirement was greeted with startled delight in Constantinople, where the Sultan immediately announced a great victory, and with anger in Petersburg. Alexander despatched an urgent message demanding to know whether the rumours of withdrawal could possibly be correct. Kutuzov sent a stubborn reply in the last days of August: 'I had firmly decided to retire from Rustchuk immediately after we had gained the victory over the Grand Vizier. This could only be done after a successful battle, or it would have been a forced move. . . . Thus, in spite of the slight loss which the retreat from Rustchuk might cause me personally, and always preferring to serve the interests of my Sire, I crossed to the left bank of the Danube.'

Kutuzov explained his reasons to his officers: he wanted an end to the war, not a repetition of the see-saw campaigns which had previously been experienced. Battle must be decisive. 'If we pursue the Turks, we shall probably reach Shumla, but what shall we do after that? We shall probably have to return, as was the case last year, and the Grand Vizier will proclaim himself the victor. Far better to encourage my friend Ahmet Bey, and he will fall into our hands again.'[24]

The Russian commander waited; he built up his strength as far as possible, deploying his regiments just north of the Danube in the vicinity of Bucharest, ready to move at minimum notice. He continued his policy of establishing close relations with his troops so that they would respond to his leadership to maximum effect. One of his officers wrote that although the summer had been very hot 'we have very few sick soldiers. The reasons for this good fortune must be that the troops have good provisions, very careful supervision, and mainly because they haven't been made weary. . . . Thanks to these cares the army has passed a very happy summer in Wallachia. Aware of Kutuzov's concern, it has become the more strongly attached to him.' As the weather grew colder, Kutuzov even found time to design a special cloth vest for his troops.[25] Meanwhile he instructed his men on the correct attitude in war. Courage could be shown in more ways than merely throwing oneself at the enemy. 'It is not hard to receive wounds,' said Kutuzov, pointing to his battered face. 'In service the main thing is to fulfil one's duty. The man who rushes into danger on a whim is not really brave.'[26]

Ahmet Bey advanced over-confidently with 70,000 men in the second half of September. Kutuzov remained in his headquarters appearing to take no interest as a succession of messengers arrived with reports of the latest enemy movements. The Turkish army began to cross the Danube. Kutuzov suddenly acted, when Turkish forces were split with 50,000 men across the river and 20,000 men still on the south bank; orders for a rapid Russian attack were issued. General Markov, a veteran of Turkish fighting under Suvorov, moved westwards with 5,000 infantry and 2,500 cavalry and Cossacks to secure a passage over the Danube upriver from the Turks; this was accomplished during darkness and the bulk of Kutuzov's remaining regiments followed, curving round behind the splintered Turkish army.

Ahmet Bey found himself surrounded. His own guns, captured on the south bank, were turned against him. Kutuzov had obtained a position of overwhelming superiority with vastly inferior numbers and with the loss of barely 400 men; immediately he switched once more from sudden action to seemingly inexhaustible patience. With insufficient troops to storm the enemy lines, he settled down to await Turkish surrender, even allowing Ahmet Bey to escape with a handful of men – Kutuzov knew that under Turkish military tradition a commander would never capitulate on the field of battle.[27]

Kutuzov waited throughout the winter. Much to Alexander's displeasure he ordered food to be supplied to the trapped Turks: the Emperor despatched repeated demands for Kutuzov to hasten the end by attacking, but the army commander considered that such an assualt would merely be a useless sacrifice of men, and the siege continued. Alexander became increasingly incensed with the stubborn Kutuzov; in early spring 1812 he listened willingly to Admiral Pavel Chichagov, one of his favourite advisers, who accused Kutuzov of dallying, 'whoring in Bucharest', and despite the Admiral's lack of soldiering experience the Emperor gave him the title of 'Commander-in-Chief Moldavia, Wallachia and the Black Sea Fleet', instructing him to supersede Kutuzov in the war against the Turks.

Unknown to Alexander peace talks had already begun.

Kutuzov reached a preliminary settlement with the enemy just twenty-four hours before Chichagov's unwelcome arrival.[28] Even the Treaty of Bucharest, eventually signed on 16 May, failed to please Alexander, and indeed the diplomatic terms seemed a disappointing return for Russia's military success: the Turks agreed to Russian control over Bessarabia, but Moldavia and Wallachia remained under Turkish authority although with the territory having limited autonomy. Alexander complained that the Turks should have been persuaded to help the Russians against the French in Dalmatia, even though such an agreement was always highly unlikely. Kutuzov was more concerned with freeing Russian forces in the Danube for employment against the French in the north.[29] Chichagov stayed to command the Danube Army; Kutuzov was to be retired. Once again his military service with the Fatherland seemed ended.

In early June Kutuzov reached his estate at Goroshki. He spent a number of days resting from the exertions of the Turkish campaign, looked after by his favourite daughter Ekaterina, Princess Kudashev, who came to stay with her children. He apparently enjoyed having youngsters around him, and his house at Goroshki during these first weeks of June was filled with a wide variety of people – the children, their parents, and adults holding long, intense discussions in the drawing room. 'I always loved to philosophize,' Kutuzov told Ekaterina, 'but now more than ever.'[30]

But dramatic reports began to arrive from Petersburg. Relations with France had deteriorated still further during the previous months, with war drawing steadily closer. Alexander had left to inspect his border fortresses early in the New Year, and the spring weather resulted in additional regiments marching into Russian Poland: by March as many as three regiments were tramping each week through the Petersburg streets. Alexander himself departed from the capital for Vilna on 21 April; Napoleon left St Cloud on 9 May, reaching Dresden on the 15th and Danzig on the 29th.

'A single blow,' declared Napoleon, 'delivered at the heart of the Russian Empire, at Moscow the Great, at Moscow the Holy, will instantly put this whole blind, apathetic mass at my mercy. I know Alexander. I once had influence over him, and it will return.'[31]

For his part, Alexander seemed to be revelling in his life with the troops on the Lithuanian border. He wrote to Catherine on 9 June: 'I scribble these lines to you having snatched forty winks after returning from a round of 60 miles, twenty of them on horseback, setting out at five in the morning. . . . Despite that, I feel fresh and am going to saddle my horse again for another reconnaissance.'[32]

Vilna had never seen such activity. The streets were jammed with troops, carriages and guns. Houses had been turned into headquarter offices, sutler stores and weapon depots; troops were billeted in almost every home. Nobles flocked to the town from Petersburg and Moscow, bringing their wives to witness the excitement . . . the fortunate few received invitations to the grand ball organized for Alexander by General Bennigsen, the Emperor's favourite, to be held on the general's estate at Zakret. A long procession of carriages travelled the five kilometres to Zakret, east of Vilna, on the night of Wednesday, 24 June, with this date chosen by Bennigsen because there would be a full moon to illuminate his lawns and fountains to best advantage.

Dancing began on these lawns and the sound of the music drifted across the peaceful fields. Alexander delighted in the occasion, smartly dressed in the uniform of the Semeonovsky Guards, first dancing with the wives of Generals Barclay de Tolly and Bennigsen then honouring the Countess Tiesenhausen. She wrote her heady impressions: 'The whole mansion ornamented with orange trees in full bloom, scenting the air . . . the musicians of the Imperial Guard playing favourite passages of music in differing parts of the park . . . the splendid uniforms with their diamond decorations . . . old trees, massively green over the Vileka, which reflected in its winding course the colours of the setting sun.'[33]

Early in the evening the weather remained so gentle that the candles on the terraces scarcely flickered. Then, towards midnight, black clouds began to roll across the velvety sky. Drops of rain splattered on the pavings, and the guests moved into the house to sit for dinner. After the banquet Alexander retired to Bennigsen's study; amongst those invited to speak with him was Michael Oginski, a Polish politician who performed diplomatic duties for the Emperor. 'I noticed he was dreamy and preoccupied,' remembered Oginski. His account continued: 'Just as I was about to leave the Czar, he received a report from the outposts of the army and appeared to be upset by what he read. Looking out of the window and seeing a downpour with hailstones and a most violent thunderstorm, he turned to me and exclaimed: "My poor wretched soldiers who are now on the march!" ' Oginski added: 'That was how I first heard that the French had crossed the Niemen.'[34]

The French Grand Army, totalling nearly half a million men, was flooding into Russian territory; Napoleon himself was only about sixty kilometres from Vilna. The gigantic 1812 campaign had at last begun. Kutuzov remained many kilometres away, ageing, infirm and apparently forgotten.

VIII

Invasion

(1812: 23 June–23 August)

French advance troops had crossed the Niemen into Russian Poland during the night of 23 June, twenty-four hours before Bennigsen's ball. Engineers threw a pontoon and pile bridge across the river at Kovno, and early in the morning of the 24th the first full regiments marched to the eastern bank, watched by Napoleon. The French Emperor stood impatiently slapping his boot with his whip, humming a catchy French tune. By the evening of the 24th the leading regiments were well on their way towards Vilna. So far they had encountered minimum opposition: Cossacks were noticed in the distance, but these horsemen wheeled away to hurry their reports back to Alexander.

The enemy were invading in four uninterrupted streams, at Kovno, Yurburg, Olit and Merech. Panic broke out in Vilna at the news. 'The tumult, the noise and the anxiety were extreme,' wrote Major Baron Woldemar von Löwenstern, a staff officer at headquarters. 'All horses were commandeered in the streets. Disorder was at its height.'[1] Similar confusion covered Russian plans. Despite the long expectation of war and the time available to make full preparations, the Russian campaign policy had still to be decided, and the chaotic atmosphere at the Russian headquarters would continue with disastrous results. Alexander's forces were far more widely dispersed than those of Napoleon. The First West Army stretched on a front of almost 100 kilometres along the Niemen around Kovno, with the headquarters at Vilna and comprising about 127,000 men under War Minister Barclay de Tolly. Barclay's northern wing, under General Ludwig von Wittgenstein, was barring the road to Riga; the southern

109

wing, Dokhturov's 6th Corps combined with General Count Peter Pahlen's 3rd Cavalry Corps, maintained contact with the Second West Army based on Volkoyysk. The latter, under Bagration, consisted of about 60,000 men. The Third West Army, 45,000 men under General Alexander Tormassov, was being assembled south of the Pripet Marshes to guard against an advance by Prince Karl Schwarzenberg's Austrian Corps allied to Napoleon. Chichagov's Danube Army remained even further south.

The Russians could adopt one of three possible plans to meet Napoleon: they could lure the French deep into the Fatherland, meet the enemy as near to the frontier as possible, withdraw to suitable defensive positions some way from the border. There seems little doubt which Kutuzov would have chosen. His

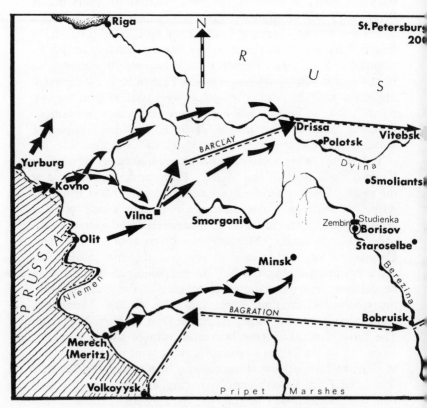

110

military activities were based on his understanding of the powers of manoeuvre, and the operation area presented excellent opportunities for such a campaign of movement: to the north lay gently rolling countryside with forests, lakes and some marshes; from Smolensk eastwards the ground lay flatter and more fertile. Numerous rivers crossed the east-west roads – the Niemen, Berezina, Dvina, the Moskva and the head waters of the Dnieper. Each provided rearguard positions similar to those used by Kutuzov in the Danube valley in 1805. Enemy communications back through Poland would be extended and extremely vulnerable; Russia's vast space could be used against the invader.

Emperor Alexander himself seemed to realize the opportunities offered by controlled withdrawal. The previous year he had told the departing French Ambassador, Caulaincourt: 'We have plenty

-**Russia's struggle**-

of open spaces in our rear, and we shall preserve a well-organized army. . . . I shall not be the first to draw my sword, but I shall be the last to sheath it.'[2] More recently Alexander had granted an interview at Vilna to Louis, Count de Narbonne, *aide-de-camp* to Napoleon, who reported the Czar as saying: 'Space is a barrier. If, after several defeats, I withdraw, sweeping the inhabitants along with me; if I let time, deserts, and climate defend Russia for me, then perhaps I shall have the last word.'[3] Napoleon himself apparently believed the Russians might attempt a withdrawal strategy. Although earlier he had said a 'single blow' would suffice, on 13 June he contradicted this statement by remarking: 'This war is not going to be a matter of a single campaign. I shall pursue the Russians as far as the Dvina and the Dnieper. I shall form a sort of bridgehead between these two rivers and behind them I shall establish 120,000 French troops.'[4]

But Alexander had to take political considerations into account. Withdrawal would have immense repercussions inside Russia; the reaction in Petersburg and Moscow might be catastrophic and the Emperor lacked sufficient courage to face the upheaval. Moreover, others urged different strategies and the indecisive Alexander listened with an over-receptive mind.

Chief among the Imperial advisers was the notorious General Ernst von Pfuehl, a Prussian-born soldier of dubious quality who had served as one of Frederick William's three chiefs of staff during the 1806 campaign when, after the defeat at Auerstedt, he had burst into hysterical, insane laughter. Carl von Clausewitz, the future Prussian military theorist and now serving with the Russians as a temporary staff officer to Pfuehl, commented: 'I never saw a man who lost his head so easily, or who, intent as he always was upon great things, was so often overwhelmed by the least intrusions of reality.'[5] Pfuehl believed the First West Army should withdraw to prepared defensive positions at Drissa, leading the French against this fortified area. Bagration's Second Army would then press forward on the right flank and rear of the enemy. But the plan posed a number of problems: the movement north-east towards Drissa from Vilna would create an even larger gap between the First and Second Russian armies through which Napoleon could strike, and no provision had been made for the concentration of other Russian forces or the possibility of further withdrawal. Clausewitz commented: 'I asked General

Pfuehl which line of retreat he contemplated, that upon Moscow or upon Petersburg? He replied: "It must depend on circumstances." [6]

Alexander favoured Pfuehl's plan. But he also listened to others. Bagration, always aggressive, sought to launch a counter-invasion with his Second Army, advancing up the Bug and the Vistula to Warsaw; Barclay de Tolly and others at the First Army headquarters insisted that either a battle should be fought as near to the frontier as possible or there should be disengagement in depth. Barclay was placed in a most unfortunate position. He still acted as War Minister besides being commander of the First Army; theoretically he held a superior position to Bagration, yet Alexander declined to provide him with the official title of commander-in-chief, and Alexander himself constantly interfered with Barclay's decision-making. Moreover the 51-year-old Barclay, born in Lithuania but from Scottish descent, lacked the character to deal with the multiple pressures placed upon him. His nickname was apt – *Boltai da i tolko*, 'all bark and no bite'.

'Everyone wanted to attract attention and make himself important,' wrote an eye-witness at the Russian headquarters. 'Suggestions and plans of campaign showered in from all sides, and Barclay needed all his equanimity not to lose his head amid all the new projects and the intrigues which were already on foot against him.' [7]

Barclay wavered; so did the Emperor, and in effect no definite plan existed by the time the French columns began to thrust into Russian Poland on 24 June. Alexander and his suite left Vilna at three o'clock in the morning, 25 June; the First Army headquarters quit the town in haste at one o'clock in the afternoon on the 28th; Napoleon entered later that Sunday evening. Alexander had already arrived at Drissa, Pfuehl's proposed site for Russian defensive positions, and it was frighteningly obvious that these entrenchments were ill-chosen, inadequate and unfinished – moreover, it seemed that the French would allow insufficient time for the Russian First Army to be fully deployed.

The unplanned retreat therefore began with all the consequent blunders and fumbling manoeuvres; Bagration displayed skill and customary courage in escaping French regiments under Davout and Jérôme, urged forward by Napoleon to trap the Russian Second Army, and after a month of desperate manoeuvring

Bagration's forces were united with those of Barclay at Smolensk on 2 August.

By now Kutuzov was in a far better position to be informed about latest events. In early July he received a deputation from Petersburg nobles inviting him to command the armed militia being raised in the Petersburg province; at first Kutuzov declined, but agreed after further persuasion from the nobles providing Alexander approved. The Emperor sent his permission, and Kutuzov stepped nearer to war, arriving in Petersburg towards the end of July. Alexander's letter of approval hinted at another advancement for the old general. 'I think it best that you should go to Petersburg, where await you rewards for all the noble services that you have performed for me and for the Fatherland.' Chief among these rewards was the title of Prince and Most Serene Highness, officially announced on 10 August after Alexander had returned to his capital. It seemed Kutuzov might be shifting further into favour.[8]

The new prince undertook militia affairs with renewed energy. He spent much time on recruiting business, on discussing details of the uniform, and on training. Kutuzov insisted that these irregulars should be as professional as time allowed. Nothing should be skimped: each militiaman had a musket, bag, knapsack, and by Kutuzov's personal demand an axe and shovel; each man had a cross on his hat with the Czar's initials and with the inscription 'For Faith and the Czar'. Training was simple: these volunteers had to know how 'to chop and to shoot'. Alexander expressed himself 'graciously pleased' with Kutuzov's efforts.[9]

An atmosphere of growing anxiety and bewilderment pervaded the Petersburg drawing-rooms: clearly the campaign was not proceeding to plan, which, the citizens believed, had merely consisted of inflicting defeat on Napoleon at the earliest moment. Instead, the Russian armies were being bundled backwards and displayed a complete lack of aggression. Rumours of defeat having been suffered by Bagration and Barclay increased almost daily, first circulated in whispers and then in the open; then came reports that the First and Second Armies were at last united and a battle would surely soon be fought. Kutuzov sat in his study late into the night, surrounded by documents relating to the enlistment and organization of the militia, and by plans and reports from the battlefront. In early August the new prince was asked to attend the Supreme State Council, moving even closer to the decision-making process and establishing more valuable contact with the conduct of the war.[10]

A battle at Smolensk appeared imminent, and for a while hopes ran high in Petersburg that this city would be the furthest the French would reach. Conditions for troops on both sides had deteriorated with savage suddenness. At first the French soldiers sang as they marched, with men of various nationalities adding their contributions; soon they trudged in silence. The countryside lay brooding and hostile around them; the weather remained hot during the day, but often became bitterly cold at night.

'Of all the unpleasant things we had to endure,' wrote a young officer in Napoleon's army, Lieutenant Karl von Suckow, 'one of the most unbearable was the thick dust which enveloped us on the march. . . . I recall that at one stage, so as to prevent anyone taking a wrong turning, a drummer was stationed at the head of each battalion, and his job was to beat the drum all the time. This fact alone will indicate just how dense the clouds of dust were.'[11]

Intelligence reports reaching the Russian headquarters revealed the suffering which the enemy were having to endure. 'In the first weeks of their advance,' wrote Clausewitz, 'the French had undergone an enormous loss in sick and stragglers, and were in a state of privation which gave early warning of their rapid consumption.'[12] News arrived at the Russian camp of roads littered with stiff and swollen carcasses of French horses and men. Rain proved as painful as the sun: sudden downpours turned the dust into mud and the heat switched to biting cold. Thousands of French horses died through eating green fodder, and the numbers of sick and wounded were simply left to die.[13] 'Worms are eating many of the wounded alive,' reported Kozodavlev, Russian Minister of the Interior.[14] And yet the horrors had only just begun.

Alexander had left his army at Polotsk on 17 July amidst emotional farewells, finally convinced he would be better employed in Moscow and Petersburg. 'Goodbye, General,' he cried to Barclay. 'Goodbye once more, *au revoir*. I commend my army to your keeping. Always remember it is the only one I have.'[15] Among Alexander's primary tasks was to soothe the increasing fears being felt in both Russian capitals; secondly, he was faced with the problem of raising troops and money for the continuing campaign. And third loomed the question of a possible change in army command. Alexander stayed eight days in Moscow, remaining within the Kremlin; he discussed the situation with the Governor-General, Count Feodor Rostopchin; a subscription list was opened to raise funds for the war; recruitment of militiamen began for service in the defence of Moscow and in the ranks of the field army.

The Emperor reached Petersburg early in the morning on 3 August. Reports continually arrived revealing the retreat of the Russian main armies, and pressure rapidly mounted for a new commander. Not only was Barclay indecisive, his relations with Bagration were deplorable. The latter had already revealed his feelings in an irate letter to Arakcheev. 'I have no cause for self-reproach. I have been stretched like catgut along the whole front. . . . Nobody in the Army or in the country will believe that we are not traitors. I cannot defend the whole of Russia on my own.'[16] Now, in early August, Bagration would barely speak to his nominal commander and resorted to written notes, some of which were extremely vicious.

Moreover, Barclay's chief adviser Colonel Wolzogen was hated by many Russian officers. Clausewitz reported: 'I heard an officer who returned from the headquarters pour out his bitterness, saying that Wolzogen sat there in a corner like a fat and poisonous spider.' He was even rumoured to be one of Napoleon's spies. 'The entire army is suspicious of *aide-de-camp* Wolzogen,' wrote Bagration. 'He is Napoleon's man more than ours.'[17] The atmosphere at headquarters had become impossibly strained. 'Secret meetings were held and plots hatched,' wrote Löwenstern. 'The operations of the commander-in-chief were criticized openly; people wanted to make him disgusted with his command by a thousand vexations which were set in train at leisure. General Bennigsen, Duke Alexander von Wurtemburg, and the Grand Duke of Oldenburg discussed freely, and with anyone who was prepared to listen, the errors that had been made and what they regarded as the incompetence of the man who had given the orders. . . .'[18] Even Barclay's chief of staff, Alexei Yermolov, intrigued against him.

The situation had deteriorated steadily after Barclay's headquarters reached Smolensk on 1 August and while the army

1a Mikhail Illarionovich Golenishchev-Kutuzov, Prince of Smolensk, Russian field marshal.

1b Alexander I, 1777–1825, Czar of Russia from 1801–1825, eldest son of Czar Paul I whom he deposed, and bitterly hostile to Kutuzov.

1c Field Marshal Count Alexander Vasilievich Suvorov, 1729–1800, Russian military hero and Kutuzov's greatest teacher.

2a Social life in Imperial Russia, to which Kutuzov was accustomed: the Empress Elizabeth and her court at the elegant Tsarskoe Selo Palace outside St Petersburg.

2b Austerlitz, 1805: Napoleon seizes upon Austrian and Russian mistakes committed despite Kutuzov's warnings.

3a General Prince Peter Ivanovich Bagration, 1765–1812, disciple of Suvorov, veteran of campaigns in Poland, Italy and Switzerland, fought at Austerlitz and bravely commanded the Russian Second Army in 1812, falling at Borodino.

3b Field Marshal Prince Mikhail Barclay de Tolly, 1761–1818, born of Scottish descent and nicknamed 'All Bark and No Bite' by his Russian critics; led the First Russian Army in 1812 but superseded by Kutuzov as overall commander prior to Borodino.

3c General Count Levin Bennigsen, 1745–1826, egocentric veteran of wars against the Turks and Poles, involved in murder of Emperor Paul and favoured by Alexander; commander of Russian forces in 1807 and acutely jealous of Kutuzov in 1812.

3d General Sir Robert Wilson, 1777–1849, brigade commander under Wellington in the Peninsular, British military commissioner to Russian army 1811–1812; highly opinionated critic of Kutuzov who did much to poison the Russian commander's reputation.

4a and b 'An astonishing similarity exists between the behaviour of Napoleon and Kutuzov during the Battle of Borodino . . . The two commanders seemed strangely detached from the turmoil around them: they sat on their chairs, for the most part silent. They appeared as two individuals alone with their thoughts . . .'

awaited Napoleon's attack on this city, begun on the 17th. Evidence of this unsatisfactory state of affairs filtered to Alexander at Petersburg. And on 17 August the Emperor received a letter from General Prince Shuvalov, a highly respected officer, who begged that another commander-in-chief should be appointed 'or Russia will be lost'.[19] Two days earlier Alexander had read a message from Rostopchin, declaring that the whole of Moscow wanted Kutuzov to command.[20]

The Emperor summoned six generals to his palace during the early evening of the 17th, including Arakcheev and General Nicholas Saltykov. He presented them with the latest reports from the battle front and told them to advise him on the command problem. The generals remained in conference for three and a half hours, then emerged with a resolution signed by all: Kutuzov must be appointed.

Kutuzov was favoured for two main reasons, equally important: first his experience and reputation, so recently enhanced by his operations against the Turks, and secondly because he was a true Russian. Too many leading generals in the Russian army were foreigners, and both people and soldiers were apparently disillusioned with this enlistment of doubtful outside aid – Barclay, Wittgenstein, Bennigsen, and scores of lesser figures. The number of foreign officers, high at Austerlitz, had increased still further in the 1812 campaign with men flocking to Russia because their own countries had been defeated. Alexander was well aware of the growing opposition to this non-Russian personnel. So too was his belligerent brother Constantine, who told peasants he met during the retreat: 'What can we do, my friends? It isn't our fault. We were not allowed to come to your rescue. It is not Russian blood that flows in the veins of the man who commands us. Painful as it is to us, we must obey him. My heart aches no less than yours.'[21] Protests had grown steadily more vocal – a Russian must save Russia. And no other commander could claim purer blood than Kutuzov, whose ancestors had fought alongside Alexander Nevsky, hero of ancient Muscovy, whose father had served Peter the Great, and who himself had served Catherine, Peter, Paul and now Alexander.

Yet the Emperor hesitated. His dislike of Kutuzov remained as strong as ever despite his elevation of the general to a princely title. According to Wolzogen, Alexander believed the old soldier to be 'a hatcher of intrigues and an immoral and thoroughly dangerous character'.[22] For three days Alexander delayed giving his decision, despite the need to rectify the appalling situation at headquarters. But increasingly depressing reports reached Petersburg from the front. The battle of Smolensk began during the afternoon of the 17th; at eleven o'clock that night, as the generals met in Alexander's palace and decided upon Kutuzov as commander, Barclay ordered evacuation from Smolensk fearing he might soon be outflanked. Retreat continued. Two days later forward French units under Ney and Murat were blocked by the Russian rearguard near Valutino Gora, eight kilometres east of Smolensk; Ney broke through at nightfall. Next morning, 20 August, the main Russian forces were withdrawing over the river Yopp towards Dorogobuzh. By now they were half-way between Vilna and Moscow. Barclay insisted in an urgent despatch to Alexander that he had withdrawn from Smolensk because he wished to save the army for the right moment – after all, Alexander's last words to him at Polotsk were a reminder that the army was the only one which Russia had.[23]

But on 20 August Alexander wrote to Catherine: 'There is great indignation here against the Minister of War who, I must confess, gives good grounds for it by indecision in conduct and by the chaos of his work.'[24] And, also on this Thursday, an *aide-de-camp* from the Czar handed a message to Kutuzov.

'Mikhail Illarionovich. Your well-known military talents, your patriotism and the repeated examples of splendid heroism which you have shown us, fully entitle you to the confidence I hereby place in you. Choosing you for this important task, I pray to the Almighty God to bless your deeds and the glory of Russian arms, and to justify the hopes our country places in you. Assuring you of my favour, Alexander.'[25]

Similar smooth sentences were spoken by the Czar during an interview with Kutuzov during the evening. The new army commander was assured of maximum support; Alexander expressed absolute confidence in him. The Emperor expressed his attitude more accurately in a letter sent to Catherine a few weeks later. 'At St Petersburg I found everybody in favour of the nomination of old Kutuzov as commander-in-chief. The knowledge of this man made him repugnant to me at first, but when Rostopchin told me in his letter of 15 August that the whole of Moscow wanted

Kutuzov to command, finding both Barclay and Bagration incapable of it, and in the midst of all this, Barclay having done as if on purpose one foolish thing after another round Smolensk, I could not help yielding to the unanimous wishes and I appointed Kutuzov. I still think at this moment that, in the circumstances in which we were, I could not have done otherwise than decide on the man who won the general vote, out of three generals equally unfitted to be commander-in-chief.'[26]

Alexander is reported to have confided in a friend at court: 'People wanted his appointment; I named him. As for myself, I wash my hands of it.'[27] At the same time Alexander was determined to keep close watch on the slippery Kutuzov: he insisted that the commander's chief-of-staff should be Bennigsen, the arrogant, opinionated Hanoverian who had played the leading role in the murder of Czar Paul, who had displayed incompetence in the 1807 campaign against Napoleon – and who considered himself better fitted to command the Russian army in 1812 than his superior. He apparently believed that only his non-Russian birth barred him from the post.

'Prince Kutuzov is old, broken, ill, and has great difficulty in staying on horseback,' wrote Bennigsen when he heard of the appointment. 'Endowed by the Creator with very considerable natural intelligence, he is very amiable in society, in particular with the fair sex by whom he has always been very sought after and who, wherever he has found himself, have conducted affairs often to his great disadvantage, which on various occasions has made him pull back posts he was occupying.' Bennigsen's diatribe continued: 'The disgust he has always felt for hard work and useful activities has, since he was a young man, got him out of the habit of application to study, so that he has no solid knowledge. Tactics is something he knows by name only. . . . You will ask me how he came to fill so eminent and important a post. I must reply that there was a general desire, not without reason, that the honour of compelling Napoleon and his army to withdraw from Russia should fall on a Russian, because he certainly did not enjoy the confidence of the Court or the Army, nor of that part of the nation who knew him.'[28]

Kutuzov drove to the Kazan Cathedral immediately after his interview with Alexander on the evening of the 20th. He lifted his decorations from his neck and placed them before the icons; he bent on to his knees, grunting from his rheumatism, and he stayed kneeling on the flags for many minutes. Then an *aide-de-camp* helped him to his feet again and he turned to leave.[29] News of his appointment was already sweeping the capital, and crowds had gathered by the cathedral steps. Men and women raised their hands to him and he wept as he walked slowly to his carriage.

Kutuzov sought further information essential to his tasks which lay ahead. On 21 August, the day after his appointment, he instructed the War Ministry in Petersburg: 'Collect as soon as possible the following: first – where are the recruiting depots, in what condition are they, and what arms are there; second – details of regular military units being formed inside the Empire; third – is there any news about the Moscow, Smolensk and other militias?'[30]

These basic questions would constantly be repeated during the next weeks, without satisfactory replies. The new army commander spent 22 August attempting to gain further information concerning resources upon which he could rely, and in arranging personal affairs. He also prayed in a succession of Petersburg churches; the Archpriest of the Kazan Cathedral presented him with a cross and with the icon of the Kazan Mother of God. Large crowds collected in the street outside his house during the night of the 22nd; early in the morning of Sunday, 23 August, Kutuzov left his wife and family and walked to his carriage through the people in the street. So thick was the throng that his aides had to clear a way for him and his carriage had difficulty in moving forward.[31]

*   *   *   *   *

So far in his military career Kutuzov had displayed amazing consistency. From this emrged his strategic principles: the avoidance of unnecessary battles, the preservation of his army, the reliance upon the power of manoeuvre, the appreciation that psychological victory over the enemy could be equally devastating as defeat inflicted upon the battlefield itself. These same principles had underlined Kutuzov's actions in 1805 against Napoleon and in 1811–1812 against the Turkish commander Ahmet Bey. In 1805 Kutuzov had been thwarted through the interference of his superiors, and without this meddling the result might have been dramatically different; in 1811–1812 Kutuzov had achieved magnificent psychological and military superiority against the Turks. Now, in September 1812, his opportunity again arose against the French. His principles would be employed once more, in exactly the same fashion as before.

IX

Back to Borodino

(1812: 23 August–7 September)

Russian regiments had retreated almost 150 kilometres since leaving Smolensk. Now, as Kutuzov left Petersburg, they neared Viazma almost half way between Smolensk and Moscow. Day after day the troops shuffled in seemingly unending lines on either edge of the wide, tree-fringed roads. Artillery and waggons rumbled and groaned two or three abreast; cavalry jingled through the fields beside the track and above the army hung a thick cloud of dust. The heat was still intense, causing extreme discomfort. Some soldiers had improvised dark spectacles out of bits of window glass; others carried their shakos under their arms and wrapped cloth round their heads, tearing a hole in the material just sufficiently large enough for them to see. Others wore garlands of leaves.

Periodically, sudden cracks sounded from the rear as French advance patrols clashed with the Russian rearguard, or as Cossacks darted in from the woods to strike the advancing enemy. Russian soldiers threw lighted branches into the doorways of cottages which they passed, and the smoke rose to mingle with the dust. Always the men maintained their march, onwards to an unknown destination. They knew nothing of overall events and were only aware of the scene immediately around them. But then a fresh rumour rippled down the lines: Kutuzov was coming.

Kutuzov's journey south from Petersburg suffered constant interruptions; at almost every village people crowded into the track and stopped his carriage, swarming over the vehicle to receive his blessing and to hold up their children for him to see. On 26 August Kutuzov had another encounter on the road, this time with General Sir Robert Wilson, on his way from the army to Petersburg. It was the first time that the two men had met; all too soon Wilson would become one of Kutuzov's most virulent critics. Sir Robert, who had served under the Duke of Wellington in the Peninsula, had been selected by the British Government to undertake a mission to the Russian army: he was to report to the Foreign Office on conditions, events and general military affairs, acting in conjunction with Lord Cathcart, Ambassador at Petersburg. The British envoy was extremely self-confident; he considered himself to be a strategic and tactical expert even though he had never commanded more than a corps. Despatches sent by him, and the diary he wrote during the 1812 campaign, were crammed with false observations. This material helped to damage the reputation of the Russian commander, and Wilson's return to the army headquarters would provide Kutuzov with acute difficulties. Fittingly, Wilson was a close friend of the equally conceited Bennigsen; and Wilson also enjoyed the full confidence of the Russian Emperor.

But the first meeting with Kutuzov apparently passed satisfactorily. The two men talked for an hour in the shade of a lean-to, and Wilson noted in his diary: 'I was much flattered by his cordial invitation to rejoin the army. Taking me by the hand, he said "Lose no time to return; I have great need of such a comrade as yourself in the Cabinet and in the field." '[1] Wilson provided a description of Kutuzov which although begrudging contrasted strongly with his later sour comments.

'A *bon vivant* – polished, courteous, shrewd as a Greek, naturally intelligent as an Asiatic and well instructed as an European – he was more disposed to trust to diplomacy for his success than to martial prowess, for which by his age and the state of his constitution he was no longer qualified. When he rejoined the army he was sixty-four years old, and though hale, so very corpulent and unwieldy that he was obliged to move about, even when in the field, in a little four-wheeled carriage with a head, called a *droshky*.'[2] In fact Kutuzov was less than a month from his sixty-seventh birthday, not aged sixty-four; he frequently suffered from ill-health, especially head pains, rather than being 'hale', and the reason he preferred to be driven in a carriage stemmed not only from his corpulence but also from rheumatism.

Next day, 27 August, Kutuzov reached the main Smolensk–

Moscow road at Gzatsk, where the local inhabitants unharnessed his horses and pulled his carriage themselves to the house prepared for him. Also at Gzatsk, Kutuzov met the first Russian regiments moving slowly down the road from Smolensk. They looked weary, filthy and demoralized, but Kutuzov nevertheless greeted them with his customary exuberance. 'My God!' he shouted. 'Who could ever have convinced me that our enemy ever dared to fight in battle with such lads as you, my brothers!'[3]

On the same day Barclay decided to abandon Viazma, sixty kilometres west along the road from Gzatsk. Once again smoke and flames gushed high as supply depots were burnt, and Barclay and his headquarters resumed their retreat. Kutuzov's carriage moved against this tide of withdrawal as he drove westwards along the road on the 28th. Everywhere the soldiers cheered him as they lined the track; gun carriages and carts were hauled to one side to allow him to pass; messengers cantered ahead to spread the news of Kutuzov's arrival. Early next morning he entered the small, dirty and overcrowded town of Czarevo-Zaimishche, latest stopping-place for the army headquarters. Barclay and his generals stood outside the house in which they were based; Kutuzov climbed down from his carriage, embraced the generals in turn, then inspected the hastily-assembled guard of honour. The soldiers in this guard were as exhausted, bedraggled and dirty as those Kutuzov had passed on the road; nevertheless the new commander murmured, as if to himself but taking care his words could be heard: 'Well well, how can we retreat with such lads!'

At that moment a rumour spread from Czarevo-Zaimishche and through the regiments: a huge, fierce eagle had flown over Kutuzov's white head, circling slowly above him as he reviewed the troops.[4] Clausewitz, then at headquarters, wrote a more realistic appreciation of Kutuzov's reception: 'The arrival of Kutuzov revived confidence in the Army. The evil genius of the foreigners was exorcized by a true Russian, a slightly reduced Suvorov; and no one doubted that the battle would take place soon and would halt the French offensive.'[5]

Kutuzov summoned his staff and his subordinate commanders to his room. Among those he asked for was Colonel Karl von Toll, who had served on the Russian staff at Austerlitz and who would now act as Kutuzov's Quartermaster-General: Kutuzov had known Toll from the latter's schooldays and placed increasing trust in him as the campaign continued.[6] The commander put repeated questions to the officers assembled before him, and yet he seemed to know the answers even before the officers spoke. 'He handled everything as if he had been managing affairs since the beginning of the campaign,' wrote one of those present. 'He seemed to know everything. He had foreseen all eventualities and he acted as a commander in every possible way.'[7] The atmosphere at headquarters changed rapidly, and within hours the staff adopted the cheerful air which Kutuzov always tried to encourage on campaign; he once wrote: 'A headquarters is not a monastery. The good humour of the soldier vouches for his bravery.'[8]

'God has kept me in good health, my dear,' wrote the commander to his wife, 'and I am full of optimism. The army is in fine fettle and we have plenty of fine officers.' Yet on the same day as Kutuzov's arrival, 29 August, Napoleon and his staff rode into abandoned Viazma, barely forty kilometres away. The Russian army was completely disorganized from its long retreat; Kutuzov, for all his apparent knowledge shown at the staff conference, was probably appalled by the losses suffered so far: the combined First and Second Armies had been reduced to less than 120,000 men, compared with a total of over 160,000 at the start of the campaign. The commander immediately sought reinforcements. During the 29th he sent an urgent letter to Rostopchin, Governor of Moscow and responsible for the militia in that area: 'The call-up of 80,000 militiamen or more . . . is a sign of the spirit of the Russians and the trust of the citizens of Moscow in their Governor. Your Excellency will no doubt maintain it [the militia] such that the army can make use of it upon occasion. . . . I will ask Your Excellency to send [the militia troops] to Mozhaisk.'[9] Kutuzov especially needed extra manpower to act as a reserve and to cover the army should he be forced to undertake a hurried withdrawal after a battle: always prudent, he had no desire to engage the French with nothing behind him. At the moment the Russian regiments were inadequate and too chaotic for a large-scale clash, yet Kutuzov knew that such an engagement was expected of him. He had to reconcile reality with this demand.

Meanwhile, after a day spent studying situation reports, Kutuzov ordered further withdrawal. No other course was open to him; as Clausewitz commented: 'Barclay had been trundled back from Vitebsk to Viazma, like someone staggering along trying to regain his balance, and to start with Kutuzov couldn't recover a firm footing for the army.'[10] The commander announced his intention to fight near Gzatsk, and Russian regiments began to deploy in this area on 31 August.

Also on the last day of August Kutuzov received a reply from Rostopchin regarding the despatch of militia reinforcements. The Governor-General's words seemed encouraging: 'If you are forced to leave your position and retreat towards Moscow, through casualties and through larger numbers of Napoleon's troops, then I will collect many hundreds of thousands of determined young men and will appear before you.'[11] Kutuzov therefore wrote to Alexander on this Monday: 'I'm gaining strength and will be in a position to leave the salvation of Moscow to the result of a battle.' But Kutuzov, with a typical attempt to remain uncommitted, added that the battle 'will only be undertaken with all care, as demanded by the important circumstances'.[12] Moreover he had already altered the proposed site for the engagement, partly to allow more time and partly because a better position had apparently been found. Bennigsen claimed he had noticed an excellent locality from his carriage window when travelling on the road from Mozhaisk: Kutuzov sent Toll to reconnoitre the area and the Quartermaster-General returned with a satisfactory report.

In a letter dated 31 August Kutuzov informed General Tormassov, commanding the 45,000-strong Third West Army south of the Pripet Marshes, that battle would be offered by the First and Second Armies at Mozhaisk. He instructed Tormassov to combine with Admiral Chichagov, still commanding the Danube Army, and to distract the enemy. His letter to Tormassov criticized the general's activities so far: 'When the enemy is actually in the heart of Russia, your object cannot be to defend our distant Polish provinces. . . .' He repeated these words in a letter to Chichagov sent the same day – and his tone further aggravated the ill-feeling between the two men which had existed since the Admiral's tardy interference in the Turkish campaign. 'My real object is to save Moscow itself. For that reason I should have no need to explain that the preservation of some distant Polish provinces has no comparison with saving the ancient capital of Moscow and the internal provinces.'[13]

The army continued to move back on 1 September, covered by a rearguard under General Konovnitsin. Sudden actions took place at Gzatsk and on the road beyond, but the bulk of the French army now slowed the advance in order to snatch rest. News of Kutuzov's arrival reached the French headquarters on about 2 September, first brought by a Frenchman living in a village by the road. 'According to this statement a complete change had just taken place in the Russian army,' reported Count Philippe-Paul de Ségur, serving on Napoleon's staff. 'All called aloud, all decided that they must have Kutuzov and a battle.'[14] Napoleon arrived in Gzatsk on 3 September. He summoned a staff conference and asked those present to tell him all they could about the new Russian commander's character and background. Ségur reported the account which the French Emperor received, and this proved to be reasonably accurate: Napoleon would be well-prepared.

'Kutuzov was described to him as an aged warrior whose reputation had originated very many years ago in the circumstances of his receiving a very singular wound. He had since shown no little tact in availing himself of circumstances. Even the defeat experienced at Austerlitz, as it had been foreseen by him, had increased his renown, which had been still further enhanced by his recent campaigns against the Turks. His valour was unquestionable. But he had been reproached with regulating his exertions by mere personal interests: for he was a cool and selfish calculator. He was dilatory, vindictive, and above all, artful; the genuine Tartar character! exercising the greatest pliability and patience, and displaying the most caressing attention, while preparing the most implacable war.

'He was more able as a courtier than a general; but he was formidable by his renown, and by the address with which he had increased it and obtained the concurrence of others in it: he had found the means to flatter the nation at large, and every individual in it, from the general down to the common soldier. It was added that there was, in his exterior, in his language, and even in his dress, in his superstitious usages, and also in his time of life, a considerable resemblance to Suvorov; that he bore the stamp of the ancient Moscovite, an air of nationality, which strongly endeared him to the Russians. At Moscow the joy that was felt at his nomination mounted almost to delirium. The inhabitants stopped to embrace and congratulate each other in the streets. They considered themselves saved.'[15]

Napoleon, according to Ségur, began to prepare for battle 'with that tranquillity which characterizes extraordinary minds'. Kutuzov also maintained his calm and apparently indolent appearance as the conflict approached. During the morning of this Thursday, 3 September, he rode with the centre regiments of the First and Second Armies from the Kolotskoi Monastery into the gentle valleys and the low rounded hills near the Moskva river. There, at the point where the Smolensk road crossed the Kolocha stream, lay a small village: its name was Borodino.

Kutuzov toured this battle site throughout the day and once again the rumour rippled through the regiments that the huge eagle had circled slowly above him wherever he went. Regiment after regiment deployed off the Smolensk highway and into the fields to the south of Borodino. The whole area seethed with jumbled, marching men, with drums beating, trumpets blaring, and a cacophony of shouted commands. Cavalry units trotted amongst the infantry – the cuirassiers on their huge horses, the gaily uniformed hussars and lancers of the light cavalry, the Cossacks on their unkempt ponies. Staff officers galloped in all directions trying to achieve cohesion from the chaos; soldiers swore as they were moved from one place to another or stood waiting for fresh instructions. Campfires were laid and lit, and soldiers piled their muskets in pyramids, rolled out their capes, and settled themselves for the night. Men clustered round the sutler waggons to obtain their gruel and heavy black bread. Denis Davidov, Bagration's *aide-de-camp* and soon to become one of the most famous partisan leaders, had grown up in this district; he wrote: 'What a sight the cradle of my youth now presented! My family house was hidden by the smoke of the campfires, rows of bayonets glittered among the helmets of the cavalry, and troops were massing among my native hills and valleys. There, on the mound where I used to play, they were throwing up the Raevsky Redoubt. The pretty little wood in front had been hewn down. . . . The village was already deserted by its inhabitants.'[16]

Kutuzov established his headquarters just behind the army positions, in a farmhouse at Tatarinovo, about two kilometres east along the road from Borodino. He stayed awake late that night dictating orders and reports. One letter was addressed to

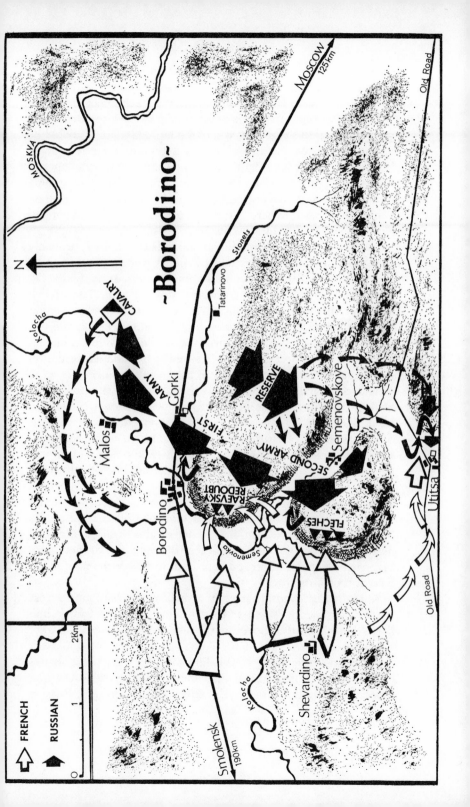

~Borodino~

FRENCH
RUSSIAN

Alexander, dated 4 September; once again Kutuzov displayed a mixture of optimism and caution. 'The position in which I've stopped at the village of Borodino, twelve kilometres before Mozhaisk, is one of the very best. . . . I will try to correct the weak point in this position, where the left flank lies. It would be desirable if the enemy attacks us here – I would then have every hope of victory. But if he thinks my position is too strong and manoeuvres himself along other roads towards Moscow, then I cannot guarantee success, and perhaps I will have to withdraw behind Mozhaisk where all these roads converge. Whatever happens I must defend Moscow.'[17]

Napoleon had no intention of avoiding battle. Indeed, probably remembering Kutuzov's withdrawal policy prior to Austerlitz, he feared that the Russians would attempt to slip away again. On 4 September he ordered the Grand Army forward. The French advance units encountered increasing opposition but by evening had reached within five kilometres of Borodino; a succession of reports informed Napoleon that the Russians were taking up position, and the French Emperor issued instructions accordingly: the Grand Army, like the Russian, deployed for battle.

The countryside at Borodino stretched in soft undulations broken only by meandering streams and occasional clusters of birch and pine. To the north of the main battle area ran the Smolensk–Moscow road down which the Russians had marched. Running parallel to the south, about three kilometres from this route, was the old Smolensk road on the far side of which lay woodland. The Kolocha stream flowed alongside the northern road, after crossing this highway at Borodino, but a thinner tributary known as the Semenovka branched off at right angles near Borodino and headed directly across almost to the old road near the hamlet of Utitsa. Another tributary, the Stonets, also branched off at Borodino and bent back to follow the road in the direction of Moscow.

Kutuzov deployed his army in a shallow arc, half lying across the new Smolensk–Moscow road just to the east of Borodino itself. He chose this position because it spread across higher ground behind the line of the Kolocha above the road and the Semenovka to the south of this highway: the steeper east banks offered some protections against infantry and cavalry charges, especially along the Semenovka. The right, or northern, Russian flank rested beyond the new Smolensk road between Borodino and the hamlets of Gorki and Tatarinovov; the centre stretched between the road and Semenovskoye hamlet situated between the two routes to Moscow; the left or southern wing lay between this hamlet and the old track. This left wing occupied an inferior position compared with the centre and right: in front of the southern sector the Semenovka stream dwindled to a series of stagnant pools and marshy patches, over which the enemy could advance with relative ease, and the old Smolensk road offered an excellent approach for guns and cavalry. It was in an attempt to guard against such an outflanking movement that Kutuzov and Toll had decided upon the positioning of the army in a shallow convex curve. The field of battle, while affording some excellent natural defences, was therefore by no means entirely satisfactory. The deficiencies were fully realized by many officers on the Russian staff. Clausewitz described the location as 'certainly not the best among the many which Toll had thought fit for battle', but he also appreciated the difficulties in finding a suitable site at short notice. 'Russia is very short of good positions. . . . If a commander, then, wishes to fight without loss of time, as was Kutuzov's case, it is evident that he must put up with what he can get.'[18] Kutuzov himself acknowledged the defect in his letter to Alexander on the 4th – 'I will try to correct the weak point in this position, where the left flank lies.'[19]

Russian regiments were placed in their allotted defensive positions late into the night on 4 September and early next morning. Barclay had continued to command the First Army following Kutuzov's arrival, and his forces would hold the right wing and part of the centre; also in this northern sector would be the main Russian cavalry under General Sergei Uvarov, together with Cossacks under Matvei Platov. Responsible for holding the bulk of the centre and the left was Bagration's Second Army, comprising about 25,000 men compared with Barclay's 75,000. The southern area would therefore be much weaker than the northern, despite the vulnerability of this sector, probably because Kutuzov expected the main French thrust to be made down the new road to Moscow through Borodino. With reserves, attached Cossacks and militiamen the Russian army totalled about 128,000 men with 640 guns; the Grand Army numbered about 130,000 with 587 guns.

To assist the centre, Russian engineers constructed the fortification which was to become famous under the names of the Raevsky or Great Redoubt. This covered almost 200 yards, comprising ramparts several yards wide and with embrasures for nineteen cannon. Its site had been skilfully chosen by Toll on the high land between Borodino and Semenovskoye, offering an excellent field of fire for several hundred yards. Further south, beyond a sudden dip in the ground, were dug three arrow-shaped redans known as the Bagration *flèches*. Few trenches or fortifications were attempted apart from these works, partly through the lack of shovels and picks – the likely need for such implements in battle had been the reason for Kutuzov's insistence that the Petersburg militia should be suitably equipped – and partly through the nature of the ground. This was often either too hard or too soft: Clausewitz referred to the difficult sandy soil in which the *flèches* were dug.

'I intend to attract the forces of the enemy,' wrote Kutuzov in his battle dispositions, 'and act according to his movement. Upon this occasion I do not consider it excessive to remind the chief commanders that the reserves must be saved as long as possible, because the general who saves his reserves remains unbeaten.'[20]

Signs of friction were already becoming apparent between Kutuzov and his chief of staff Bennigsen. The latter criticized the commander's plans, resented the general's reliance upon Toll, and attempted to interfere with the dispositions; he still believed he would have been a far better leader for the army. Yet now, on 5 September, close cooperation was more essential than ever before: during this Saturday afternoon the French began to probe forward north-east towards Borodino from the village of Yelnia.

Almost one kilometre in front of the main Russian positions lay an isolated earthwork known as the Shevardino Redoubt. This had been constructed after Toll suggested the need for a defended observation post to 'discover the direction from which the French were advancing their forces, and possibly to discover Napoleon's intention'.[21] The Shevardino Redoubt hindered the deployment of the French right wing: Napoleon studied the position through his telescope during the afternoon, then ordered the post to be eliminated. Battalion columns from the

French First Corps, commanded by General Jean-Dominique Compans, marched forward to undertake this task followed by strong cavalry detachments. The Russians in the redoubt, mainly comprising Neverovski's 27th Infantry Division as part of Prince Gorchakov's Corps, were outnumbered by over two to one. They nevertheless repulsed the first French assault; the second managed to gain a foothold but was swept out again.

Fighting threatened to spread into a general engagement between the whole French right and Russian left wings; the French seized the fortifications, only to be thrown out once more by Russian reinforcements. Not until nightfall did the Russians give way, after having suffered about 5,000 casualties – slightly more than their enemy. Napoleon was surprised to discover that no Russian prisoners had been taken: the defenders refused to allow themselves to be seized alive, and soon this Russian determination to fight to the last would become commonplace.

Shevardino Redoubt had in fact been badly sited and held far too long. 'Bennigsen had chosen the position.' claimed Barclay, 'and he did not want to lose face. . . . He therefore sacrificed six or seven thousand brave soldiers and three guns.'[22] During this action Kutuzov made one important alteration to his main battle plan – and this too would later be a source of conflict between the commander and his chief of staff. Kutuzov detached General Ivan Tuchkov's Third Corps from the reserve, 8,000 men, and sent this with 1,500 Cossacks and 7,000 Moscow militiamen to help protect the old Smolensk road: these were positioned under cover of thick woods near the village of Utitsa, intended to act as a surprise striking force. Kutuzov planned that 'when the enemy commit their last reserve against Bagration's left flank, I shall be able to strike them in the flank and rear with my concealed forces'. Further forward from Tuchkov's ambush were deployed four rifle regiments as a covering screen.[23]

Rain had started to fall during the fighting at the Shevardino Redoubt and this continued into the night. Soldiers lay shivering beneath their coats, the moisture wet upon their faces and hair, and the rain hissed on the campfires. Napoleon constantly asked his aides whether the Russian fires could still be seen, fearing Kutuzov might still intend to slip away, but the French Emperor need scarcely have asked. 'The whole of their camp was one vast uninterrupted blaze of light,' wrote the French officer Major

Eugène Labaume, 'which, as it presented a magnificent appearance, contrasted sharply with our resting place, where the soldiers were unable to gather wood and lay in complete darkness, hearing nothing but the moans of the wounded.'[24] French troops also lacked food and especially drink: some took the flasks from the Russian corpses at Shevardino and found these bottles contained bad brandy, strongly flavoured with pepper and vitriol which burnt the mouth.

Kutuzov's camp-chair had been placed by the fire at his Tatarinova farmhouse, and he sat late into the night alternatively dozing and listening to latest reports. Everything seemed satisfactory in the actual battle position, but one point was giving him anxiety: Rostopchin had failed to send substantial Moscow militiamen as promised. So far less than 15,000 had arrived, described by one Russian officer as 'raw Russian peasants clutching pikes and muskets which they scarcely knew how to wield'.[25] Half of these were now deployed in the woods near Utitsa with Tuchkov's ambush force; protection to cover any subsequent withdrawal was therefore still lacking, and Kutuzov despatched another note to the Moscow Governor: 'I am depending on Your Excellency to furnish me as much as possible from the troops under your command.'[26]

Forward Russian regiments were called to arms before first light on Sunday, 6 September, in the expectation of a French attack. But none came. The sun arched slowly through the clear autumn sky as both armies continued to wait. The Russian regiments presented an impressive, colourful sight in full view of the French: indeed, their lack of concealment meant that they would soon be exposed to unremitting bombardment from the massed French guns without chance of reply. Rather than seeking protection, the Russian lines were extremely vulnerable on the forward slopes and summit of the hills. Infantrymen were positioned in two close rows of battalion columns, with cavalry densely packed in similar pairs of lines; behind them were massed the reserves. Protests had been made to the Russian command over this exposed arrangement, which would inevitably result in terrible casualties, but Bennigsen insisted that the 'deep and compact order of battle is the best means to avoid being crushed by Napoleon'.[27] Kutuzov himself may have had sound reasons for standing his regiments in full sight of the enemy: he believed his troops fought best when they could see their opposition. Moreover, the enemy must be tempted to strike direct rather than outside the weaker left flank.

This scheme apparently worked. Napoleon's plans for the battle reveal that he failed to realize the full strength of the Russian position. The Emperor scanned the enemy lines through his telescope during the morning of the 6th, but was prevented from reconnoitring too close by the thick screen of riflemen which Kutuzov had sent out along the Semenovka stream; as a result Napoleon made a number of mistakes in his assessment of the Russian line. He believed the 'Bagration' *flèches* to be smaller than they actually were, and that these fortifications were situated on the same ridge as the Raevsky Redoubt, not appreciating that a tributary of the Semenovka ran between the two, cutting a significant dip in the high ground. Napoleon therefore intended to attack all the Russian fortifications simultaneously with a direct assault across the Semenovka. He refused to consider a wide flanking movement proposed by Davout, declaring: 'The movement is altogether too great. It would lead me away from my objective and make me lose too much time.'[28]

The respective plans by Kutuzov and Napoleon could only result in carnage. The two armies would clash face to face south of the road to Moscow; victory would go to the troops which withstood the shock the longest. Kutuzov retained his faith in his men, and during the 6th he gave them further encouragement. Towards noon he mounted a huge white horse and proceeded round his regiments; unlike Napoleon he had no intention of issuing an impersonal proclamation to his army as a whole, and instead he spoke a few words to each regiment in turn.

'Fulfil your duties,' said Kutuzov to one group. 'Think of the sacrifices of your cities to the flames – of your children who implore your protection. Think of your Emperor who looks on you as the source of his strength. And tomorrow, before the sun sets, you will have traced your faith and loyalty to your Emperor and Fatherland in the blood of the invader.'[29]

To the Simbirsk infantry, part of Neverovsky's battered division, Kutuzov declared: 'You have the task of defending our native soil. Serve loyally and honourably to the last drop of your blood!' Mixed with the emotional phrases were practicalities. 'Each regiment will be committed to the battle, but you will be relieved regularily every two hours.'[30] Unlike many commanders who insisted that their troops should spend their last hours smartening themselves as if for parade, Kutuzov ordered that the men should be allowed to rest, and if possible they should sleep. He once came across a party of soldiers brushing their uniforms, pipe-claying their belts and polishing their buttons; riding up to them he called: 'I don't want any of that. I want to see whether you're in good health my children. A soldier has no time for smartness during a campaign. He must rest after his tiring efforts and prepare for victory.'[31]

Just before evening a sudden stir spread among the Russian regiments. Amongst the troops moved a strange and colourful procession: the priests and archimandrites were carrying round the Holy Ikon of the Black Virgin, rescued during the fighting at Smolensk in August. The ikon, held aloft by the priests, swayed above the kneeling troops; regimental colours were sprinkled with holy water, and soldiers bowed their shaven heads to receive the blessing.

Last orders were issued. Russian commanders sent messages to their troops, as practical as those which Kutuzov himself had issued. Barclay instructed his corps commanders 'to restrain their men from letting off their muskets carelessly, and to make gunners economize with their ammunition as much as possible'.[32]

Night fell. Napoleon issued his proclamation to the Grand Army, to be read to his troops just before battle began next morning. 'Soldiers! The moment for the long-awaited battle has come. Victory depends on you. We have need of it. Victory will give us plentiful supplies, good winter quarters, and an early return home. Fight as you did at Austerlitz, Friedland, Vitebsk and Smolensk, and future generations will remember with pride your conduct on this historic day. May it be said of each of us: "He fought in that great battle under the walls of Moscow!" '

Once again the Russian soldiers settled by their fires. Few managed to sleep and instead they played cards, tossed dice, cleaned their weapons one last time. They took out their clay pipes and discussed old campaigns. Some infantrymen tried to find comfort in song. 'The soldiers were in fairly good order,' wrote a staff officer, 'and, as they had had a rest during the last few days, they now sat, wrapped in their long grey coats, round the fires – and often joined in chorus to sing the monotonous, melancholy, dirge-like, yet not unpleasing national songs which the Russian people are so fond of. This singing before the battle had a strange effect on me, and I listened to it for several hours until I fell asleep, exhausted, beside my horse.'[33] At one Russian fire the soldiers were discussing the countryside around them, and especially the strangely-appropriate names of the streams and villages, all of which seemed to have warlike connections: *Ognik*, Fire, *Kolocha*, Stab, *Voyna*, War, *Stonets*, Groans.[34]

Napoleon stayed awake for most of the night. At three o'clock in the morning, Monday, 7 September, he summoned his valet and had punch brought in; then he turned to his *aide-de-camp*, General Jean Rapp.

'Today we shall have to deal with this celebrated Kutuzov,' he said. 'No doubt you remember that it was he who commanded at Braunau during the Austerlitz campaign. He stayed in that place for three weeks without leaving his room once. He didn't even mount his horse to go and inspect the fortifications. General Bennigson, although he is old, is a much more energetic fellow. I cannot understand why Alexander did not send this Hanoverian to replace Barclay.' Napoleon took another glass of punch. A little later he said: 'Fortune is a shameless courtesan. I have often said it, and I am beginning to experience it.' He read more reports then turned to Rapp again. 'This poor army is sadly depleted, but what remains is good.'[35]

Kutuzov's staff officers had left him alone in his room at the Tatarinovo farmhouse. The young officers in the hall outside could hear the general pacing up and down and the occasional shuffle of a map. His orderly at the door listened to Kutuzov grunting and coughing, and sometimes talking to himself in jerky exclamations: 'Like that. . . . No no not that, not like that. . . .' Kutuzov was working out Napoleon's possible moves.[36]

Shortly before dawn the Russian commander emerged from the farmhouse parlour. He told his staff to follow once they had breakfasted, and he left the building, mounted his Cossack pony and rode towards his command post in the village of Gorki. With him went a single Cossack carrying the commander's stool. Their horses walked slowly between the dying campfires, where men moved like shadows in the half-light. At Gorki, Kutuzov bent forward in his saddle and grunted as he dismounted to sit on the stool which the Cossack hastily placed ready. Kutuzov wore his customary simple tunic, although in honour of battle a sash fell across his huge stomach, and today his flat peaked cap was white. There he sat patiently waiting, his hands on his knees, staring in front.[37]

At precisely six o'clock on the morning of this Monday, 7 September, the first cannon fired on the right of the French line. Others immediately followed. The battle which Napoleon would later describe as the most terrible in all his career had at last begun.

X

Borodino

(1812: 7–8 September)

Single artillery shots merged into one continuous roll of thunder; the Russian guns replied, and the cannon balls and shells arched high over the marshy ground between the two armies. 'Thick clouds of smoke,' wrote a Russian eye-witness, 'billowed from the batteries into the sky and darkened the sun, which seemed covered by a blood-red shroud.'[1] Then, amidst the roar of the guns, waiting Russian soldiers could hear the sharp staccato rap of a French drum; others answered further down the enemy line, and the first French infantrymen began to march steadily forward.

Napoleon had arrived at his command post by the Shevardino Redoubt. An aide brought him a chair which he twisted round and sat astride, his arms resting on the back. Kutuzov still sat on the hill by Gorki, his huge body seeming to overflow the narrow wooden stool. Between these two men, Napoleon and Kutuzov, over 255,000 troops prepared to throw themselves at each other in an increasing frenzy of slaughter.

French guns tried to carve a way for the infantry. 'The enemy shot flew towards us or falling short then rolling on through the grass. Shells burst in the air and showered fragments, making a horrible clatter.'[2] The exposed Russian regiments suffered one barrage after another, with the men trying to keep in line ready for the advancing infantry; they shuffled together each time a gap was torn in the ranks, their feet stumbling against the remains of those who had already fallen; officers shouted above the noise of the guns, ordering the men to face the front, to stand steady, to check their weapons. From the rolling black smoke came the first line of blue-coated French infantrymen, bayonets held rigid in front of them and glinting in the sun. Closer they came, a swaying mass; at 200 yards the waiting Russians raised their muskets; at 100 yards the first volleys were fired. The French charged, and the two opposing lines locked tight together in a confused, shrieking maul. The initial French assault was directed against the village of Borodino itself; reports of this action seemed to confirm Kutuzov's belief that the main enemy thrust would be down the Smolensk–Moscow road.

But within thirty minutes adjutants galloped to Kutuzov with information from Bagration's left wing: the French had launched a general attack on the *flèches*; other enemy troops seemed to be attempting an outflanking movement along the old Smolensk road towards the village of Utitsa. And now Kutuzov learnt that Tuchkov's troops, which he had ordered to be concealed to ambush such an attempt, had been taken out into the open where they would be exposed to far greater numbers of French. Kutuzov's deception plan had been ruined – only later would he learn that Bennigsen was responsible for this alteration.[3]

More messengers arrived, one after the other. All confirmed that the Russian left wing was Napoleon's primary target – not the stronger right as Kutuzov had envisaged. Yet battle had only just begun: the possibility existed that the threat to the left was a diversion. A premature reaction by Kutuzov could be disastrous. His aides remembered afterwards how the commander had sat listening to the alarming reports, saying little; now and then he lent forward or tilted his head as if trying to judge how the battle swayed by the changes in the intensity of the sounds.[4]

Grapeshot from the guns immediately in front of the *flèches* managed to block the first French assault. 'The execution inflicted by our batteries was terrifying,' reported Löwenstern to Kutuzov, 'and the enemy columns disintegrated despite continual reinforcements. The more enemy that came, the more bodies piled up before us.'[5] But French infantrymen from Compans' division managed to batter an entrance into the *flèches* on the second attempt. Meanwhile General Prince Poniatowski's French 5th Corps pushed against Russian troops holding Utitsa village; Tuchkov was thrust back to the hill behind the blazing houses where he ordered his artillery to be dragged into line – these guns immediately opened devastating fire on the advancing French, who ran for cover in the ruins of Utitsa.

Bagration despatched two brigades of Konovnitsin's division to retake the *flèches*: the Russians ran forward in a dense mass and fell upon the exhausted French with bayonets fixed, and within minutes the fortifications had been seized back again. Konovnitsin's blood-splattered men piled up the bodies of the Russian and French dead on to the breastworks to provide greater protection, and then they awaited the next attack.

The time was now just before eight o'clock. Battle had been in progress almost two hours. To the north the French had abandoned the village of Borodino seized in the opening minutes; a heavy artillery attack on Gorki had failed to silence the Russian guns; Bagration's left wing still held, but this remained the most threatened sector. Originally, Napoleon probably never intended his main preliminary thrust to be aimed so far south, in just the same way that Kutuzov had never expected it to be so strong in this area. Ségur wrote: 'It was Napoleon himself who had just given the order to his left wing to make a violent attack. Perhaps he . . . merely wished to detain the attention of the enemy on that side. But he multiplied his orders, and pushed to excess his instructions and exhortations, and brought on a battle in front, while his plan had been to conduct it in an oblique direction.'[6]

The higher ground outside the battered village of Utitsa assumed increasing importance. 'The hill there commanded the whole neighbourhood,' commented Kutuzov later, 'and if the enemy had seized it they would have been able to strike our left wing in the flank, making it impossible for us to block the old Smolensk road.'[7] Kutuzov now began to shift forces from his right flank to the centre and left. Orders were hurried to General Baggovut's Second Infantry Corps, part of Barclay's First Army: these troops were to march as soon as possible behind the Russian line and then act in support of Generals Borozdin and Tuchkov, respectively defending the *flèches* and Utitsa hill. Baggovut asked the messenger for details of the situation. 'They could hardly be worse,' replied the adjutant. 'If you don't hurry we'll all be finished, Bagration's army is battered into the ground, and it's a wonder Tuchkov still holds.'[8]

Immediately Baggovut's regiments had begun to march they became entangled in the continuing barrage of cannister fire, shot and shells from the French guns. 'Soon we lost all count of the casualties,' wrote one of the officers.[9] It became obvious that this corps would never reach the left flank and Utitsa hill in time. Kutuzov had already foreseen this danger: he took the drastic step of summoning up units of the reserve, including three cavalry regiments, eight grenadier battalions in a mixed division, and three artillery companies.[10] Even this extra strength had still to reach the *flèches* when the French launched another violent assault from both front and flank. Line upon line of infantrymen advanced up the slope against the corpse-strewn fortifications; frenzied Russian gunners loaded, fired and re-loaded and round shot shattered whole sections of the approaching enemy. Still they came on. Russian soldiers of the 7th Combined Grenadier Division, commanded by General Vorontsov, stood to meet them and the bayonets clashed and thrust, but more French hammered in behind. The central and southern *flèches* fell with the enemy bayoneting virtually all surviving members of Vorontsov's grenadier division – which, he declared later, 'disappeared not from but on the battlefield. . . . It simply ceased to exist.'[11] Only now did the French find that a third *flèche* existed. And at that moment the Russian reinforcements ran screaming into the battle, bayonets jabbing, and hurled the French away again.

Meanwhile Baggovut's reinforcement reached Utitsa hill, just in time to prevent Poniatowski's troops from hacking aside the outnumbered Russians under Tuchkov. The latter fell mortally wounded; Baggovut himself assumed command. Further left the ghastly struggle for the *flèches* was resumed with charge after charge against the Russian defenders. Bagration, in the thick of the fight, stood and clapped his hands shouting 'Bravo! Bravo!', perhaps in admiration of the French courage.

Then, at about ten o'clock, the enemy began to threaten the Great Redoubt in the Russian centre; Raevsky's troops at this fortification were already depleted through having to send help to the left wing. The first assault, by Broussier's division, was beaten back, but this only appeared to be a reconnaissance in force, and on the far side of the Semenovka the French could be seen massing for the main attack, drums beating above the crashing cannon. Russian troops stood silently, watching; gunners waited with linstocks in their hands ready to apply them to the ignition powder; behind stood the long lines of Russian infantry, and on the slopes further back were massed the restless cavalry.

At that moment, further along the line, Bagration was leading a counter-attack by his Cuirassier Division against the French at the *flèches*; his men were being slaughtered around him. Bagration noticed his surgeon Gangart, who had stayed beside him, thrown violently to the ground as his horse was shot beneath him. 'Save Gangart!' shouted Bagration. And then a bullet struck the general in the leg, smashing into the bone; he struggled to remain in the saddle, knowing that if he left the field the effect on his men might be disastrous. But his knees could no longer grip. Bagration drooped over his horse's neck then slid to the ground. His *aides* propped their commander against a bank, where he lay with his uniform tunic unbuttoned, his clothes soaked in blood and a gaping wound above one knee. First he refused to leave the battle, and still protested as soldiers carried him to the rear.

News of the loss of their general was already causing consternation in the left wing. The French secured a foothold in the *flèches*, and it seemed as if the Russian Second Army was about to collapse. An adjutant galloped up to Kutuzov and told him Bagration was gone. Kutuzov's aides noticed him shudder, then he turned to the Prince of Wurtemburg and asked: 'Will Your Highness be pleased to take over the command?' The Prince hurried off. But the situation at the *flèches* had become increasingly desperate, with Konovnitsin, temporary commander of the Second Army, rushing about trying to restore some kind of order – this officer still wore his nightcap. Wurtemburg sent back a panicked plea for reinforcements and Kutuzov changed his mind over the prince's fitness to command: he replaced him with the far tougher Dokhturov.[12]

Meanwhile the full French assault on the Raevsky Redoubt had been launched. Raevsky had already received a frenzied message from Konovnitsin asking for his personal presence at the *flèches* to help maintain control, but had refused knowing his own redoubt would soon be under heavy attack.

'My guns began to roar immediately the enemy stepped within range,' wrote Raevsky afterwards. 'The smoke hid the French so completely that nothing could be seen of them. One of my orderlies was standing just to the left of me, and after another volley he shouted: "Your Excellency – save yourself!" I spun round and saw French grenadiers pouring into my redoubt with fixed bayonets fifteen yards away.'[13]

'We dashed towards the redoubt and clambered through the

embrasures,' wrote one of the French grenadier officers, Captain Charles Francois. 'I myself went into an embrasure just after the gun in it had fired. The Russian gunners tried to beat us back with spikes and ramrods. We fought hand-to-hand and they were truly formidable opponents. . . . Once inside the redoubt I fought the Russian gunners with my sword and cut down more than one of them in the process.'[14]

The redoubt was taken. The French stood amongst the dead and wounded and attempted to organize themselves for the expected Russian counter-attack. Further to the left the *flèches* still held, commanded by the exhausted Dokhturov, despite a massive attack by Napoleon's famous 'Iron Division' of cuirassiers. Kutuzov again drew on his dwindling reserves, and ordered Ermolov, Barclay's chief of staff, to launch the counter-attack. This began almost immediately, with the Russians striking towards the redoubt in four main columns which approached in excellent order.

'The separate columns came towards the hill in perfect step to the beat of the drum,' wrote Wolzogen. 'Not a single shout came from the men. All this was so frightening for the French that we could see some of them fleeing and the strength at the redoubt dwindled.'[15] The French at the fortification, commanded by General Charles Bonnamy, had expended most of their ammunition in their seizure of the position; nor had they been given sufficient time to bring up many guns. The Russian lines advanced steadily up the slope; the troops began to shout, and now they ran forward with bayonets levelled. Back they thrust the French, through the embrasures and down the slope inflicting dreadful casualties.

'The French lost at least 3,000 dead in this incident,' claimed Barclay. 'The hill and the surrounding ground were scattered with enemy bodies for a distance of several hundred paces.'[16]

A bloody, half-dead French officer was brought before Kutuzov – General Bonnamy, whose 30th Regiment had been annihilated by the Russian counter-attack. Bonnamy was 'in a frightfully battered state and reeling from side to side, whether from wounds or other causes. "Doctor!" was Kutuzov's cry on seeing him, and after exchanging a few words with the wounded man he had him carried away. Under the uniform of the French hero were found two undershirts, and beneath them again his whole body was ripped with wounds.'[17] Bonnamy had been slashed by Russian bayonets in at least thirteen places.

Kutuzov had few reserves on which he could now draw; Barclay's First Army had been weakened to provide greater strength for the centre and left. The Raevsky Redoubt had been re-taken but the French were battering forward again on almost the entire length of the Russian line; the cannonade continued. And now, at about eleven o'clock, the *flèches* on the left finally fell, after about five hours of almost constant hand-to-hand fighting. French and Russian dead were heaped so high that the attackers could hardly clamber over them, and the filthy smoke billowed so thick that men found difficulty in gasping for breath.

A new threat suddenly emerged from the smoke between the *flèches* and the Raevsky Redoubt. Kutuzov received frantic reports that a massive assault was being launched towards Semenovskoye village, comprising elements of two French corps plus powerful artillery and cavalry support. Russian defenders consisted of forces which Kutuzov had already taken from the reserves: these units included the Ismailov, Lithuanian and Finnish regiments, just to the south of Semenovskoye village, and the eight battalions of the Second Combined Grenadier Division positioned to the front of the burning, artillery-battered houses. Further back waited Russian cavalry, mainly the First Cuirassier Division.

The attack began with a renewed artillery bombardment, even more terrifying than previous barrages. Shells, shot and cannister fire poured from the blackened sky and struck the Russian ranks, scattering soil and bodies. Then enemy cavalry trotted from the smoking valley, formed ranks and began to move forward with the horses picking their way through the dead. Officers in the Grenadier Division screamed at their men to form squares, and the Russian troops rushed backwards and forwards as they tried to obey. The first French cavalry reached them before a square could be organized, with the enemy charging in amongst the grenadiers, sabres slashing, trampling men beneath the hooves, then thrusting onwards. But by now the rest of the grenadiers had managed to form two defensive groups which caught the French cavalry in terrible cross-fire: scores of horses fell shrieking; the survivors spurred their animals desperately forward, trying to escape the Russian musket volleys, only to be attacked by Russian cuirassiers to the rear of Semenovskoye. South of the

145

village the Ismailov, Lithuanian and Finnish regiments had also come under attack from French cavalry, but these magnificent regiments formed squares before the enemy could reach them. The French suffered fearful loss. Moreover, Russian troops threw out a ragged yet determined line to face the hordes of French infantrymen now marching against them, and volley after volley shattered the approaching foot soldiers: the French commander, Count Louis Friant, forced his men onwards; the Russian commander, Dokhturov, ordered forward men from the Moscow and Astrakan regiments to bolster the thin Russian line. The defenders held their ground; the enemy began to fall back.

Murat, the French cavalry leader, rode amongst the retreating infantrymen shouting at them to turn about again. He grabbed one colonel by the collar, slewed him round to face the Russians and told him he must continue to fight. The colonel obeyed; he shouted to his men: 'Soldiers, face front! Let's go and get killed!'[18]

And at last the French managed to pierce their way upwards, up the dreadful slope, over the bodies of the Russian defenders, through the burning ruins of Semenovskoye. The Russians were forced on to the plateau beyond, where they finally managed to hold the enemy advance. Another hole had been ripped in the Russian line: first the *flèches*, now the Semenovskoye sector, both of them on the left of the Russian deployment. It seemed that the French could begin to push northwards, rolling up the entire enemy army. Moreover, Napoleon had still to commit his elite Imperial Guard, comprising 47,000 crack troops, the pride of his Grand Army.

But the Russians had already begun a counter-attack in an entirely unexpected direction. The movement of this assault would be critical. Kutuzov's cavalry on the right flank, like Napoleon's Guard, had been unemployed throughout the bitter six hours of fighting. These powerful horsemen were positioned close to Kutuzov's command post at Gorki, comprising Uvarov's 2,500 regular cavalry and Platov's 5,500 Don Cossacks. Platov had taken a detachment to explore the position further north, beyond the extreme right near the hamlet of Malos, and he discovered two important facts: first, the Kolocha proved to be easily fordable at this point, even for small artillery pieces; secondly, the French had apparently left the area undefended. The opportunity existed for a Russian flanking movement behind

Borodino. Platov galloped towards Gorki to inform the Russian High Command.

On his way he met Toll, to whom he explained his proposal, and Kutuzov's quartermaster-general reacted enthusiastically, hurrying back to his commander. Clausewitz, on Uvarov's staff and standing near the command post, heard Kutuzov declare: *'Eh Bien! Prenez-le!'* 'Enthusiasm blazed up like lighted straw,' remembered Clausewitz. The Russian cavalry began to move, a clattering body of yellow-uniformed hussars, dark green dragoons and Cossacks in their blue and red.[19]

Uvarov's regulars led the way, crossing the Kolocha then heading directly towards Borodino itself. Clausewitz, riding close to the commander, had serious doubts about the whole operation: he knew from previous experience how dangerous it might be to attempt a movement with only cavalry against a possible combination of enemy cavalry and infantry. 'We know well what happens when a single arm is opposed to two others.' His gloom proved justified. Uvarov's advance inclined to the right owing to swampy ground outside Borodino: the Russians surprised a French cavalry detachment, but then came against infantry from the Italian division, commanded by General Alexis-Joseph Delzons. These enemy infantrymen only amounted to about one regiment according to Clausewitz, but they nevertheless organized themselves into a strong defensive square with their backs against a small brook. Three charges by Uvarov's Elizabetgrad Hussars were repulsed, and only when the square had been shattered by horse artillery could Uvarov's advance continue – and by now the French had been alerted to the threat on the flank. Platov's Cossacks had moved in an arc further north, aiming to the west of Borodino. Powerful groups of French cavalry streamed out to meet them and enemy infantrymen scattered into the thick brushwood covering this area. Neither the Cossacks nor the regular Russian cavalrymen were able to filter further forward and the offensive slowed: the result was nothing more than Clausewitz had expected. Small cavalry detachments attempted to force a way through led by 'some young fire-eater who had a reputation to make', but few of these attackers survived.

Kutuzov had placed high hopes on this attack. As Clausewitz commented: 'The Russians could not carry out any offensive movement other than that led by General Uvarov. All eyes were

147

now turned upon him.' And as Kutuzov wrote in his report to Alexander after the battle: 'The enemy were approaching our left flank in great force. In order to draw off his attack I ordered Adjutant-General Uvarov with his First Cavalry Corps to cross the Kolocha river and attack the enemy on his left flank.'[20] The Russian commander relied upon the operation to redress the imbalance in the general situation; he constantly asked for fresh news of Uvarov's progress, only to find that the cavalry had been brought to a halt.

The Russians still clung to the Raevsky Redoubt, but the French had strengthened their hold on the abandoned positions further left and on the plateau behind Semenovskoye village. The Imperial Guard might be thrown into the battle at any moment. From where he stood Clausewitz could see this awesome force 'standing motionless in heavy columns like a thunder cloud'.[21]

Napoleon still sat at his command post at Shevardino. Repeated requests were made for the Guard to be ordered forward; each time Napoleon snapped his curt refusal. His decision seemed inexplicable to those clustered around him, who believed the intervention of the Guard would be decisive especially against the reeling Russian centre. Napoleon ignored all pleas. And among his reasons for maintaining the Guard intact was the threat now posed by the Russian cavalry on his left flank: already the presence of this force had proved enough to commit seventeen French cavalry regiments in the defence of the area, plus possibly 10,000 infantrymen. Napoleon could never be sure that this deployment would be enough; the Guard must be kept as reserve.

Uvarov and Platov therefore succeeded to a far greater extent than was immediately noticeable – and certainly more fully than Kutuzov would admit. The Russian cavalry finally pulled back in the mid-afternoon; when Uvarov reported to Kutuzov he received an abrupt reprimand: 'May God forgive you!'[22] Kutuzov's reaction was unjust, but by then other pressures were building up at an alarming rate.

Napoleon had delayed sending reinforcements to his forces threatening the Russian centre at the Raevsky Redoubt. Now, with the danger to his left flank removed, the French prepared to strike in overwhelming strength although still without the Guard: thousands of infantrymen and cavalry shuffled into line for the advance. These forces comprised three infantry divisions from

Eugène's Fourth Corps, supported to the north by General Emmanuel de Grouchy's Third Cavalry and to the south by the Second and Fourth Reserve Cavalry Corps.

Russian defenders at the redoubt had already been decimated. Corpses marked the ruins of whole regiments. Among these bodies lay the remains of a detachment of Wurtemburg cuirassiers which, according to an eye-witness, 'seemed to have been singled out as a special target, and their shattered helmets and cuirasses flew in splinters through the whole formation'. Prince Eugène of Wurtemburg had himself been in the midst of the artillery bombardments which had massacred many of those around him: at one time an *aide* had tried to attract his attention, waving an arm because he was unable to make himself heard in the din, only to have the limb torn off by a cannonball; thrown from his horse, the *aide* raised the other arm, still trying to gain his commander's attention. The prince had one horse shot under him and mounted another which was killed almost immediately; Eugène fell among two writhing officers and a soldier whose face had been ripped away. An adjutant ran forward with another mount, but the prince had scarcely time to put his foot in the stirrup before another shell landed, blowing up the animal. Yet Eugène still survived.[23]

And now the shell-shocked remnants of the regiments saw the French forming for another attack on the Raevsky Redoubt. The filthy, bloody Russians cowered beneath the shattered parapets while nearly 200 French guns attempted to smash all remaining resistance. Behind, Barclay scratched together all available reserves – just two cuirassier regiments.

The French began to move. 'From a distance it seemed that a gigantic iron-clad caterpillar was creeping towards the battery, covering the whole mound, its yellow, scaly armour glistening in the sun.'[24] In front rode the cavalry, led by Napoleon's *aide-de-camp* General Auguste de Caulaincourt, brother of the ex-Ambassador to Moscow. So strong was this enemy cavalry, and so weak the Russian mounted troops in the area, that Barclay decided he must preserve his cuirassier regiments: the defence of the redoubt had to be undertaken first by the gunners in the fortifications themselves, and then by the infantry standing behind.

The rest of the battle seemed to pause as the monstrous French

149

caterpillar crept forward: all attention was fixed on the Russian centre. The bombardment slackened as the cavalry approached; the earth ceased to shake from the thudding cannon balls and now trembled from the hundreds of hooves. The situation was immediately noticeable to those at Kutuzov's command post at Gorki: an officer reported afterwards: 'The rays of the half-obscured sun reflected on the sabres, swords, bayonets, helmets and armour, providing a fearful yet sublime picture.' The French neared the redoubt. 'Our guns fired a final salvo. Then they fell silent. A muffled cheering informed us that the enemy had burst over the defences and were thrusting forward with their weapons.'[25]

French cavalrymen swept over the bodies of the Russian gunners – 'there were dead and mutilated men and horses lying six or eight deep' wrote a Polish officer – and out onto the plateau behind the wrecked Russian position. Russian infantrymen struggled into line to meet them. Volley after volley flashed vivid from the swirling smoke, and Kutuzov's constant faith in the courage of his peasant soldiers proved justified once again. Ragged and weakened, the Russians fought in a half-crazed fury to check the French advance: one line loaded whilst another fired; the volleys continued to spit into the French until the last moment, and then the Russians used their muskets as clubs, and when these were broken and splintered, they used their bare hands. The French advance slowed. Incredibly, for the moment those reeling Russian regiments still held. The exhausted French and Russian soldiers pulled slightly apart, almost too weary to fight, and the pulse of battle began at last to slow.

'I can still see the weariness and exhaustion which the struggle assumed,' wrote Clausewitz. 'The infantry masses were so reduced that perhaps no more than a third of the original strength remained. The rest were either killed, wounded, engaged in removing the wounded, or rallying in the rear. Large gaps were everywhere apparent. The massive artillery engagements, undertaken by nearly 2,000 guns, was now only heard in single shots; and even these seemed to have lost the force and thunder of their original voice, and now coughed in a hoarse and hollow fashion. The cavalry made its attacks at a weary trot.'[26]

By now the sun was sinking steadily behind the clouds of black cannon smoke and swirling dust. Riderless horses galloped

in scores backwards and forwards across the battlefield, whinny-
ing in terror. On the plateau behind the Raevsky Redoubt the
dust hung so thick that men could see no further than ten paces.
Soldiers threw themselves on the ground, sobbing with exhaustion; others leant on their muskets, peering into the murk with
bloodshot eyes. Cavalrymen drooped over their horses' necks;
gunners were slumped over their artillery pieces.

A decision had still to be reached. The Russian army retained
just sufficient cohesion to cling to remaining ground; the French
army had suffered equal damage. And in this bloody stalemate
all rested upon the actions and attitudes of the two opposing
commanders, Napoleon and Kutuzov.

$$* \quad * \quad * \quad * \quad *$$

An astonishing similarity exists between the behaviour of
Napoleon and Kutuzov during the Battle of Borodino – behaviour
which resulted in both receiving the same accusations from their
critics. Throughout this massive conflict the two commanders
seemed strangely detached from the turmoil around them: they
sat on their chairs, for the most part silent. They appeared as two
individuals alone with their thoughts, apparently taking scant
interest while in front of them thousands upon thousands of men
fought and died under their command.

Ségur provided this description of Napoleon. 'Almost the
whole of the day he sat on his chair or walked slowly forward and
backward in advance and a little to the left of the redoubt taken
on the 5th, on the bank of a ravine far from the field of battle,
which he could scarcely see anything of after it had passed beyond
the heights: showing no agitation . . . and no impatience with
respect to his own troops or the enemy. He merely exhibited a
few gestures indicative of melancholy resignation, when every
now and then, in quick succession, he was informed of the loss of
his best generals. He rose many times, in order to take a few steps,
and then sat down again. Everyone around him observed him
with astonishment. Hitherto, in such momentous issues, he had
displayed a calm activity; but, in this instance, it was the coolness
of indolence, or the calm of lethargy.'[27]

'Had he not waved his horsewhip to and fro from time to
time,' wrote one commentator, describing Kutuzov, 'or traced

patterns on the ground with the handle, the generals and adjutants surrounding him would have thought that he was asleep.'[28]

Wolzogen also described Kutuzov during the battle. 'Barclay instructed me to find Prince Kutuzov, who had not appeared in the battle-line all day. . . . I rode a long way before I found the prince. I eventually met him – and his suite, who were so numerous that they looked to me like reinforcements – on the Moscow road about half an hour's ride behind the army. This suite consisted almost entirely of rich young Russian noblemen, who indulged in all kinds of pleasures and had taken no part whatever in the terrible and earnest events of the day. Colonel Toll was with them and busily eating a capon. . . . I knew that Kutuzov had spent the whole day in rear of the army among champagne bottles and delicatessen.'[29]

Kutuzov was closer than Wolzogen claimed and had been throughout the day; there is no evidence to substantiate the inference that Kutuzov spent his time swilling down champagne; Colonel Toll was in fact the most active member of Kutuzov's staff. The commander's post was less than half a kilometre away from the front line. Nevertheless Wolzogen's description contains some elements of truth: other eye-witnesses confirmed that Kutuzov appeared to give minimum attention to events around him; he seemed sunk in apathy; his actual involvement in the issue of orders was mainly confined to summoning up the reserves.

Critics of both Napoleon and Kutuzov failed to understand the realities of command at Borodino. Once the armies had been deployed, the basic plans formulated and the battle begun, the two leaders were extremely restricted in the amount which they could have altered the detailed course of fighting. The holocaust had been set in motion; now they could only await the result. They had to rely on others, apart from two critically important decisions which only they could make: first, the use of the reserves, and secondly when to bring the battle to an end.

With both these decisions Napoleon and Kutuzov adopted a parallel approach. This emerged not through their actions but their attitudes. They may have seemed detached, but both were drawing on their abilities in command derived partly through experience and partly through instinct. The conflict was more than a clash between opposing armies: it was also a struggle of will between the respective commanders. Both Napoleon and Kutuzov were reaching out towards one another over the chaos and inferno which lay between them.

Napoleon needed to sense whether or not to send the Imperial Guard forward. His decision had to be based on factors even more important than the actual state of the fighting at a particular time, more important than the fact that if the Imperial Guard had marched when the *flèches*, the Raevsky Redoubt or Semenovskoye had fallen then the Russian army might have had to retreat. He had to be able to divine whether this retreat would mean the end of the Russian commander's ability to resist the whole French campaign, not merely the French army at Borodino. Unless he could be sure, his despatch of the Guard might mean the weakening of this last intact French force without conclusive result, and the Grand Army would have been stranded miles inside hostile territory. General Count Pierre Daru received this reply from Napoleon when he pleaded for the Guard to be used: 'Tell me – who will fight if there is a battle tomorrow?'

Kutuzov, for his part, had to determine whether his army could still hold after Raevsky Redoubt had fallen. And his attitude at this point revealed his strength as a commander. He depended on other factors than casualty figures, reports of regimental positions, information brought by the succession of adjutants: these told him that the Russian army was in a perilous position with Bagration mortally wounded, the *flèches* taken, Semenovskoye seized, all reserves committed, and now Raevsky Redoubt possessed by the French. But beyond these facts was another. Kutuzov knew that his army was a living body, composed of thousands of individual soldiers who he understood so well; now all depended upon whether this body remained sufficiently alive to fight.

Even Wolzogen, among Kutuzov's harshest critics, sensed something of this attitude. Barclay had sent him to the commander because the situation was extremely desperate; urgent orders were required – and it seems clear that Barclay felt these orders should be for retreat. Wolzogen eventually found Kutuzov and poured out his information. He wrote: 'I began my report with an account of the positions and state of the army and said all important posts had been lost, except for the right wing on and to the left of the Smolensk road, and every regiment was in a condition of extreme exhaustion and chaos. Kutuzov interrupted me, shouting: "You must have been getting drunk with a flea-ridden sutler woman to present a report like that! The French have been thrown back along the entire length of the army. Tomorrow I'll place myself at the head of the army and drive the enemy from the sacred soil of Russia without any trouble." '

Wolzogen, choking down his anger, claimed he 'saw through Kutuzov's sly, unfair reasons for treating me like that'. Wolzogen realized that Kutuzov's diatribe was a sham, although the colonel believed the prince had acted in such a fashion to claim credit for a glorious, fictitious victory.[30]

Kutuzov's atttitude was simple. The troops must fight to the last; there would be no retreat from the battlefield that night. Barclay was instructed to withdraw only about a thousand yards to straighten the Russian line, with the right resting on Gorki Hill and the left stretching across towards Utitsa woods. Kutuzov declared: 'The enemy movements show that they have suffered just as much in action as we have. I therefore intend to continue the battle.' Full-scale operations would be resumed next day; Barclay commented: 'I don't know whether we could ever summon up the strength.'[31]

The news of Kutuzov's attitude soon spread. His soldiers heard that not only did they stand undefeated, but they were strong enough to battle again. These troops, aware of nothing beyond their immediate vicinity, where everything seemed so desperate and confused, were therefore told that the army as a whole still lived. And with this encouragement the individual regiments began to breathe again, exactly as Kutuzov had intended.

$*$ $*$ $*$ $*$ $*$

Russian regiments moved back at about six o'clock, bringing them to about the position where the reserve artillery had stood during the battle. Soon afterwards the French also retired, behind the Kolocha. Raiding Cossacks swarmed on to the battle-field once night had fallen, ranging over the ruins of the Raevsky Redoubt and the *flèches* and venturing to the fringe of the French lines. A light rain began to fall, and the fearful aftermath of battle spread over both armies. Wounded men lay in their thousands behind the respective lines; others shrieked and groaned throughout the night from the battlefield itself. Campfires acted as regrouping signals for the various units; mutilated men tried to crawl from the darkness to these beckoning lights. Conditions were exactly the same for both French and Russian, and no one could tell who were the victors and who the vanquished.

It is impossible to judge whether Kutuzov in fact intended to fight a second day's battle at Borodino, or whether he merely announced such a plan to rally his men. Certainly he considered Borodino to be a defensive victory. But whatever his original motives for his order to Barclay to prepare for renewed struggle, it soon became abundantly apparent that the Russian army must withdraw completely. Kutuzov returned to his quarters at the Tatarinovo farmhouse after dusk; already he had instructed Toll and Golitsyn, another member of his staff, to investigate the condition of the army. Toll reported back to the farmhouse soon after ten o'clock: his information proved intensely depressing. The Sixth Jaeger Regiment – 910 non-commissioned officers and men killed or wounded; the Litovsk Regiment – 741; the Ismail Regiment – 777. . . . And so the lists continued.

Total Russian casualties are difficult to determine with any real accuracy, and estimates vary between 38,500 dead and wounded and as many as 50,000. Most Russian historians have accepted the figure of about 44,000, representing more than one man in every three. Over 60,000 rounds of artillery were fired, and by nightfall on the 7th the Russian ammunition stocks were extremely low; many gun carriages were so battered through the constant recoil that they were held together by rope.[32] Kutuzov knew that French losses were also extremely high. In fact, Napoleon's casualties were probably over 30,000, including forty-eight generals dead and wounded; French guns probably fired about the same amount of rounds as the Russian; cavalry losses were higher than those of the enemy.[33]

Kutuzov soon reached the conclusion that his army was in no fit state to fight in the immediate future. Moreover, he felt strong apprehension over the lack of reinforcements being sent to him, either in the form of militiamen or regulars: no more men had arrived from Rostopchin, despite the Governor's promises, and Kutuzov had inadequate cover for his army should he be forced into a precipitate retreat following renewed battle. A planned withdrawal was the only wise step to take, during which reinforcements could be collected and regiments reorganized. The army must be preserved.

Russian commanders assembled at the dingy farmhouse were therefore ordered to prepare their regiments for the march. But Kutuzov was anxious to avoid any impression that the army had suffered a defeat: his orders specified that the troops would move in four columns and battle would be renewed at the first available opportunity. Once again it is impossible to assess how far Kutuzov attempted to deceive and how far he really believed that battle would soon be resumed. Whichever the case might have been, his subsequent despatch to Alexander created a strong impression in St Petersburg that Borodino had resulted in the virtual defeat of the French, and when this was shown not to be the truth Kutuzov would be branded as a liar and a fraud.

Yet the report to Alexander, sent on the day after Borodino, contained no more than Kutuzov's conviction that the French could not be considered the victors of the battle: the enemy had attacked and finally had been obliged to retire without gaining control of the battlefield; Kutuzov had therefore succeeded in his defensive battle. 'Beaten at all points, the enemy retreated in the middle of the night, and we were left the masters of the field of war.' According to Kutuzov 'a cruel cannonade from both sides continued into the depths of the night. Our artillery inflicted immense damage with roundshot and silenced the enemy batteries, after which all the French infantry and cavalry withdrew.'[34]

Kutuzov undoubtedly exaggerated, from a number of causes. The outcome of the day's fighting left him both exhausted and elevated; the latter emotion was revealed in a note to his wife: 'My dear, I am in good health, thank God, and I have not been beaten, and I won the battle with Bonaparte.'[35] Moreover, Kutuzov clearly attempted to bolster morale in both his army and in St Petersburg: soldiers and citizens must appreciate the massive blow which had been inflicted on Napoleon's vaunted Grand Army. Perhaps, for this reason, Kutuzov's first message to Alexander after the battle failed to make clear that the Russian army would now withdraw, although his earlier report on 4 September had warned: 'Perhaps I will have to withdraw behind

Mozhaisk.' Alexander should have been prepared; as it was, news of retreat would come as a shattering shock – why, if Borodino had been a victory, should the Russians now flee?

Napoleon later provided a comment which proved the most suitable verdict on the battle of Borodino: 'The French showed themselves worthy of victory and the Russians of being invincible.'[36] These words reveal the real result of the battle: in the conflict of wills between Napoleon and Kutuzov the latter emerged the stronger – even though this psychological victory had still to become apparent. The seeds of the French Emperor's ultimate destruction were sown in the bloody field of Borodino.

XI

MOSCOW

(1812: 8–15 September)

By dawn on Tuesday, 8 September, the Russian regiments were moving along the road eastwards towards Mozhaisk. Troops staggered with weariness; many of them had been unable to snatch even a few minutes' sleep since the battle, and now they marched on again, ignorant of the army's plans, still trusting in Kutuzov.

Behind them lay a scene of horror fully revealed by the light of day. French troops, as exhausted as their enemy, had been under constant alert throughout the night as a result of Cossack raids; now they sat by their dreary fires too weary to move, or wandered like spectres over the battlefield. Napoleon had been informed in the early hours that the Russians seemed to be withdrawing; with his own regiments so shattered he could do nothing to stop this retirement. Instead he rode forward to inspect the field of conflict.

'Everything concurred to increase the horrors of it,' wrote Ségur. 'A lowering sky, a cold rain, a violent wind, habitations in ashes, a plain completely torn up and covered with fragments and ruins; all round the horizon the dark and funereal verdure of the trees of the north.'

Napoleon sought some sign of victory – trophies, captured guns, standards – but could find nothing. He demanded to know the number of prisoners taken, and was astonished to hear that only about 800 could be assembled: as before, the Russians had preferred to die rather than be seized. Ségur's account continued: 'The Emperor could appreciate his victory only by the number of the slain. The ground of the redoubt was so thickly strewn with slaughtered Frenchmen that they appeared rather to belong to

158

them than to those who still survived. There seemed on those spots to be more dead than living conquerors.'[1]

Clerks were attempting to assess casualties. In one part of the battlefield these officials 'used a dead horse as a writing table, and the orderlies even dragged up a few Russian corpses to act as chairs for the scribes, who were re-fighting the battle with their pens'.[2] Surgeons were still labouring amongst the thousands of wounded. Amputated limbs were piled high, overflowing the banks of baskets. Baron Domique Larrey, the Grand Army's Surgeon-General, had himself performed 200 amputations during the night, of which an astonishing 74 per cent were successful.

Napoleon's army was both severely weakened by the casualties of Borodino and shaken by the bitterness of supposed victory. Officers and men were more aware than ever before how far they were from home, and how deep into hostile territory. 'We had never suffered such heavy losses,' commented Colonel Raymond de Montesquiou, Duke of Fezensac. 'Never had the army's morale been so damaged. I no longer found the soldiers' old gaiety: a gloomy silence had replaced the songs and amusing stories which previously had helped them to forget the fatigue. . . . Even the officers appeared anxious. . . . This depression, natural in a defeated army, was remarkable after a decisive action, after a victory which opened to us the gates of Moscow.'[3]

The main French army began to move from Borodino during the afternoon of this Tuesday, 8 September. Meanwhile, the advance guard under Murat hurried eastwards after the Russians. By this time Kutuzov had moved through Mozhaisk, issuing no orders for a stand to be made at this town even though less than a hundred kilometres remained before Moscow. Reinforcements had still to arrive, especially the militiamen promised by Rostopchin, and added to this question of numbers was a deeper reason for Kutuzov's continued withdrawal: he reported to Alexander: 'It is not just a business of the glorious victory in battles, but the whole aim must be directed at the utter destruction of the French Army.'[4] Napoleon must not merely be blocked, but annihilated.

The French advance guard therefore entered Mozhaisk on the morning of 9 September after a delaying action by the Russian rearguard under Miloradovich. Napoleon rode into the town later in the day, with his staff officers appalled by the fresh horrors revealed in the dirty streets: Russian wounded had been left, too weak to march, and now they lay in hundreds among the corpses of their comrades. Napoleon established his headquarters in a half-built, windowless house and attempted to catch up on neglected paper-work. 'He lost his voice so completely,' wrote one of his secretaries, Baron Fain, 'that he was not able to dictate or even to talk. This was the result of a heavy cold aggravated by spending the last few cold nights in a tent. In this embarrassing situation he had recourse to his pen. . . .'[5]

Among the letters written by Napoleon this Wednesday was a highly inaccurate despatch to the Austrian Emperor, Francis. 'I hasten to announce to Your Imperial Majesty the happy issue of the battle of the Moskova. . . . Knowing the personal interest that Your Majesty is good enough to take in me, I thought I ought to announce this memorable event to you in my own hand, and to tell you that I am in good health. I reckon the enemy's losses at 40–50,000 men: he had between 120–130,000 men engaged. I lost from 8–10,000 killed or wounded. I took sixty guns, and a great number of prisoners.'[6]

News of the battle had reached Moscow but without details of the result, and a solemn Te Deum was offered for the success of the Russian army. Yet many leading citizens were already packing their belongings ready for the flight to St Petersburg. Hour by hour the Russian regiments approached the city. Miloradovich's rearguard fought off a strong attack by Murat's forces on 10 September, with the engagement lasting into the night, although Clausewitz noticed that the French troops appeared to be showing increasing signs of exhaustion.[7]

Next day, 11 September, Kutuzov ordered a halt. His forces lay across the road in the vicinity of Zvenigorod, less than fifty kilometres from Moscow itself; Napoleon had remained in Mozhaisk but many of his regiments were pushing steadily up the road behind Murat's advance cavalry. Kutuzov still sought reinforcements: he wrote on this Friday: 'The army has come to a halt near Moscow. . . . Although I hope for superiority, the situation regarding weapons is uncertain.'[8] Yet during the day he received information from St Petersburg despatched the previous week: regular reserve regiments would not reach him in the immediate future, and it also became apparent that no fresh militia levies were being prepared.[9] Instead, Rostopchin posted a proclamation in Moscow urging citizens to join him in an unofficial, ill-organized crusade against the approaching French. 'Arm yourselves as best you can. Come on foot or on horseback. Bring only three days' supply of bread with you. Mass together on Three Mountains [Sparrow Hills, outside the city], and I shall be with you. Together we shall exterminate the Villain. Glory to those who resist. Eternal memory to those who fall. Woe at the Last Judgement to those who evade their duty!'[10]

Count Theodore Rostopchin, Moscow's Governor-General since 24 June, had served as Czar Paul's Foreign Minister until dismissed during one of the Emperor's erratic moments. His direction of foreign affairs had been marked by a policy of alliance with France but now his actions were fired with a patriotism which bordered on hysteria. Impatient, nervous and highly excitable, Rostopchin was also characterized by a gift of high-flown rhetoric – and by an unfortunate tendency to make promises which he was unable to fulfil, notably with the supply of militiamen to Kutuzov. Soon this crop-haired, bulbous-eyed count would be among Kutuzov's most virulent critics; moreover he owed his present position to Catherine Pavlovna, sister of Czar Alexander, and this highly influential female also entertained acute suspicions of the Russian commander's actions.

Rostopchin's proclamation posted on the 11th met with massive response. Thousands of peasants and townsmen flocked to the Sparrow Hills fired with a fanatical zeal to repel the invaders. The military value of this unorganized, almost unarmed horde was extremely questionable; in the event these patriots found themselves without a leader – Rostopchin was detained in business at Moscow and failed to appear before his amateur army. The crowd waited for him until nightfall then shuffled miserably back into the city.[11] Meanwhile, also on 11 September, Kutuzov's first account of Borodino reached St Petersburg, and the reaction in the capital marked a startling contrast to the gloom and growing panic in Moscow. The French had apparently been thrown back – Kutuzov had claimed 'we remained masters of the field of battle'. This Friday represented the feast of Alexander Nevsky, the great Russian saint, and the Emperor used the occasion to announce the news to his people with the commander's great words read to the assembled congregation in the great cathedral.

'The effect was glorious,' wrote Sir Robert Wilson, still in Petersburg. The British envoy immediately sought to finish his affairs in the capital so that he could return to the Russian army and 'pursue the career of true glory'.[12] Alexander declared that Kutuzov would be honoured with the rank of Marshal and would receive 100,000 silver roubles; twenty-five roubles would be given to each private soldier in his army. Celebrations continued in the capital far into the night, with bells pealing from the churches, fireworks flaring, and with hopes high that Napoleon might soon be dragged to Petersburg in a cage.

On 12 September Kutuzov moved his headquarters to Mano-novo, even closer to Moscow, although his order of the day inferred that a battle would soon be fought.[13] Reinforcements had still to arrive from the Moscow militia. Kutuzov wrote to Rostopchin, asking him to come to the army headquarters for discussions; the Moscow governor immediately took this to mean that the commander intended to explain his battle plans and he posted another bombastic, misleading notice in the city streets: 'I leave tomorrow to visit HH Prince Kutuzov to take, jointly with him, the measures to exterminate our enemies. We shall send these visitors packing and we shall make them give up the ghost! I shall return for dinner and we shall all lend a hand to make mincemeat of these traitors!'[14]

By now Moscow was within sight of the Russian army, and in the city the terrified inhabitants could see the soldiers' campfires burning in the low hills to the west. The number of families fleeing soared steadily higher; hundreds of carts, carriages and litters were filling the roads to Yaroslavl, Vladimir and Ryazan, and the fear felt by these refugees was increased by the scores of wounded soldiers travelling with them – including the dying hero of Borodino, Prince Bagration.

But Rostopchin retained his inflated optimism when he reached Kutuzov at ten o'clock on the morning of 13 September. The governor's subsequent account of this meeting is extremely un-trustworthy, but nevertheless it is clear he received the definite impression that Kutuzov intended to fight before Moscow. Rostopchin found the prince sitting by a fire. 'He was surrounded by generals and *aides-de-camp*, who asked for orders. One by one he sent them off, now to Barclay, now to Bennigsen, some-times to Count Toll. . . . The prince received me with great courtesy and took me to one side. We stayed alone together for half an hour. . . . He told me that it had been decided to give battle to Napoleon at the very spot where we now stood.'[15]

Bennigsen had prepared a battle plan which envisaged the army taking up defensive positions south-west of Moscow. The right flank would be the curve of the Moskva in front of the village of Fili, which lay almost in the Moscow suburbs at the point where the Smolensk road entered the capital; the left wing would rest in the Sparrow Hills around Vorobievo almost twenty kilometres away. To defend this line Kutuzov would be able to deploy fewer than 80,000 men; French strength was unknown, but reports indicated that reinforcements had been rushed to the Grand Army from Smolensk. In fact Napoleon's army probably totalled about 100,000 at this stage.[16] Relations between Kutuzov and Bennigsen had continued to worsen since Borodino: the chief of staff disagreed with the decision to withdraw from Mozhaisk, and once further retirement commenced he increasingly quarrelled with his commander over the movement of the different regiments on the road. But it soon became apparent that the deployment now suggested by Bennigsen would be extremely dangerous: the front would be extended; the line would incline south of Moscow, allowing Napoleon to push directly with concentrated forces down the Smolensk road against the Russian right wing; attempts to avoid this massed effort against the Russian right, by moving the entire line further north, were rendered impossible by the river Moskva; any subsequent withdrawal from the battle position would be perilous, because of the steep slopes towards Moscow, the curving Moskva, and the city itself.[17]

Early this Sunday morning Barclay undertook his usual practice of reconnoitring the army positions in person. The First Army commander, suffering from fever and exhaustion, reported back after an hour's inspection. He found Kutuzov sitting on a camp-chair on a small hillock beside the road at Fili; the prince listened in silence to Barclay's gloomy assessment. Staff officers were sent to re-examine the ground, and at the same time Kutuzov began to explore alternatives, despatching Barclay and the First Army chief of staff, Alexei Yermolov, to reconnoitre the roads south.[18]

The officers returned to Kutuzov's improvised headquarters during the mid-afternoon; the prince listened quietly to respective reports. Discussion was interrupted by heavy firing from the Russian rearguard, indicating the enemy's imminent approach. Kutuzov's generals and staff officers began to hurry away, instructed to return for a full war council at five o'clock, and the old prince rose ponderously from his chair. He beckoned Duke Eugène von Wurtemburg to him and whispered in French: 'It's all on my head. Whether for good or bad, only it can decide.'[19]

The generals assembled for the war council at five o'clock. Already, the sky had begun to darken as the officers dismounted outside a peasant's small log cottage which Kutuzov had commandeered at Fili. Inside, the prince sat in an armchair placed in the centre of the room; beside him stood a table strewn with maps. A fire had been lit in the hearth, and the smoke from the wet wood gusted into the room. Present were Bennigsen – according to some reports the start of the meeting was delayed because he dallied with a meal – Barclay, Dokhturov, Ostermann-Tolstoy, Konovnitsin, Yermolov, Toll, Raevsky and one or two other senior officers.

Bennigsen spoke almost immediately, demanding to know whether the army would fight beneath the walls of Moscow or surrender the city to the enemy. Kutuzov impatiently interrupted. This was not the issue, he declared. The point to be settled was whether to engage the enemy in a position which could not be defended and thus take the risk of losing the entire army, or manoeuvre the army into a better position even though Moscow would be temporarily abandoned. The difference between the commander and his chief of staff was therefore subtle, but sufficient: Kutuzov placed first priority on his army; Bennigsen on Moscow. Opinion proved to be sharply divided. Barclay repeated that the present positions were entirely unsatisfactory; Konovnitsin wanted to move forward into the attack; Raevsky and Ostermann-Tolstoy urged a withdrawal through the capital. Bennigsen continued to insist that the plan prepared by him was perfectly feasible and should be adopted, and he expressed surprise that his dispositions should be criticized; Dokhturov apparently agreed with the chief of staff. Yermolov wavered. Toll favoured withdrawal.

Kutuzov conducted the war council entirely according to the regulations of Peter the Great which specified that senior army commanders should be consulted. He himself said only a few words while his subordinates presented their opinions, but witnesses noticed that he appeared tense; a messenger arrived with a fresh report of French movements and Kutuzov merely

164

commented 'Very good' in a low voice. Finally, after about ninety minutes, Kutuzov declared his decision.

'I know all the blame will be on my head. But I must sacrifice myself for the good of the Fatherland. I order the retreat.' Kutuzov added: 'The loss of Moscow is not the loss of Russia. My first obligation is to preserve the army, to get nearer to those troops approaching as reinforcements, and by the very act of leaving Moscow to prepare inescapable ruin for the enemy.' The army would withdraw through Moscow, marching south-east to be in a position to cover Ryazan or Tula, even though this would uncover the road north towards Petersburg. Kutuzov made to move from his chair. The officers stood. The old prince declared: 'Now gentlemen. No more talk. Everyone to his post.'[20]

Also on 13 September Napoleon sent an illuminating message to Murat. 'The Emperor is worried at not having news of the enemy. If you do not find him in front of you, it is to be feared that he is on your right on the road to Kaluga and he would be in a position to hurl himself on our rear. . . . His Majesty awaits your news impatiently, with special reference to what is happening on your right, i.e., on the road from Kaluga to Moscow.'[21] By moving south-east towards Ryazan, Kutuzov would in fact be placing his army in a position to switch into the area which Napoleon most feared.

Once again, it is almost impossible to read Kutuzov's mind and to judge whether he in fact had ever planned to fight before Moscow. His deviousness, and his skill in cloaking his own opinion until he made a definite decision, made any assessment entirely speculative. But it is clear that Kutuzov seized upon the strategic implications to a far greater extent than his subordinate commanders. He is reported to have commented after the war council: 'You fear a retreat through Moscow, but I regard it as far-sighted. It will save the army. Napoleon is like a stormy torrent which we are as yet unable to stop. Moscow will be the sponge that sucks him in.'[22] And as Clausewitz wrote: 'The cleverness of this old fox was more useful at the moment than Barclay's honesty.'[23]

The army must be preserved. This principle was repeated in Kutuzov's letters immediately after the war council. 'I won the battle before Moscow,' he told one of his daughters, 'but it was necessary to save the army, and soon all our armies – Tormassov,

Chichagov, Wittgenstein and some others – will begin to act towards one aim. Napoleon will not be long in Moscow.'[24] Kutuzov's decision to abandon the capital reinforced the steadily growing psychological superiority which he had won over Napoleon at Borodino. Moreover, by moving south-east the Russian army would be able to guard the fertile southern provinces and the manufacturing town of Tula. The latter, 'the Sheffield of Russia', produced items ranging from exquisite snuff-boxes to massive cannons, and by 1812 was able to turn out over 1,300 muskets each week.[25]

But first the army had to manoeuvre through Moscow. Russian troops began to filter through the streets during the night of 13–14 September, and thousands more citizens joined the retreat. 'I found the capital in a woeful state,' wrote a young officer named Nikolai Muravyev, later to become a general in the Crimean War, 'with weeping and clamour everywhere. Along the streets lay dead and wounded soldiers. . . . Disorders had already broken out. Crowds of people stood everywhere. . . . Almost all the nobility had left.'[26] Flickering lanterns lit the retreat. Raevsky's adjutant was riding beside his tough, battle-scarred corps commander: 'Suddenly, in the silence of the night, I heard our beloved hero quietly sobbing.'[27] The chaos seemed all the more horrific in contrast to the serenity of the buildings, described by the French-woman Madame de Staël just a few days before as 'green, yellow, pink, and sculptured like dessert decorations'. Some citizens were attempting to dismantle a huge cross which stood proudly on one of the churches and which the people were unwilling to let fall into French hands: then it was seen that a vulture had become entangled in the chains around the cross, and the crowd cheered, believing the capture of the bird represented an excellent omen.

But for the most part the people shuffled in silence as they herded over the cobbles towards the city's southern gates. Occasional panic broke out among the crowds as sudden rumours spread that the French cavalry were close behind. And indeed, a French attack at this moment could have been disastrous, with Kutuzov's regiments split and entangled with the fleeing civilians. The Russians attempted to gain time through a short armistice. Kutuzov ordered Miloradovich, commanding the rearguard, to obtain a twenty-four-hour truce with Murat while Moscow was cleared: the Russian general was instructed to inform the French vanguard commander that if this was refused, the people of Moscow would put up a desperate and costly defence of their city.

Miloradovich accordingly sent forward the white flag to the French advance positions, and the Russian request received a favourable response. Clausewitz, still with the Russian rearguard, commented: 'It was clear that the French wanted Moscow in a complete state, and if the Russian request was agreed to, any Russian plan to set the city ablaze would be avoided.'[28] If this in fact was the French motive for agreeing to a temporary ceasefire, then the subsequent tragedy must have been received with an even more shattering shock.

The final Russian regiments moved through Moscow unmolested by the French. A military band began to beat out a defiant tune in an attempt to lift the spirits of the soldiers, but Miloradovich rode in a fury to the commander, thrusting forward his prominent jaw and shouting: 'What idiot told your band to play?' The band officer replied that a garrison must play suitable music when leaving a fortress, under a regulation laid down by Peter the Great. 'Where do the regulations of Peter the Great provide for the surrender of Moscow?' bellowed back Miloradovich. 'Order that damned music to be stopped!'[29]

Kutuzov entered Moscow at nine o'clock in the morning of the 14th, escorted by his staff. He apparently asked an aide: 'Show me a roundabout route to avoid meeting anyone.' In fact most of the citizens were already pushing through the gates on the opposite side of the city and the streets were now almost deserted. 'We rode across Moscow in a melancholy silence,' wrote Prince Nicholas Boris-Golitsyn on Kutuzov's staff, 'nobody expressing what was in his thoughts, and each apparently absorbed in sombre reflections. The solemnity of this silent march, of which no one except the commander-in-chief knew either the destination or the duration, had something sinister about it as we passed through these streets, usually so thronged now all but empty.'

Count Rostopchin had acted in a frenzy since his return to Moscow late the previous night, organizing evacuation, instructing officials to burn papers, collect treasures, protect the religious relics. And according to many subsequent accounts, the Governor-General had also been preparing to set the capital alight. At Fili he had confided to Würtemburg that he would rather see Moscow destroyed than fall into French hands – some historians claim

Rostopchin actually said 'burnt' not destroyed. He is also reported to have told his son Sergei: 'Salute Moscow for the last time. In an hour it will be in flames.'[30] The previous night Rostopchin had sent an angry letter to Alexander, denouncing Kutuzov. 'The commander-in-chief's resolution decides the fate of Your Empire, which will foam with rage when it learns that the city which contains the grandeur of Russia and in which rests the ashes of your ancestors is to be handed over to the enemy.' The Governor added: 'I vouch for it with my life, Sire, that Bonaparte will find Moscow as deserted as Smolensk. Everything has been taken away. Moscow will be a desert in his hands – if fire does not consume it – and may become his tomb.'[31]

Now, at midday on the 14th, Rostopchin was almost ready to depart. Kutuzov met the person he most wanted to avoid: the army commander and the Governor encountered one another at the bridge over the Yauza, close to the Kolomna-Ryazan Gate from the city. Rostopchin sat on his horse wearing a military frock-coat and with a whip twitching in his fist; he seemed even more highly-charged than usual, his movements jerky, his lips pulled back from his teeth. Kutuzov sat slumped in his saddle and his Cossack mount plodded on. The two men barely spoke: Rostopchin glared at the prince, then pulled round his horse and trotted back into the city.

Kutuzov stopped at the Old Believers' Cemetery, not far outside the Kolomna Gate, and dismounted. He stood for a while beside the road, then climbed laboriously into a droshky but still waited. Troops were marching past him, among them Sergei Glinka serving in a militia regiment. 'Slowly the regiments marched past their commander,' wrote Glinka. 'Anger and grief burned in their eyes, their mouths uttered loud cries of "Where are we being led?" "Where has he brought us?" His right hand resting on his knee, Kutuzov sat motionless, as though seeing nothing, hearing nothing.'[32]

Napoleon had ridden forward to join his advance guard during the morning. Gradually the Emperor and his staff approached the city. 'At length,' wrote Ségur, 'the last height that had remained to be passed over was gained . . . it is called the "Mount of Salvation" because from the top of it, at the sight of their holy city, the inhabitants make the sign of the cross and prostrate themselves on the ground. Our light troops soon gained the

168

summit. It was two o'clock, and the great city was glittering with a thousand colours in the sun. Struck with astonishment at the spectacle, they halted, and exclaimed in admiration, 'Moscow! Moscow!' ... At the sight of this golden city, this brilliant clasp of Europe and Asia, this superb rendezvous, where the luxury, the customs, and the arts of the two finest divisions of the world meet all together, we halted with feelings of contemplative and proud elevation. What a day of glory had at last arrived!'[33]

Napoleon reined his horse beside his men. 'There it is at last,' he said. 'And high time.'[34]

The French advance guard cautiously entered the city; the Russian rearguard took up position on the opposite outskirts. The roads stretching southwards were still crammed with refugees: people were crying, their faces dust-covered and stained; babies were being pushed in wheel-barrows; household belongings were piled upon backs; the old men and women were helped or carried in litters or left to stagger on alone. Among those watching the pitiful sight was Clausewitz; he suddenly noticed something else, beyond the refugees. 'I saw wreaths of smoke rising from several places in the furthest suburbs.' The fire of Moscow had begun.[35]

Napoleon and his staff waited for a deputation to approach from the city. A member of the Emperor's entourage, Captain Brandt, overheard a veteran soldier whisper to a comrade: 'They will wait a long time. All those Russians will emigrate to Siberia rather than surrender.'[36] Napoleon heeled his horse forward and began to descend the hill to the gate.

Kutuzov still waited near the southern suburbs. Colonel Toll rode up to his commander and reported that the French had entered Moscow. 'God be praised,' answered Kutuzov. 'That is their last triumph.' He gave the order to his driver and the droshky began to move along the bumpy road south, while behind Kutuzov the smoke from Moscow rose steadily into the afternoon sky. Explosions could be heard, one after another in the distance; Russian soldiers turned to gaze back at their capital. 'Mother Moscow is burning!' they exclaimed.[37] The smoke billowed thicker and the wind fanned the flames as night approached. At first the French were blamed for the dreadful fire of Moscow; Clausewitz wrote: 'On this march I saw Moscow burning without interruption, and although we were ten kilometres distant, the wind sometimes covered us with ashes. Even though the Russians were already broken in to sacrifices of this kind, after the burning of Smolensk and other towns, yet this one filled them with terrible sorrow, and incensed them against an enemy who they held responsible for this act of barbarity, a result of the enemy's hate, insolence and cruelty.' Rostopchin would claim credit for the fire after it became a symbol of Russian resistance. His claim seemed well-supported: his known actions before the event, his public statements, even the fact that he had ordered the fire-tenders to be taken from the city before the French arrived. Later, in 1823, Rostopchin tried to deny responsibility and his son wrote: 'My father never gave a direct order to anyone to set fire to Moscow, but he took all kinds of measures to see that it did burn.'[38]

Tolstoy believed the fire started by accident: fires were common at that time of year amongst the dry wooden houses. Clausewitz agreed, although years later he tended to the view that Rostopchin was perhaps the author. At the time Clausewitz wrote: 'The confusion which I saw in the streets as the rearguard moved out; the fact that the smoke was first seen to rise from the outer edge of the suburbs where the Cossacks were active, both convinced me that the Moscow fire was a result of the chaos, and of the habit the Cossacks had of first thoroughly pillaging and then setting fire to all the houses before the enemy could make use of them.'[39] Napoleon's officers were convinced that the fire was a massive and carefully planned operation, and for days afterwards Russian 'incendiaries' would be executed by the occupying army.

Kutuzov's opinion is unknown. It would have been in character for the old Marshal to have kept his belief hidden; certainly he profited from the fire, because it reduced the comfort which Moscow could offer the French and increased the hatred felt by his soldiers against the enemy. Most likely he simply accepted the fire as a fact, and he would have agreed with a later French commentator: 'The truth about the burning of Moscow is that Moscow has burnt.'[40]

Meanwhile, the Russian withdrawal continued; the next step had to be decided. By nightfall on the 14th Kutuzov had reached the village of Panki, about fifteen kilometres south-east of Moscow, where he established a temporary headquarters. A succession of staff officers reported on the state of the regiments, which seemed to be improving almost by the hour. Yermolov, who had previously wavered over the decision to leave Moscow, commented: 'I observed very carefully the effect which the abandonment of Moscow had produced on the troops, and contrary to expectation I noticed that the private soldier had not lost heart and was by no means disposed to grumble.' Another officer, Löwenstern, also noticed this upsurge of spirits. 'Quite spontaneously everyone forgot his personal concerns and thought only of the affront the enemy had just inflicted on us, and, far from being disheartened, we felt more passionately determined than ever to continue the war and to make every conceivable sacrifice. One felt as if a burden had been lifted. After the capture of Moscow we had the Empire to save, not just a town; and from this moment everybody said: "The war is only just beginning!" '[41]

This was precisely the reaction which Kutuzov had hoped to obtain, and no one felt the lifting of the burden more than he: no longer would Kutuzov be tied to the defence of Moscow, as he had been since joining the army and as Barclay had been almost since the campaign began. Now Kutuzov could manoeuvre for the destruction of Napoleon. Orders were despatched to other Russian armies: Chichagov was instructed to move his Danube Army into the Mogilev region, south-west of Smolensk, to threaten the enemy's rear and sever communications; Wittgenstein was told to unite with Chichagov as soon as possible.[42]

Kutuzov had so far neglected to inform Alexander of the abandonment of Moscow. But even before the news reached Petersburg the Emperor had begun to interfere with the commander-in-chief's future plans by despatching orders to Chichagov and Wittgenstein. These two subordinate commanders were told to operate farther west than Kutuzov intended, in a more independent role, and this divergence soon led to a complaint from Kutuzov to Alexander: 'It is necessary to point out that distant diversions from the main war cannot have as much influence on it as near ones.'[43] Chichagov responded far more readily to Alexander's requests than to Kutuzov's commands; the burden of Moscow may have been removed from Kutuzov's shoulders, but the burden of Alexander and his favourites remained as heavy as ever.

Napoleon entered Moscow next day, 15 September. Only about 15,000 of the 250,000 inhabitants of the city had stayed. Small groups stood beside the road as the French Emperor rode in; Napoleon was dressed plainly in the green uniform of a Chasseur colonel, and appeared overshadowed by the magnificent apparel worn by Murat – pale pink riding breeches, bright yellow leather boots, four ostrich feathers and an aigrette of heron's plumes fluttering from his hat. The conqueror of Moscow established his headquarters in an Italian-style palace forming part of the Kremlin. But the fires in the city were steadily spreading, eating up street after street, and that night Napoleon reluctantly agreed to move to safety. He barely escaped. 'We walked upon a blazing earth,' wrote Ségur, 'under a blazing sky, between blazing walls.' The Emperor managed to reach the Moskva, then left the city to take up temporary residence at the Petrovsky Palace ten kilometres north. From his windows he could see Moscow engulfed in flames. 'What a frightful spectacle!' he exclaimed. 'To have done it themselves! Such a number of palaces! What extraordinary resolution! What a people! They are genuine Scythians!'[44]

The French Emperor nevertheless felt reassured over the position of the main Russian army. Before Moscow he had feared the Russians might lurk near the Kaluga road, thereby threatening his communications from Smolensk. Napoleon had anxiously awaited news from Murat, sent out with his cavalry along the path of the retreating Russians, and was relieved to find that Kutuzov was leaving the Kaluga road untouched; instead, the Russian army took the Ryazan road much further to the south-east. This route, Napoleon believed, could not have suited the French better: the Russians were wandering aimlessly in a direction which would leave his own communications intact and which would leave the route to Petersburg wide open. Napoleon therefore relaxed, allowing the bulk of his army to rest in the environs of Moscow, and he believed the Russian movement to be a virtual admission of defeat.

Kutuzov celebrated his 67th birthday on 15 September still travelling southwards on the Ryazan road. He was well-content. He had won the psychological advantage over Napoleon; now he could make use of this to seize the most critical weapon in any campaign – the initiative. The Russian move towards Ryazan only amounted to a feint. Kutuzov planned a daring cross-country manoeuvre which would enable his army to side-step Murat's probing cavalry; the Russian army would disappear from view, until it suddenly emerged in the most dangerous position of all. Kutuzov was about to launch the decisive operation which settled the entire campaign of 1812.

XII

The Tomb of an Army

(1812: 15 September–17 October)

'I intend tomorrow to make a march along the Ryazan road,' wrote Kutuzov to Count Wintzingerod on the 15th, 'but then a second march to come out on to the Tula road, and from there on to the Kaluga road to Podolsk.' By this sudden manoeuvre the Russian army would inscribe a half-circle round the south of Moscow. Kutuzov added: 'I hope to attract all the enemy's attention on to my army threatening his rear.'[1]

By nightfall on Wednesday, 16 September, the army lay about three kilometres south of Bronniski, itself about twenty-five kilometres south-east of Moscow. At this point the dart across country began. Leading regiments moved northwards almost back on their tracks for a few kilometres, then they swung abruptly westwards towards the river Pakra. Some detachments had already cut westwards while the main regiments continued to move south: these now covered the route along the Pakra for the movement of the main army. The rearguard remained as a covering screen under Miloradovich, situated in the vicinity of Bronniski. Kutuzov informed Alexander of the operation in a despatch dated 16 September: the manoeuvre, wrote the marshal, would also have the value of protecting the Tula weapons factory and the important foundry further south at Briansk. This report from Kutuzov also contained the commander's first reference to the abandonment of Moscow.

'After the battle of 7 September,' wrote Kutuzov, 'which though bloody was a victory for us, I was nevertheless obliged to abandon the position near Borodino for the reasons which I have previously had the honour of explaining to Your Imperial

Majesty. After this battle the army was in great disorder. The Second Army in particular was considerably weakened. Our forces approached Moscow in this exhausted state, having daily to endure fighting with the enemy vanguard, and being so hard pressed could find no position from which we could await the enemy with confidence. . . . I could therefore not risk a battle which might have had unfortunate results – not only the destruction of what remained of the army, but also the destruction of Moscow, threatened with being reduced to a heap of ashes. In this extremely critical situation I decided to leave the enemy free to enter Moscow, after having deliberated with my principal generals of whom some were of contrary opinion.'

Kutuzov continued: 'I very humbly dare to suggest to Your Very Gracious Lord and Sovereign, that the entry of the army into Moscow was far from being the submission of Russia. On the contrary, with the troops which I have been able to save I moved towards the Tula road, thus securing the prepared resources of our very rich Government. In all other directions I would have been cut off, as would Tormassov and Chichagov. . . . The loss of Moscow is reparable and does not mean the loss of the Fatherland. . . . Your Imperial Majesty will not deny that this is the inevitable result of the loss of Smolensk and of the disorganized state in which I found the army.'[2]

This despatch would not arrive in Petersburg until 20 September, four days away, and by then Alexander had been informed of Moscow's fate from other sources. On 18 September the Emperor received a letter from his sister writing from Yaroslavl. 'Moscow is taken,' announced Catherine. 'It is one of those inexplicable things.' The letter proceeded to lecture Alexander on the correct attitude to adopt. 'Do not forget your resolution: no peace and you still have the hope of recovering your honour. . . . My dear friend, no peace. . . .'[3]

Alexander was stricken with grief. He condemned Kutuzov as the 'one-eyed satyr'. His dislike of the commander-in-chief had already intensified as a result of the Borodino despatch which seemed such a flagrant deception; the Emperor now sought means of increasing his vigilance over Kutuzov – existing favourites at the army headquarters, notably Bennigsen, were clearly insufficient. Alexander therefore seized upon the services offered by the British envoy, General Sir Robert Wilson, about to leave

Petersburg and join the army. The Emperor asked this British visitor to report back to him; according to Wilson's account: 'The Emperor had expressed himself on that subject in the most decisive manner, and has authorized me to repeat to *him* and to my *Government* whatever opinions or statements I may deem it expedient to communicate.'[4] Meanwhile Alexander replied to Catherine on the 18th: 'Admittedly there are things that it is impossible to imagine. But be sure that my resolution to fight is more steadfast than ever; I would rather cease to be what I am than come to terms with the monster who is causing the world's misfortune.'[5]

This 'monster' Napoleon returned to his quarters in the Kremlin on the 18th. He continued to believe his military position to be excellent, with the Russian army somewhere south-east towards Ryazan. The fire still burnt in Moscow and would continue to do so for another week, although the main blazes were under control by the 19th. A foul stench covered the city; troops bivouacked amongst the charred rubble or on the wet fields besides the Moskva; torrential rain began to fall on the 17th to add to the discomfort of the soldiers.

'All that time pillage continued,' wrote a Russian postal official, Andrei Karfachevsky. 'The French entered houses and, committing gross acts of violence, took from their owners not only their money, gold and silver, but even boots, linen, and – most ludicrous of all – cassocks, women's furs and cloaks, in which they stood on guard and rode on horseback. . . . After pillaging churches they stabled horses, slaughtered cattle, and lodged wounded soldiers there; and having stripped the sacred ikons of their frames they bayoneted them and poured filth on them; they also committed other abominations which the tongue cannot mention.'[6]

Corpses were rotting in the blackened Moscow streets – citizens executed or beaten to death by the French, soldiers of the Grand Army who had died of their wounds, French troops murdered by gangs of Moscow partisans. The city looked like a battlefield. 'Some houses appeared to have been levelled to the ground,' wrote Colonel de Fezensac, 'others still retained a few pieces of smoke-blackened wall. Rubble of all sorts cluttered up the streets. A fearful smell of burnt matter came from all sides. . . . Most of the inhabitants, driven by our soldiers from the houses which had been spared by the flames, had taken refuge in the churches. These wretched people, wandering like phantoms in the ruins, and dressed in rags, had recourse to the most melancholy expedients for prolonging their miserable existence. Now they chewed a few vegetables still to be found in gardens, now they tore strips of flesh from animals dead in the street.'[7]

Napoleon let his troops do virtually as they wished. Soon, he believed, all would be ended: the target had been reached, peace would follow, just as it had done after his occupation of Vienna and Berlin. Meanwhile Kutuzov's cross-country march continued. The Russian commander despatched a report to Alexander on the 18th: 'The army . . . is plunging the enemy into uncertainty at each halting-place, while making for a definite goal, but at the same time concealing it by sham manoeuvres by the light forces. The enemy, having lost sight of our army and being still perplexed, is sending strong reconnaissance missions to various points in order to discover us.'[8] By this Friday the main Russian regiments were moving steadily west along the Pakra river; Kutuzov's headquarters had reached the neighbourhood of Podolsk, situated where the Pakra crossed the main Moscow–Tula road about thirty kilometres from Moscow itself. Murat's forces, led by General Count Horace Sébastiani, still believed the Russian army to be on the Ryazan road covered by the rearguard at Bronniski.

This rearguard slipped away westwards on about the 18th, following the bulk of the Russian regiments. Kutuzov had ordered a light Cossack screen to remain behind, comprising two regiments; these horsemen lured the French cavalry further down the Ryazan road during the 19th, and during this lull in fighting the opposing troops even engaged in conversation. Murat, duped by Kutuzov in the 1805 campaign, was being fooled again: the Cossacks played upon his vanity, exclaiming with delight at his magnificent uniforms and insisting that they admired his military prowess – at one point Murat even believed that these wily enemies might make him king of the Cossacks.

On 19 September the main Russian army reached the next road radiating south from Moscow – the route to Kaluga. Next day Kutuzov established his headquarters at Krasnoi Pakra, a small town on this road. His operation had almost been completed; the army was in a position to strike north against the Smolensk-Moscow communications; contact could be more easily established with the armies under Tormassov and Chichagov; Tula,

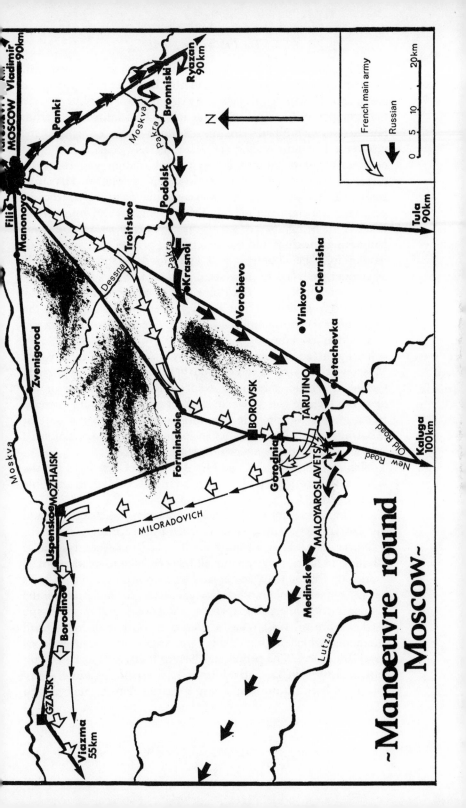

~Manoeuvre round Moscow~

French main army

Russian

0 5 10 20km

N

MOSCOW Vladimir 90km

Fili

Manonovo

Panki

Moskva

Pakra

Bronniski

Ryazan 90km

Podolsk

Troitskoe

Dessna

Pakra

Krasndi

Vorobievo

Vinkovo

Chernisha

Tula 90km

Zvenigorod

BOROVSK

Forminskoie

TARUTINO

Letachevka

Kaluga 100km

Moskva

Uspenskoe MOZHAISK

Gorodnia

New Road

Old Road

MILORADOVICH

MALOYAROSLAVETS

Medinsk

Borodino

GZATSK

Viazma 55km

Lutza

Briansk and the southern fertile regions could be protected. Moreover, the Russian army would now be better placed to move north should Napoleon attempt a march on St Petersburg.

Alexander still complained over the lack of information from Kutuzov. 'I've not had a line from Kutuzov since 10 September,' wrote the Emperor on the 19th. 'It's scarcely credible.'[9] Instead he received more gloomy letters from Catherine and from the displaced Governor-General of Moscow, Rostopchin. His sister wrote: 'The taking of Moscow has put the finishing touches to peoples' exasperation; discontent is at its highest and your person is far from being spared. . . . You are openly accused of your Empire's misfortune and the general and private ruin, in short of having lost the country's and your own personal honour.'[10] Alexander believed he had acted in the best possible manner: Kutuzov was to blame. The Emperor's opinion was reinforced by the letter from Rostopchin dated 13 September, in which the Governor-General complained bitterly over Kutuzov's decision to abandon Moscow.

Then, on 20 September, Kutuzov's account of the loss of Moscow at last arrived in Petersburg, brought by an *aide-de-camp*, Colonel Michaud. Alexander wept at this confirmation of the news – which he had so far kept secret from Petersburg citizens. But Michaud also provided an optimistic report on the state of the army, revealed in dramatic fashion, according to the Colonel's later account of the conversation with Alexander.

'Sire, my heart bleeds,' said Michaud to the Czar, 'but I felt the whole army, from the leaders down to the last soldier, in a terrible state of fear!'

Alexander exclaimed: 'What are you saying, Michaud? Would my Russians let themselves be crushed by misfortune?'

'Never, Sire! They are only afraid that Your Majesty, out of kindness of heart, may let yourself be persuaded to make peace.'[11]

Also on this Sunday, 20 September, Napoleon sat in the Czar's palace at the Kremlin and addressed a letter to 'My Brother, the Emperor Alexander.' Bonaparte's ambiguous, cautious message used the fire of Moscow as a pretext to open a dialogue with Alexander which he hoped his opponent might seize upon to negotiate peace. 'The proud and beautiful city of Moscow is no more. Rostopchin had had it burnt. . . . Three houses out of every four have been burnt down: only a quarter remain. Such a deed

178

is as useless as it is atrocious. . . . I made war on Your Majesty without any hostile feelings. A single letter from you, before or after the last battle, would have stopped my advance, and I would willingly have surrendered the advantage of occupying Moscow. If Your Majesty still retains some part of your old feelings for me, you will take this letter in good part. In any case you cannot but agree that I was right in reporting what is happening at Moscow.'[12] The letter was entrusted to Ivan Yakovlev, a prominent Moscow citizen, who was asked to take the message to Petersburg with all possible speed.

Napoleon was becoming increasingly anxious over the where-abouts of the Russian army. Reports sent to him by Murat assured him that many of the Russian regiments were scattered and no longer fit to fight; the French Emperor himself had declared soon after his arrival in Moscow that the Russian troops 'are in no fit state to conduct a campaign'. Then his doubts began to rise. He knew his brother-in-law Murat to be brave in battle – but also headstrong and often unreliable. And Murat, King of Naples, had been deceived by Kutuzov in the past. Now Napoleon told his staff in the Kremlin: 'The King [of Naples] has visions of the Russian army taking flight on the road. . . . the soldiers deserting, disbanding by troops, the Cossacks even preparing to make common cause with the conqueror.'[13] The Emperor awaited each report from Murat with rising apprehension.

Kutuzov's manoeuvre was finished successfully on 21 September. His army lay round the village of Tarutino, about seventy kilometres from Moscow – and seventy kilometres across country from Murat on the Ryazan road. Miloradovich's advance guard was positioned northwards at Dessna; Raevsky covered the right flank near the Pakra; on the left lay a detached corps under General Ivan Dorokov, ordered to watch and operate against the Smolensk–Moscow road. Kutuzov established his staff head-quarters at Letachevka, five kilometres south of Tarutino.

'For the moment, not a step further,' declared the Russian commander. 'We are going to prepare for our task and remember that the whole of Europe and our beloved Fatherland are watching us.'[14]

The entire character of the campaign had been altered, with the Russian army no longer in retreat but poised to take the offensive, hovering in the most suitable strategic position. Yet Kutuzov's achievement between 15–21 September has been ignored, belittled or begrudged. Ségur merely commented: 'The winding march which Kutuzov performed, either through indecision or through stratagem, was highly advantageous.'[15] Wilson believed the commander only undertook the manoeuvre after he had 'at length become sensible of the mischiefs that must result from a continuance of retreat in the direction of Ryazan'.[16] Clausewitz, about to leave the main army to journey to Wittgenstein's force, was told by Barclay: 'Thank your God you are called away from here. No good can come of all this.'[17] Others have credited Toll with the operation, and indeed Toll had suggested a move on to the Kaluga road at the time of the Fili conference. But the execution was Kutuzov's, together with the timing, and the latter was one of the most important aspects of the manoeuvre. An attempted deployment on the Kaluga road immediately after Fili would have been far less effective: Napoleon would have been alerted to this danger and could have reacted accordingly. The feint towards Ryazan amounted to a typical Kutuzov scheme, catching Napoleon and his army off-balance, and strengthening the psychological hold which the Russian commander was increasingly exerting over his opponent: the deception, the slippery manoeuvre, the unexpected reappearance in a position of strength, would have immense impact on Napoleon and would influence his attitude in the days leading to the French retreat. Now, instead of feeling like a conqueror in the enemy's captured capital, Napoleon's actions revealed that he sensed himself being trapped: Moscow seemed almost claustrophobic.

On 21 September Napoleon's suspicions became unbearable. He instructed Marshal Jean-Baptiste Bessières, Duke of Istria, to lead a strong 'corps of observation' and explore the region around Podolsk; Murat was ordered to probe forward with greater vigour beyond the Cossacks.[18]

Also on 21 September rumours of the fall of Moscow were rippling through St Petersburg. Alexander still avoided issuing an official statement and instead impatiently awaited some report of operations by Kutuzov which he could present to the people as encouragement. But Kutuzov could afford to wait: his forces would grow stronger while the French declined, cooped in Moscow with their communications under increasing pressure. Bennigsen and Barclay urged aggressive action, but Kutuzov dismissed their demands as premature. Bennigsen also complained of the army deployment at Tarutino, which he termed 'regrettable'; Kutuzov replied: 'Was your position at Friedland such a good one? Eh? As for mine here, it suits me and I shall stick to it.'[19]

At last, on 23 September, Murat discovered that no Russian forces were deployed behind the Cossack regiments. The unfortunate king of Naples hurried his men towards Podolsk along roads which were now thick with mud from continued rain. The news reached Napoleon during the late evening of the 23rd or early on the 24th: the Emperor immediately tried to organize forces to cover the Russian army front: troops under Poniatowski were ordered to join Murat at Podolsk while Bessières moved towards the Russian advance guard at Dessna. But containing the main Russian army was merely one of the two vital military problems which Napoleon had to overcome, and the other would be even more difficult. Cossacks and partisans were becoming increasingly active against French detachments and supplies: on 23 September partisans seized a convoy of fourteen waggons on the Podolsk road; elsewhere this Wednesday sixty powder waggons were blown up by the French to prevent their seizure.[20]

Next day stimulating reports reached the Russian headquarters: Wellington's army had apparently recaptured Madrid from the French on 12 August. Kutuzov immediately issued the information in an Order of the Day to his troops. 'The French have been driven from Madrid. The arm of the Almighty weighs heavily on Napoleon. Moscow will be his prison, his tomb, and the tomb of his army!' Kutuzov repeated virtually the same words in a letter to Alexander dated this Thursday, 24 September, and his despatch also provided important details regarding his own policy and plans:

'Disorder that reigns in the enemy army prevents it from attempting any move against us; Bonaparte's remoteness from the countries under his domination deprives him of any help he could get from them; he only manages to procure provisions with the greatest difficulty. The horses of his artillery and cavalry are suffering even more. The great majority of the cavalry perished in previous combats, especially on the memorable day of 7 September, so glorious for Russian arms; the remainder, surrounded on all sides by our partisans, is experiencing a terrible shortage of fodder. Our main detachments are on the road to

Mozhaisk, St Petersburg, Kolomna and Serpukhov; a day seldom passes without more than 300 prisoners being taken.

'Today the Russians, distinguished at all times by their love for their Sovereign, are burning to defend the throne of their Emperor and to fight the oppressor of their Fatherland. The peasants are arming and organizing themselves; they post sentries on the tops of mountains and on belfries to spy out the enemy's approach. Every day we see these worthy sons of the Fatherland arriving at headquarters and asking for arms. . . . Thus the aggressors are driven back everywhere and, while they are being cut down in their thousands at the other end of Europe, their tombs are being dug on the soil of this Empire, which they will have threatened with destruction in vain.'[21]

Within hours after writing these words, amounting to an energetic and uncompromising declaration of his determination to defeat the French, Kutuzov welcomed Sir Robert Wilson to his headquarters, and almost immediately Wilson began informing Alexander that Kutuzov was utterly lazy, incompetent and perhaps even a friend of the French. 'My headquarters are with Prince Kutuzov,' wrote Wilson in his diary on his arrival, 'but as he is very unequal to much exertion in society, and likes to be retired, I generally take my seat at Bennigsen's table, where I have a regular cover at all times. . . .'

Wilson and the Russian chief of staff soon became close friends and confidants: both agreed that the army commander could only be described as a 'dotard'. Intrigues rapidly increased at the army headquarters – even Toll criticized Kutuzov behind his back. Barclay observed Bennigsen's underhand actions against Kutuzov, similar to those which this same officer had practised against Barclay himself: the First Army commander, soon to retire, kept silent. In this increasingly unpleasant atmosphere Kutuzov withdrew to his room, spending hours alone with his maps. He treated Bennigsen with contempt; with Wilson he remained polite, but distant; to Alexander he displayed an attitude of ironic paternalism.

Alexander's relationship with those around him also rapidly deteriorated. The loss of Moscow had still to be formally announced, and some people found guilty of spreading the rumour were punished by being made to sweep the Petersburg streets, but the fate of Russia's second capital was in fact common knowledge. Fears increased that Alexander would seek peace. On 27 September the Emperor attended a service at the Kazan Cathedral to mark the eleventh anniversary of his coronation; he drove to the cathedral in a closed coach to avoid the hostile stares of his people. 'Never shall I forget those minutes,' wrote Roxane Stourdza, one of his wife's ladies-in-waiting. 'We ascended the cathedral steps between two ranks of onlookers who did not give a single cheer. . . . I happened to glance at the Czar and, sensing the agony of spirit he was undergoing, I felt my knees begin to tremble beneath me.'[22]

Snowflakes fell softly outside Napoleon's study window in the Kremlin this Sunday, although they melted immediately. The Emperor knew that insufficient days had passed since his letter left for the Czar, yet his impatience for a reply was becoming unbearable. Reports of damage being inflicted by Cossacks and partisans were increasing at an alarming rate; only a few hours before, Napoleon had been informed that Cossacks had intercepted a convoy, two army mail coaches, and had captured a courier on the Smolensk road only about fifteen kilometres from Moscow. The main Russian army remained poised scarcely more than a day's march from the city. Disturbing reports were also arriving from further back along his threatened communication link: Maret, Duke of Bassano, wrote to Napoleon from Vilna that the foreign troops at this garrison were looting and deserting.[23]

Citizens in St Petersburg were officially informed on 29 September that Moscow had been abandoned to the French. Almost immediately Alexander slipped away to his villa on Kammionyi Island, five kilometres from Petersburg; the Emperor would stay in this retreat for much of the next four weeks, nursing his raw nerves and an infected leg. And Alexander would display a mental strength which surprised many who knew him, a firmness of character – or perhaps a recognition that he had no real choice – which precluded any negotiation with Napoleon. The French Emperor's letter, dated 20 September, went unanswered although it may never even have arrived.

So the three-cornered battle of wills continued: Napoleon, Alexander, Kutuzov. The latter felt entirely satisfied. 'We fight with small units every day,' wrote the marshal to his daughter Praskov'ya on 1 October, 'and until now we have been successful everywhere. Every day we take up to 300 men captive and we lose so few that they amount to nothing.'[24] Next day he wrote to St Petersburg: 'The regiments have been brought up to strength by the recruits coming from the different provinces. Training of recruits – who are burning with zeal to fight – continues in the camps. Cavalry horses are in much improved condition, having received food in sufficient quantity and being quartered in a healthy watering place. Provisions are so plentiful that the army wants for nothing.'[25] Exactly the reverse applied to the enemy; also on 2 October Kutuzov reported to Wittgenstein: 'The enemy was so weakened after the glorious battle of Borodino that until now it has not been able to heal itself and for that reason cannot undertake anything against us.'[26]

Yet Alexander began to feel growing disquiet at Kutuzov's unwillingness to open a full offensive. His sister shared similar fears, expressing her criticism of Kutuzov in offensive terms in a letter to the Czar dated 3 October: 'His physique must be pre-judical to him in his present post, for, with that grotesque body, he cannot like activity, and the inaction of the army is only the result of his personal laziness.'[27] But in Moscow the French Emperor could stand his own inactivity no longer. On 3 October, after a sleepless night, he suddenly summoned his army commanders to the Kremlin.

Napoleon announced that he would lead the Grand Army against St Petersburg. The war must be brought to an end. Ségur described the scene: 'The Emperor, with great animation, fixed his sparkling eyes upon his generals, whose grave countenances and unbroken silence expressed nothing but astonishment.' The army commanders began to voice their objections – the season was too late, supplies too short, the Petersburg road stretched barren and vulnerable to partisan attacks, the enemy army lay too near. 'What was to become of the 6,000 wounded still at Moscow? These unfortunate men, then, were to be delivered up to Kutuzov! That general, moreover, would press closely on the army in its march, and harass it without intermission! It would be necessary for it to attack and defend at the same moment, they would be marching to a conquest like men who fled from battle!' Various plans were pressed as alternatives, including an immediate withdrawal from Moscow southwards towards Kaluga. To this Napoleon replied that 'he liked plans

184

that were simple, routes the least indirect, high-roads – such as the road which had brought him to Moscow – but which he was determined not to tread again until he had secured peace.'

From the discussion emerged the proposal to open negotiations. At first Napoleon asked Caulaincourt to take a letter to Alexander: Caulaincourt argued that his arrival in St Petersburg would merely convince Alexander of the weakness of the French situation – someone of lesser stature should be sent. The choice fell on the Marquis de Lauriston, Caulaincourt's successor as Ambassador to the Russian Court. Lauriston was therefore ordered to approach Kutuzov to obtain a safe-conduct for the journey to Petersburg, after which he would take the letter to Alexander; the emissary left Napoleon's presence with the French Emperor's last words following him to the door: 'I want peace. I must have peace. I will have peace, at the expense of everything but honour.'[28]

Lauriston reached Murat's headquarters next day, 4 October, with this French vanguard now established in the vicinity of Vinkovo close to the Russian advance positions. Early in the morning of 5 October Lauriston presented himself at the Russian outposts under flag of truce, requesting permission to speak with Kutuzov. His arrival immediately precipitated a violent clash between Wilson and Kutuzov over the correct procedure to be adopted by the Russian army commander. The British general's subsequent account of this quarrel constituted a scandalous smear on Kutuzov – and at least some of Wilson's fabrications were believed by Alexander himself.

According to Wilson, Kutuzov intended to betray the Russian army. The accusation stemmed from Kutuzov's apparent willingness to meet Lauriston in person at a secret rendezvous on the road to Moscow. Wilson claimed he received word of this proposal in a note sent to him by Bennigsen early in the morning; he pulled on his clothes and 'hastened to Bennigsen, whom he [Wilson] found with a dozen generals, anxiously awaiting his arrival. They afforded him proof that Kutuzov, in answer to a proposition made by Lauriston on behalf of Napoleon, had agreed to meet him this same night at a station several miles from his most advanced *videttes*, on the road to Moscow, there to confer on the terms of a convention "for the immediate retreat of the whole invading army from the territories of Russia, which convention was also to serve as the basis of a peace, to which it was to be the preliminary". They added that "Napoleon himself might be expected at the interview".'

Napoleon was therefore to be allowed to escape unmolested. Wilson took it upon himself to confront Kutuzov: he felt that 'he had a duty to perform from which he could not shrink with honour'. The British general accordingly put the charges to the Russian marshal, and 'the marshal's countenance confirmed the allegation'. Wilson warned his host that Alexander had given him instructions 'to report on any attempt to negotiate' and he threatened such a report would now be sent. Eventually, according to Wilson, he persuaded Kutuzov only to see Lauriston at his own headquarters and with witnesses near by.[29] The British general sent a self-satisfied despatch to Alexander: 'I have the honour to inform Your Majesty that this morning Field-Marshal Kutuzov communicated to me his intention to grant an interview at the Russian outposts to the *aide-de-camp* general of Bonaparte. I have believed it my duty to put forward very firm and clearcut objections to this idea, the realization of which is not in keeping with Your Majesty's dignity, for it will encourage the enemy, sow discontent in the army and provoke the distrust of foreign States.'[30] Wilson wrote in his diary: 'I have rendered most important service, and prevented a successful negotiation for the retreat of the army.'[31]

Wilson's account is woven from lies which were either perpetrated by himself or by Kutuzov's enemies at the camp – probably a mixture of both: the English general most likely became entangled in Bennigsen's intrigues against Kutuzov which were being waged in daily more active fashion. Wilson's story therefore acts as a useful indication of the difficulties under which Kutuzov had to work. There is no evidence whatsoever that Kutuzov ever intended to meet Lauriston at a secret rendezvouz. Lauriston had no brief from Napoleon to discuss a French retreat, and the idea that Napoleon himself might have been present is fanciful in the extreme, revealing the unreliability of the rest of the accusation against Kutuzov. It is highly improbable that Kutuzov wanted to enter into negotiations at all, let alone allow for an unmolested French retreat, and his subsequent treatment of both the emissary and Napoleon's letter indicates his full realization that nothing could be gained from talks. Since his military position remained extremely strong, Kutuzov had no need of discussions with the enemy, except as a means of further deceiving the French – which he now attempted to do.

Kutuzov received Lauriston at the Russian headquarters during the late evening of the 5th, but only after the French emissary refused to talk to any other representative of the Emperor. Wilson, the Prince of Oldenburg and the Prince of Würtemburg insisted on being close at hand in order to preserve 'the strictest forms of etiquette' – this trio, none of whom was Russian, amounted to a virtual guard over Kutuzov: he referred to them as 'these foreign gentlemen'. Unfortunately, Wilson's own position had been undermined earlier in the day: his friend Bennigsen had misbehaved by engaging in friendly conversations with Murat at the outposts.

The old marshal proceeded to display all his deviousness: according to Langeron he showed 'that artfulness which particularly distinguished his character'. He greeted Lauriston courteously, taking Napoleon's letter from him and tossing it casually on a side-table; he then chatted sociably about the old days in St Petersburg when Lauriston had been a welcomed guest at his house; he talked of the weather, the roads and other inconsequential matters. Lauriston could contain his impatience no longer and implored Kutuzov to read Napoleon's letter. Kutuzov took it up, skimmed the pages with his one good eye, then flipped the communication back on the table without reply and seemed about to continue the small-talk.

Lauriston exclaimed: 'His Majesty, the Emperor, my master, wants to see the end of this cruel war!' Kutuzov still made no reply. The French emissary then voiced his indignation at the cruelty of the partisans. Kutuzov answered politely that he could not civilize a nation in three months who regarded the enemy as a marauding force of Tartars under a Genghis Khan. Stung by this insult, Lauriston insisted that Napoleon's Grand Army could not be considered equivalent to those ancient invaders. 'There is some difference,' he declared. 'There may be,' replied Kutuzov, 'but none in the eyes of the people.'

According to Kutuzov's own private account of the meeting Lauriston tried to claim that French affairs were by no means unsatisfactory. 'Don't think that Napoleon desires peace with the Russian Emperor as a result of the unfortunate results in Spain

187

or as a result of the declared English intention of a landing on the western shores of France. Entirely to the contrary, we will go into Madrid when we wish to, and the English will never dare to land on French soil. If this happened all the French would rise as one man and the ocean would be the tomb of the English.' Lauriston continued to insist that the Peninsular War was progressing well, and that recent French setbacks were purely temporary.

Soon afterwards Kutuzov led the conversation back to Spanish affairs and to the English threat. Lauriston was amazed by his apparent knowledge of events. 'How do you know all these details?' Kutuzov replied: 'Why, from you, General – I didn't know them before.'

The door to the room swung open to admit General Platov, the Cossack commander, escorted by troops as if under arrest. Kutuzov demanded his sabre and subjected him to a strict reprimand, adding that in spite of his authority as chief commander he didn't wish to hand Platov over to a military court but would send him to Alexander who would decide his fate. The trick worked: Lauriston apparently reported to Napoleon that Platov had been replaced and the Cossacks were therefore without a leader and in disarray; in fact, Platov would soon show that he was in full command.

Kutuzov did agree with Lauriston that there should be a partial armistice between French and Russian troops: outposts in the centre of the opposing lines would cease sniping for a fortnight, but the ceasefire would not apply to the wings of the armies – the Cossacks and partisans would thus still be able to operate. Either side would give a two hours' notice before the truce ended; Lauriston apparently wanted a full armistice, which Kutuzov refused. The Marshal withheld permission for Lauriston to travel to St Petersburg; instead the Russian commander said he would see that Alexander received Napoleon's letter – the Czar himself would decide whether the French envoy should be allowed to visit the Russian capital. Kutuzov therefore acted with diplomatic dexterity, attempting to avoid any accusation that he acted as an intermediary between the two Emperors; he carried this caution to the extreme, even insisting that Napoleon's letter should be copied: the copy went to Petersburg and Kutuzov probably destroyed the original, thus severing a direct link between Napoleon and Alexander. Kutuzov described his meeting with

Lauriston in a report to Alexander, taken to Petersburg by Prince Peter Volkonsky who would also provide a verbal account of the interview.

'He began to talk about peace,' wrote Kutuzov, 'saying that the friendship that had existed between Your Imperial Majesty and the Emperor Napoleon had unfortunately been broken by purely external circumstances; this present moment offered a good opportunity for re-establishing this friendship. "Must this strange war, this unique war, last eternally then? My master the Emperor has a sincere desire to end this dispute between two great and generous nations, and to end it for ever." I replied that I had no instructions on this subject and that at my departure to join the armies even the word peace had not been mentioned once; moreover, I had no desire to communicate one iota of all this conversation to my Sovereign, regardless of whether all the words that I had heard from his mouth came from him, as the result of his personal reflections, or of whether they had a higher source; that "I would be cursed by posterity if I was regarded as the prime mover in any kind of settlement, for such is the prevailing frame of mind of my nation". At this moment, he handed me a letter from the Emperor Napoleon, a copy of which is enclosed, and asked me to request Your Majesty's authorization for him, Lauriston, to go to St Petersburg with it; and proposed an armistice (which I refused him) while waiting for a reply. Here he impatiently calculated the time it would take for a reply to arrive. I promised to comply with his request, which amounted to making the Emperor Napoleon's desire known to Your Majesty. . . .'[32]

Lauriston hurried back to the Kremlin, arriving on the 6th. Napoleon reacted with delight at the news that his letter was on its way to Alexander; he summoned his generals and, according to Ségur, 'announced to them the approach of peace! They had only to wait a fortnight for it! He alone had been acquainted with the Russian character! On the receipt of his letter all Petersburg would be lit up with bonfires.'[33]

Kutuzov was also well-satisfied. Lauriston's visit had revealed the growing discomfiture of the French. Time remained entirely on his side – time during which his raw recruits could be moulded into fighting regiments, his partisans could bleed the French, and the enemy would become increasingly anxious. Winter approached. Kutuzov welcomed a lull in military activities, with

189

fighting dwindling to such an extent that frequent peaceful exchanges took place between the respective advance posts, but at the same time he knew the French could never be certain this unofficial armistice in the centre of the two lines might not suddenly be ended by a Russian offensive. As Ségur commented: 'At once fierce and artful, he [Kutuzov] could prepare with all necessary caution and concealment for the most sudden and ferocious attacks, and disguise the most baleful projects by honeyed words and flattering caresses.'[34]

The marshal therefore remained highly active, preparing for the resumption of full-scale war. He issued detailed instructions regarding recruit training: 'Teach them to turn and to march as a front in platoons and in sections. Do not look for any kind of beauty.'[35] Officers were warned not to burden their men with unnecessary duties, equipment or rules and regulations – nothing should be allowed to detract from 'the essentials of business'. Discipline should be obtained through the infusion of 'warrior spirit and patriotic fervour' rather than through punishment.[36]

The camp at Tarutino bustled throughout the first two weeks of October. A visiting artist provided this description: 'From all sides reserves are passing through, together with Cossack regiments, supply convoys. The field-marshal stands by his hut. . . . At his hut people of different kinds are crowding round him – nobility, merchants with bread and salt, priests with icons, peasants fall at his feet begging for weapons, wives and children robbed by the miscreants beg for help and defence.'[37] The atmosphere was always informal. The partisan leader Colonel Davidov described how he once walked up to Kutuzov at the camp wearing filthy peasant clothing. 'Taking advantage of his agreeable welcome, I begged forgiveness for daring to appear before him in my peasant's dress. He replied: "In a people's war it is necessary. Act as you are acting, with your head and your heart. It doesn't matter to me that the one is covered with a cap and not with a shako, and the other beats under a yamak and not under a uniform." '[38]

Kutuzov, the courtier, diplomat, professional soldier, now revealed another attribute: his skill at promoting guerrilla warfare. He grasped the essence of this type of conflict, which showed such a contrast to the rigid battlefield tactics normally employed. He instructed one partisan leader, who had had the misfortune to be surrounded by the enemy: 'The partisan should never find himself in this position, because he must only stay in one spot for as long as it takes to feed his men and horses. The partisan must march secretly along the small tracks. Having arrived at a village he must let no one out of it so that no one will be able to give news of him. In the daytime he should hide in the woods or in low-lying places. In a word the partisan must be decisive, quick, and tireless.'[39]

Controversy was already arising over the question of arming the peasants. Many members of the Russian hierarchy – including Alexander himself – feared these partisans might make use of the opportunity to rise against the state; memories of the Serf Revolt under Pugachev had remained strong during the intervening thirty-nine years. Kutuzov appreciated the military value of armed peasant groups, although he preferred the strongest of them to be led by regular army officers. The latter included some colourful figures, all of whom worked in cooperation with the main army: Davidov, who organized his first partisan unit after witnessing the French occupation of his family estate at Borodino; Prince Nikolai Kudashev, Kutuzov's son-in-law through the marriage of his daughter Ekaterina, Captain Sesslavin and Captain Figner. The activities of these highly mobile groups were often atrociously cruel. 'Figner and others thought they were acting heroically by massacring all their prisoners,' wrote Löwenstern, serving on Kutuzov's staff. 'Fortunately their ferocity had no imitators, and almost nobody except a few young men, as inexperienced as they were unprincipled, committed acts of cruelty in mood of exaltation. . . . Figner and his associates had difficulty in finding in their units men willing to undertake these massacres, and it was usually the Cossacks of the Bug who did so, being fiercer than the rest and eager for the booty they received.'[40] Despite this barbarism, Kutuzov gave Figner support and found in him a valuable guerrilla commander. At one time he entrusted Figner with a letter to his wife, and in the letter Kutuzov wrote: 'Look hard at him [Figner] – this is an unusual man. I have never before seen such a noble spirit. He is fanatically brave and patriotic, and God knows what he would not undertake.'[41]

Kutuzov therefore used the guerrillas and the peasants to the maximum amount possible both before and during the French retreat, while appreciating that the partisans could never be controlled in similar fashion to regular troops; he knew that by unleashing the peasants there would be a sharp rise in atrocities committed, but this situation must be accepted. He explained his attitude in a letter to Alexander during October, referring to the peasants in the Kaluga and Moscow provinces.

'They suffered all blows inflicted by the enemy's invasion with a martyr's firmness. They hid their families and small children in the woods, but they themselves, armed, sought to defeat the robbers who appeared at their peaceful villages. Frequently even the women punished the enemy with death. Often the armed villagers, having joined themselves to our garrison, helped us a great deal in the extermination of the enemy, and I may say without exaggeration that many thousands of the enemy were slaughtered by the peasants.' Kutuzov also explained his policy of arming the peasants despite misgivings felt by other Russian nobles: 'Respecting their just necessity, and the spirit of their general zeal to inflict harm on the enemy everywhere, I not only did not attempt to discourage them, but on the contrary . . . I encouraged this desire in them and strengthened them with weapons from the enemy. In this way the inhabitants of these places received arms from my main headquarters and from other partisans. Others took them from the French, whom they killed with their bare hands, and others even bought them from the Cossacks, eagerly paying money for them.'[42]

To help gain peasant support – and perhaps to persuade the serfs from turning against their masters – Kutuzov issued strict instructions that foraging parties should always leave food for the villagers. Supplies taken should be limited, even though the regular troops might go hungry as a result. At the same time the commander attempted to improve the welfare of his own men. As early as 24 September the senior army surgeon reported that the soldiers would soon be suffering from the approaching winter: 'The larger part of the army is wearing summer trousers and many of their overcoats are so thin that they cannot protect themselves from the damp and the colder weather.' Kutuzov sent repeated requests to provincial governors for essential supplies, but the response proved unsatisfactory. The commander-in-chief could only attempt to instil a spirit in his men sufficiently strong to overcome these material deficiencies: in one Order of the Day he declared: 'Winter is coming on, blizzards and frosts – are you afraid of them, children of the North? Your iron breasts do not fear either the severity of the weather or the wickedness of the enemy. It is the truest war of the Fatherland, against which everything crumbles. Let each one remember Suvorov. He showed us how to bear hunger and cold when it was an affair of victory and of the Russian people.'[43]

But one problem emerged stronger than ever before during these weeks, for which Kutuzov could find no solution. The most valid criticism against him related to his absence of a suitable staff system. This lack had already hampered his handling of the Borodino battle and would always prove a hindrance. At Borodino, Kutuzov had been allowed insufficient time to collect an efficient team beneath him; now, in October, this team was still unformed. Kutuzov himself was partly to blame: his secretive nature precluded a close working relationship with subordinates – he once said that 'even the pillow on which a commander sleeps must never know his thoughts'.[44] Yet even without this attitude Kutuzov would have had great difficulty in establishing a trustworthy staff system. The atmosphere at headquarters continued to be corrupted by intrigue. Barclay retired on 4 October, prompting Wilson to write in his diary: 'His departure will do good by removing a spirit of dissension that was injurious to the general interests.' But the Wilson-Bennigsen cabal continued, with the British general convinced that Bennigsen would have made a far better commander-in-chief. Wilson wrote: 'If General Bennigsen ever fulfils his promise to me, I think I may venture to say that his continuance here will prove most advantageous.'[45] The presence of Alexander's two spies at the headquarters robbed Kutuzov of any chance of creating a staff structure.

On 16 October the Russian Emperor received Napoleon's letter, sent by Kutuzov in the hands of Prince Volkonsky. Alexander displayed immediate anger; by this time he had already received Wilson's report of Kutuzov's alleged behaviour with Lauriston. Alexander condemned the marshal's handling of the situation and declared in brave words – which have also been attributed to Kutuzov – 'Peace? But we haven't waged war yet. My campaign is only beginning!'[46] The Emperor decided to despatch a reply – not to Napoleon, whom he would continue to ignore, but to Kutuzov, whom he continued to distrust and whose words he disbelieved in favour of Wilson's.

Also on 16 October Napoleon attempted another overture. He

had already been warned by Caulaincourt that Kutuzov was perhaps 'trying to lull Your Majesty to sleep in Moscow'.[47] Preliminary plans had been prepared for a French departure from the capital, and Marshal Victor was instructed to concentrate on Vilna and then take up position between Orsha and Smolensk as 'a general reserve'. Now, on the 16th, Napoleon addressed a letter to Kutuzov via Berthier which he presumably hoped would prompt some information on Alexander's attitude: behind the sentences lurked a question to which Napoleon desperately sought an answer – would Alexander negotiate?

'General Lauriston was given the mission of proposing to Your Highness the making of arrangements to give the war a character in conformity with the established rules and the taking of indispensable measures resulting from the state of war. In fact, the devastation of her own country is harmful to Russia, as much as it affects the Emperor painfully; Your Highness will readily feel the interest I have in ascertaining the definitive decision of his Government.'[48]

Lauriston presented the message later in the day; Kutuzov made no reply. The absence of reaction by the Russian commander failed to prevent Wilson from sending another despatch, this time to Lord Cathcart although most of the content would most likely reach Alexander.

'The Field-Marshal would not dare to begin negotiations, without risking his life . . . but the impression of these reports is so harmful from the internal, external, political and military point of view that their consequences may become disastrous. . . . The Field-Marshal is undoubtedly disposed to woo the enemy, the French compliments delight him. He esteems these birds of prey. . . .'[49]

The situation at the Russian headquarters had become intolerable. Kutuzov ignored Bennigsen and could barely stand being in the same room; Wilson threatened to leave the camp – which Kutuzov would have welcomed. Rostopchin had attached himself to the headquarters, after having burnt his own country house on 1 October – 'What patriotic virtue!' Wilson had exclaimed. 'What nobility of spirit!'[50] Since then he had allied himself closer to Bennigsen. Now Rostopchin finally quit the camp, heading towards his protectress, Grand-Duchess Catherine, at Yaroslavl, who was another sniping critic of Kutuzov; *en route* Rostopchin

194

sent a final tirade to the army leader. 'As I do not wish to remain inactive nor contemplate the destruction of the province of Kaluga, nor hear all day that you are busy sleeping, I leave for Yaroslavl and St Petersburg. In my capacity as a loyal and true servant of the Fatherland, I desire you to pay more attention to Russia, the troops entrusted to you and the enemy. As for me, I thank you that it does not fall to me to deliver a capital or a province to anyone, and that you do not let me enjoy your confidence in any way.'[51]

Back at headquarters the pressure increased for Kutuzov to move against the French. Bennigsen, Wilson, and even Toll and other previous Kutuzov supporters, insisted that the present military inactivity must end. Kutuzov had continued to declare that: 'I will play for time, lull Napoleon as much as possible and not disturb him in Moscow. Every device which contributes to this object is preferable to the empty pursuit of glory.'[52]

But on 17 October Kutuzov received a report from partisans, sent by Dorokov, that Napoleon seemed to be on the point of leaving Moscow. At any moment Kutuzov's policy might be vindicated. And now Kutuzov agreed to a battle; Russian forces would attack although in restricted number, sufficiently strong to satisfy those who wanted to fight but not too many to weaken the Russian army for the decisive clash. Perhaps Kutuzov believed a limited engagement might tempt Napoleon out from the security of Moscow, a move which the French already seemed to be considering. Whether or not the devious Kutuzov had such a motive, this was in fact the result: the 1812 campaign exploded into life again.

XIII

Maloyaroslavets

(1812: 18–25 October)

Russian and French positions lay entangled amidst the fields and copses south of Moscow. 'The position of the mutual outposts was the most extraordinary I had ever seen in war,' wrote Wilson in his diary, 'for they were so interwoven as to present fronts on all points of the compass.'[1] This close proximity had led to peaceful contact between the two armies during the temporary truce; sometimes French and Russian soldiers played cards or drank together; at night the songs from one campfire were answered by a chorus from the enemy. Both armies knew war might be resumed at any moment, and ambushes continued on the flanks, but the two-week truce covering the central positions had lulled Murat's cavalrymen into a feeling of false security.

The two weeks ended on 18 October. At five o'clock this Sunday morning Russian regular cavalry and Cossacks erupted from the misty woods above the small river of Chernishna, seven kilometres west of Vinkovo; the attackers comprised eleven mounted regiments and twelve mobile guns under Denisov, who directed them forward to curve round to the left of French positions held by Murat's vanguard commander Sébastiani. At the same time the enemy came under accurate fire from six Russian guns positioned further to the right: shells landed amongst French cavalrymen as they ran half-dressed from their tents and attempted to mount their horses. Almost immediately Sébastiani's troops began to retreat; Russian infantrymen under Baggovut ran to intercept.

Russian forces in this action were entrusted to Bennigsen, with Kutuzov having finally allowed his chief of staff to wage a

196

limited offensive. The Russians swept through the French camp; Murat himself barely escaped capture, and Bennigsen believed the moment had come for further decisive action which would turn the enemy's retreat into rout. He called to Wilson, riding by his side, and asked him to gallop back to Kutuzov.

'Beg the marshal to give no time to the enemy to rally or make any new disposition!' shouted Bennigsen. 'He's only to roll him back . . . in his present disorder on Spass Kouplia, while I hurry there to intercept.'

Kutuzov, watching from a distance, refused. Instead he ordered the action to end. Bennigsen, almost beside himself with rage, confronted the commander and demanded more troops, more cavalry, more guns. Kutuzov shrugged him aside. Murat recovered slightly, ordering his carabineers into a charge which he led personally – 'his plume was seen waving in the thickest of the fray,' commented Wilson – and the fighting faded.[2] Bennigsen and Wilson were incapable of understanding Kutuzov's decision. 'I can't get over it!' exclaimed the Russian chief of staff in a letter to his wife. 'This magnificent, this brilliant day could have had incalculable consequences if I had been supported. Before the eyes of the whole army, Kutuzov forbids the sending of a single man to my aid, those are his own words. . . . Imagine my situation: I have to wrangle with him whenever it is a question of making a move against the enemy. His cowardice exceeds even the limits accepted for poltroons. . . .'

Bennigsen spat out his hatred in an insolent note to Kutuzov. 'The troops of His Imperial Majesty had won this victory in a style such as one only sees on manoeuvres. It is regrettable that Your Highness was much too far from the battlefield and could not see the splendid spectacle of the enemy's defeat.'[3]

Kutuzov had seen enough. The state of the enemy camp where horsemeat and dead cats had been prepared for food, the remarks by prisoners indicating shortages in ammunition and equipment, the cavalry mounts with their ribs showing and haunches angled sharp through lack of fodder, the inefficiency of the enemy – all these told Kutuzov that his strategy was working. And he knew he could employ his forces to better purpose than merely smashing Murat's vanguard – the entire French army might soon be moving against him. Kutuzov's very calmness in the face of Bennigsen's frenzy increased his chief of staff's loathing.

'God has given me a victory,' wrote Kutuzov to his wife. 'The king of Naples commanded. They were from 45–50,000 men. It wasn't so difficult to beat them, but it was necessary to beat them cheaply for us, and we only lost about 300 men including the wounded. With just a little more luck it would have been an entirely charming little battle. It was the first time that the French lost so many cannon and the first time they ran like hares.'[4]

Among the captives taken on 18 October was the French general Beauvollier, seized by the Cossacks under Kutuzov's son-in-law Kudashev. The latter brought the Frenchman to Kutuzov, who received him courteously and surprised his prisoner by his excellent French and by his knowledge of Beauvollier's family background. After a long discussion on the history of the French Revolution the Russian commander turned to the Frenchman and asked: 'Well, what does the Emperor Napoleon think of me?'

'He fears you,' replied Beauvollier. 'He refers to you as the sly Old Fox of the North.'

'Then I'll try to show he's not mistaken,' commented Kutuzov.[5]

That Sunday evening Napoleon received news of the defeat inflicted on Murat. He immediately decided to take the field against Kutuzov. 'We must wash out the insult!' he shouted; he would leave Moscow at once. Final preparations for evacuation were hurried forward, but then Napoleon had slight second thoughts – he would stay just one more night in the Kremlin. His aides noticed his acute agitation; he seemed to find it impossible to sit still but continually jumped up to ask questions, check papers, or merely to stride with jerky paces across the room; he hardly touched his food. He declared repeatedly that the army must depart 'in the manner of an enemy who is performing a manoeuvre, and not that of an enemy who is beating a retreat', and he addressed a despatch to the garrison commander at Vilna saying he intended to strike towards Kaluga, smashing the Russian army if attempts were made to stop him, after which he would seize Tula or move north towards Viazma. 'In any case, towards the first weeks of November, I will have brought my troops into the square which lies between Smolensk, Mogilev, Minsk and Vitebsk. I am deciding on this movement because Moscow is no longer a military position. I am going to seek another more favourable one at the beginning of the next campaign.

The operation will then be directed towards St Petersburg or Kiev.'[6]

Napoleon's plans were in considerable confusion; Kutuzov's were startlingly clear. On 16 October he had despatched a letter to Alexander: 'The enemy intends to retreat along the Smolensk road. Our present position will give us the opportunity to come closer to that road if necessary. If the suspicions are well-founded that the enemy is to retreat along the Smolensk road, then as soon as possible I will march parallel to this route to the Ugra. The enemy will certainly look for the road which is not yet destroyed – that is to the right or to the left of Smolensk. From this point it will be convenient to act against him in either of these two cases.'[7] In other words Napoleon would be trapped. Kutuzov's forces would march to the south of him; to the north waited Russian forces under Wittgenstein. Napoleon would either have to move from the Smolensk road to face one or the other, or would have to continue the retreat on the same highway which he had used to invade Russia – despite the destruction wrought in this area during the first weeks of the campaign.

Kutuzov had seized the initiative – indeed, he had done so through the decision to abandon Moscow on 13 September followed by his cross-country march – and he intended to make use of this crucial advantage. The date of his despatch to Alexander revealing his plan is important: Kutuzov had decided upon his movements at least two days before the clash with Murat's advance regiments. Now he had to make sure that the French commander acted as he, Kutuzov, wished him to do. Kutuzov increasingly became the cat, and Napoleon the mouse.

Regiments of the Grand Army began to file from Moscow at two o'clock in the morning, Monday, 19 October. They presented an astonishing spectacle. 'It was not only the number of fighting men who made up the endless procession,' wrote an eye-witness, Captain von Kurz, 'but the innumerable waggons, carts, droshkys, chaises, often laden with booty. And the number of guns, ammunition waggons, vans, and the like, moving in eight or ten parallel columns, took up an incalculable stretch of the road. Besides the artillery, powder-waggons, and carts, the rest of the many vehicles were loaded with provisions of all sorts: wine, brandy, sugar, coffee, tea, tobacco, salt meat, dried fish, etc. . . . Other waggons contained booty in the form of gold, silver, precious stones, and valuable furs. . . . The enormous clutter of transport became jammed, and it was impossible for individuals to find room. The great crowd had become so intermingled that to make one's way forward required a tremendous effort. The great congestion of waggons and troops poured through the fields in three wide columns.'[8]

Napoleon left Moscow on the 19th, managing to extricate himself from the swollen flood of his army. He rode south on the old Kaluga road during the 20th. The weather had turned fine, with the sky bright and clear, and he shrugged aside those who warned him that winter lay not far ahead. He pointed to the sky and said: 'In that brilliant sun do you not recognize my star?' Once again he remembered the sun of Austerlitz and of Borodino.[9]

But rain fell heavily later in the day, hindering the progress of the march. The foul weather proved a blessing for the Russians: Napoleon was attempting to direct his army westward from the old to the new Kaluga roads, and the switch in direction threatened to catch Kutuzov unawares. But the rain hampered the movement of the guns and the thousands of French carts after the change of direction at Troitskoe on 21 October. At the same time the weather delayed reports reaching Kutuzov of both the French movement from Moscow and the subsequent enemy route. Not until the night of 21 October did a Cossack arrive at Tarutino with the news that strong French forces had moved into Forminskoie on the new Kaluga road barely thirty kilometres away. At first Kutuzov apparently believed the enemy comprised a strong foraging party: he summoned General Dokhturov and ordered him to lead 3,000 cavalry, 12,000 infantry and eighty-four guns in the direction of Forminskoie; his instructions were to guard the road from this town but 'on no account to engage in a combat which might require further aid from the main army . . . and perhaps bring on a general battle under disadvantageous circumstances'.[10]

Also on 21 October Kutuzov at last replied to the message received from Napoleon on the 16th. The Russian commander addressed his answer to Berthier, the French chief of staff; he said that insufficient time had lapsed for a reply to reach him from Alexander concerning the original letter brought by Lauriston, but he continued: 'I will repeat here a truth, the full force of which you will undoubtedly appreciate my Prince, namely that it is difficult, however much one may desire it, to stop a people embittered by what it sees, a people that has never known war on its own territory for 300 years, that is ready to sacrifice itself for its Fatherland and that is quite insensitive to those distinctions between what is or is not customary in ordinary wars. As for the armies I command, I flatter myself, my Prince, that everyone will recognize in the way they act, the principles that characterize every loyal, brave and generous nation. . . .'[11]

This message, taken by a Russian envoy to Napoleon within a few hours, represented an unequivocal declaration of continued war. Yet Alexander also put his pen to paper on this Wednesday, expressing his criticism of Kutuzov's handling of the French negotiation attempts.

'Prince Mikhail Illarionovich. By your report sent with Prince Volkonsky, I learn of the interview that has taken place between yourself and the French *aide-de-camp* General Lauriston. At the very moment of your departure for the armies that were entrusted to you, you knew, from the explanations I gave you personally, of my firm and insistent desire to abstain from all negotiations and all relations with the adversary that might have tended to produce a peace. But today, after these events, I must repeat with the same firmness that the rule established by me must be respected strictly and resolutely in its entirety.'[12]

By the time this unnecessary Imperial reprimand reached Kutuzov it would be even more irrelevant. Napoleon was obliged to rest his forces at Forminskoie on 22 October and he attempted to organize his leading regiments. French troops began to leave the town on Friday, 23 October, with Napoleon aiming for Kaluga via Borovsk and Maloyaroslavets; Dokhturov's Cossacks hovered near by and discovered that the force in front of them represented far more than a foraging party, although they still did not realize that the whole of the Grand Army was in the area. Messengers were despatched to inform Kutuzov, and Cossacks were hurried to Borovsk, only to find the French there before them. Kutuzov immediately ordered Dokhturov to head for Maloyaroslavets and at about three o'clock in the afternoon of the 23rd he himself began moving with his regiments towards this town, explaining his actions in an urgent despatch to Alexander: 'The enemy is doing his utmost to circumvent me in order to hurl himself on Kaluga and penetrate into our fertile provinces.'[13] To reach the town of Maloyaroslavets the main Russian regiments had to march about thirty kilometres south-west, moving across rough tracks from the old Kaluga road to the new; meanwhile Dokhturov would have to block the French with his outnumbered forces.

Maloyaroslavets offered an excellent site for a defensive battle. The small town lay on a hill above the Lutza; the road through the town ran alongside the river, winding through a succession of ravines. The approaching enemy would have to narrow its front through the gap, but an area of wasteland stretched at the southern edge of the town upon which defending forces could be deployed. The critical point would be the bridge where the road bent over the Lutza, situated in Maloyaroslavets itself.

French advance troops seized this bridge first, early in the morning of Saturday, 24 October. Dokhturov's Cossacks, who had been shadowing the enemy, failed to prise this small enemy advance guard from the crossing, and 20,000 French reinforcements from Eugène's Corps rapidly approached. General Wilson, with Dokhturov, saw Eugène's troops begin their advance towards the bridge – 'a dense body flocking forward'. His account continued: 'I shall only say that I had the honour to open the ball and plant the first guns that saved the town, for the enemy were pouring in. . . . I pushed the guns into short grape distance. After the first four rounds the enemy's columns broke, and *sauve qui peut* was the general effort up and down the hill. The slaughter must have been considerable.'[14] This bombardment did indeed halt the first French advance, but the outnumbered Russians were still unable to seize the bridge and were obliged to fall back to the wasteland at the southern edge of the town, where Dokhturov had established his headquarters.

More French arrived, and with enemy pressure gradually building up, Dokhturov anxiously searched for signs of Kutuzov and the bulk of the Russian army; he received no reports of approaching Russian regiments, and once again Wilson used the occasion to attack Kutuzov's ability as a commander. 'The Russians only accuse *one person* of being *deficient in example*,' wrote the British general, 'in addition to the heavy charges which can be brought against him for ignorance in the conduct of the troops, for sloth, for indecision of counsels, for panic operations, and for "a desire to let the enemy pass unmolested". Marshal Kutuzov affords a memorable instance of incapacity in a chief, of an absence of any quality that ought to distinguish a commander.'[15]

Once again Wilson's charges – which were repeated to Alexander and which have been repeated down through the years – were totally without foundation. Wilson claimed that Kutuzov had only ten miles to march to the battle, yet 'perseveringly turned a deaf ear to every messenger and entreaty' and allowed Dokhturov's fragile force to suffer terrible casualties while he dallied on the way. In fact Kutuzov had to march double the distance which Wilson claimed, along foul roads and during darkness; his main regiments reached the vicinity in about twenty-four hours, and Kutuzov took the precaution of hurrying Raevsky's corps on ahead – these troops arrived during the morning of the 24th, within two hours of the start of the battle.

Kutuzov fully realized the importance of Maloyaroslavets. To Alexander he wrote: 'This day is one of the most notable in the whole bloodthirsty war, because if the battle at Maloyaroslavets had been lost, it would have had the most disastrous consequences and opened a route for the enemy.'[16] At the same time, although Kutuzov advanced to the battle as quickly as possible, he also proceeded cautiously. Unlike Wilson, whose account reveals signs of panic, Kutuzov retained his characteristic calm; he believed that Maloyaroslavets could be held by Dokhturov's gallant corps and by Raevsky's troops – the ground strongly favoured the defence. More men might be superfluous; Marshal Bessières reached a similar conclusion when he later carried out a reconnaissance for Napoleon and reported: 'Three hundred grenadiers placed there could keep a whole army in check.' Above all, Kutuzov wanted to keep his main army uncommitted simply because he was still unaware that Moscow had actually been abandoned: Napoleon might only be moving part of his army against him while the rest remained in the capital or even struck elsewhere.

This calculated reasoning was lost to Wilson and to many of those Russians fighting in the inferno of Maloyaroslavets. The ravines gushed filthy black smoke and the thunder of the cannon echoed from the slopes; Raevsky's regiments ran into the attack as soon as they arrived with orders 'to penetrate into and carry the town by storm'; this they managed to do, driving over the burning timbers and the piles of rubble, but only to be forced out again during the afternoon by fresh French troops. The Russians continued to hold the southern exit; they lined the walls and gullies with shells and grapeshot smashing into their battered positions, and each time the French infantry attempted to advance the Russian volleys drove them back again.

Napoleon, like Kutuzov, had been absent from the main battle. The French Emperor arrived in the afternoon and expressed astonishment: he seemed unable to believe that any Russian troops could have reached the town in time to block his advancing regiments. Then, at about four o'clock, Kutuzov's main force appeared to the south: through his glass Napoleon could see the Russians deploying in a dark, undulating mass. The French had lost their chance of victory; Kutuzov, who had never sought a decisive pitched battle, had achieved his object of simply blocking the enemy.

Bombardments by both armies continued into the night. 'After sunset the spectacle had been indescribably magnificent and interesting,' wrote Wilson. 'The crackling flames – the dark shadows of the combatants flitting amongst them – the hissing ring of the grape as it flew from the licornes – the rattling of musketry – the ignited shells traversing and crossing in the atmosphere – the wild shouts . . .'[17] Cannonades were fired intermittently next day, Sunday, 25 October, although the Russians pulled slightly back south of the town. French casualties in the battle totalled about 5,000 killed and wounded, the Russians slightly more. Napoleon rode through the ruin of Maloyaroslavets, then undertook a reconnaissance expedition, from which he only just survived a sudden attack by Cossacks. For much of the day Kutuzov stayed inside the farmhouse which he used as a head-quarters.

As at Borodino, the two commanders seemed to set themselves strangely apart from their entangled troops. At the great battle they had sat attempting to understand the mind of the other commander; now they behaved in similar fashion, and the outcome would be even more important: the next move had to be executed, the most fateful of all.

Napoleon returned to his headquarters at the village of Gorodnia at five o'clock this Sunday evening. The Emperor was quartered in a miserable weaver's cabin, stinking of rats and damp.

And as Ségur wrote: 'In this crumbling hovel, in a dark and dirty chamber, divided into two by means of a cloth, the fate of the army and of Europe was to be decided.'[18] Discussions continued into the night. Kutuzov's army was intact, blocking the road ahead; the Russian commander was avoiding full pitched battle – and whilst the enemy army remained in being Napoleon knew he could never be safe; he lacked a secure base, and Kutuzov could lead him into unknown territory with the winter threatening to engulf the Grand Army. Food was already short; the cavalry lacked fodder; French communications were stretched and would become more so with every move forward. In the dark hours of the night Napoleon reached his decision. Retreat.

Kutuzov lay on his camp-bed in his farmhouse headquarters. As usual during a campaign he remained fully dressed; his decorations were still pinned to his simple tunic. Outside a small group of Cossacks dismounted from their ponies: across some of the saddles were slumped bound French captives. Dokhturov's orderly, Bolgovsky, brought in astonishing news: the leader of the Cossacks, Lieutenant Yazikov, had just come back from Moscow. And the capital had been deserted by the enemy, even by the last garrison. No French remained.

Kutuzov refused to believe Bolgovsky's words. 'Have the French abandoned Moscow? Is it true?' The orderly repeated the information in greater detail, with Kutuzov urging him to talk faster so that he might reach the wonderful conclusion. His subtle, stubborn strategy had been successful. Napoleon's complete departure from Moscow was an admission of defeat, just as his seizure of Moscow had seemed a victorious conclusion to the French campaign. Now the Grand Army could be dealt with by the Russian forces and by the ally which Kutuzov called 'General Winter'.

The old marshal sobbed. Then he turned to an icon on the wall and exclaimed: 'God my Creator! Thou has granted our prayers at last! Russia is saved!'[19]

The battle of 24 October proved more decisive than Borodino. In later years the Russians placed a small plaque in the town of Maloyaroslavets, and the eleven words carved upon it stated the simple truth: 'End of offensive. Beginning of rout and ruin of the enemy.'[20]

XIV

Retreat

(1812: 26 October–13 December)

Kutuzov had imposed his will upon Napoleon as no other single commander had done before. Now he could reap the benefits. But first, reaction set in. The tension had affected Kutuzov during the last weeks although few suspected it; he cloaked his mental stress beneath his usual silence: while others might have revealed their agitation, as Napoleon had done during his last night at the Kremlin, Kutuzov appeared to be almost asleep. But the same strain was being suffered, and now, on 26 October, Kutuzov could scarcely believe the news that the French were at last retreating.

The Russian commander therefore acted cautiously, withdrawing southwards slightly towards Kaluga while the Grand Army retreated in the opposite direction towards Mozhaisk. The two armies pulled apart, and the mists and the snow-swollen clouds rolled across the wet countryside between them – already, on 27 October, the temperature dropped to minus four degrees and the weather was closing in.

Kutuzov had apparently let slip the opportunity to deal the French a heavy blow, and Alexander, Bennigsen and Sir Robert Wilson would never forgive him. The British general declared his feelings in an indignant letter to Alexander on 26 October; he also noted in his diary: 'This morning the enemy was retreating, probably to gain the Smolensk road. The marshal will sing *Te Deum*, but the rest of the army "hymns of lamentation". . . . By a false movement, occasioned by his personal terror rather than by an error of judgement, he has made a circuit of near eighty versts [about eighty kilometres] and has lost sight of the enemy. . . . I can scarcely behave with common decency in his presence.'[1] Bennigsen revealed his feelings in a letter to Alexander denouncing Kutuzov: the communication accused the commander of abandoning the Russians to their fate, of not attending to any army business and of 'living in ease and luxury' while his troops suffered. Alexander, who valued Bennigsen's opinion highly, decided he should send this letter to Kutuzov – it would arrive in the last week of November.[2]

News of the enemy's abandonment of Moscow reached St Petersburg at noon on 27 October. Ceremonial cannon fired triumphant salvoes from the fortress of St Peter and St Paul, with the sound of these guns echoing across the waters of the Baltic; citizens wept in the streets and the noble ladies took out their ball-gowns for the ecstatic celebrations. Alexander acknowledged the cheers of the crowd; he prepared to attend a magnificent ceremony at the Kazan Cathedral, and at the same time despatched a vicious letter to the deliverer of Russia, Kutuzov: 'I see with extreme displeasure that the whole aim of cutting off the enemy's retreat has entirely disappeared. Your inexplicable lack of action after the successful battle of the 18th near Tarutino, in which you lost those advantages which presented themselves, and the unnecessary and pernicious retreat after the battle of Maloyaroslavets have annihilated all the advantages of your position.'[3]

Kutuzov's actions were motivated by his caution: he had to be certain that the enemy movements were not merely part of a deception plan, and he had to be sure of the exact route being taken by Napoleon – the French might have attempted to reach Smolensk via Kaluga, which Kutuzov now covered. The direction of the retreat had been the subject of detailed and painful discussion at the French headquarters on the night of the 25th, when Napoleon had reached the decision to retreat. Smolensk marked the principal objective, promising plentiful stores, a winter base for future operations or an exit from Russia. To reach the city the Grand Army could attempt one of three routes: southwards via Kaluga; north-west via Medinsk, or directly north to Mozhaisk and then west along the road which the Grand Army had used to reach Moscow. Murat proposed battering the Russians out of the way to reach the fertile country around Kaluga – but by now Napoleon knew that Kutuzov guarded this route: the Russians could deploy in defensive positions of their own choosing, or could merely step to one side and then strike when the Grand Army was least prepared. Davout urged a move north-west, via Medinsk, where the countryside had been untouched by war – but even Murat realized this route would expose the army to flank attacks from Kutuzov's near-by army, and progress would be slow through the unknown territory. Kutuzov had therefore positioned himself in such a way that there seemed no alternative route for the French other than via Mozhaisk, even though the road between Mozhaisk and Smolensk had been damaged and stripped of provisions during the French invasion. And so the French moved north.

By late afternoon on the 27th the position was clear to Kutuzov, with the situation exactly as he had hoped. His guard across the Kaluga road had proved successful; the enemy were taking the route which would be most profitable for the Russians. Kutuzov had no intention of striking at the French while the enemy could act 'like a wild boar harried by hunters': first the Grand Army must be weakened. The marshal had already explained in his letter to Alexander dated 16 October that if the enemy attempted to reach Smolensk the Russian army would march parallel, preventing any French attempts to leave the road in search of supplies. Kutuzov added latest details in a despatch to Alexander on the 27th: 'The enemy, forestalled on all the roads, began to retreat through the area to the Mozhaisk road, and therefore I have been obliged to issue the following orders: the army is directed along the right-hand route towards the city of Viazma; the detachment of General Miloradovich is strengthened, and will go parallel between me and the Mozhaisk road.' Chichagov would be instructed to forestall the enemy as much as possible with his Danube Army further west, 'to destroy all bridges and fords and inflict all conceivable harm'.[4]

By Wednesday, 28 October, the Russians had begun the pursuit. Kutuzov ordered his regiments forward with a stirring Order of the Day: 'From his very entry into Moscow the Enemy was cruelly deceived in his hopes there to find abundance and even victory. He has now undertaken a hasty retreat, not seeing in front of him anything but continued terrible war . . . able to discern a warrior in each Russian. . . . I have ordered this army to put out the fire of Moscow with the blood of the enemy.'[5]

In front of Kutuzov's regular regiments rode the Cossacks,

with parties of fifty or more men ranging far ahead to strike at the retreating enemy. Kutuzov provided detailed instructions to the Cossack commander, Platov: 'Try to gain a march over the enemy in such a way that with your main forces you can make suitable attacks on the retreating heads of his columns, combined with constant night alarms. The same orders have been given to General Orlov Denisov to perform similar operations on the left of the high road. This kind of pursuit will bring the enemy into an extreme position and will deprive him of the major part of his artillery and baggage waggons.'[6]

'We had them swarming round us constantly,' wrote an officer in Napoleon's army, Heinrich Vossler. 'Officers or men on their own, even if they strayed no more than a hundred yards from the main body, paid for their carelessness with their lives.'[7]

Behind these Cossacks marched the bulk of the Russian army, directed along the narrow tracks north-west towards Medinsk after which Kutuzov intended to swerve north and intercept the Grand Army at Viazma: the French, taking the longer route due north via Mozhaisk, would presumably arrive too late at Viazma to prevent the Russians reaching this town first. French troops were suffering at a rapidly increasing rate. 'We were almost without provisions,' noted Ségur, 'and winter had overtaken us. Some of the men had already sunk under these complicated evils.' Many waggons had been burnt at the start of the retreat because the horses were too weak to pull them, and the smoke from these bonfires rose black against the grey, overcast sky.

'The whole road to Mozhaisk was enveloped in smoke,' wrote Wilson, now with Miloradovich's vanguard. 'We saw various explosions of powder waggons. . . . The peasants of the village in which we now are have wreaked dreadful vengeance on many of the enemy. Fifty were seized here and buried alive. . . . All the peasants, and the few prisoners who escape death, declare that famine makes great havoc. Their only nourishment is horse-flesh, which many cannot eat as it produces dysentery.'[8]

But early on 28 October the first French troops reached Mozhaisk; Napoleon entered the town later in the day and his spirits began to revive: apart from Cossacks no sign had been seen of the enemy, and now his army could march on a familiar road. Perhaps Kutuzov had declined to enter into pursuit. Almost immediately the French Emperor suffered renewed depression: Davout sent him a Russian chasseur, captured earlier in the day, and during the course of interrogation this captive let slip that 'the whole Russian army was marching upon Viazma, by way of Medinsk.' Napoleon's reaction was described by Ségur:' Did Kutuzov mean to outstrip him there, as he had done at Maloyaroslavets, cut off his retreat upon Smolensk, without provisions, without shelter, and surrounded by an armed and hostile population?' Ségur's account continued: 'His first impulse led him to reject this idea with contempt.'[9] Napoleon nevertheless ordered his Guard forward at maximum speed to cover the retreat, and he himself left Mozhaisk almost immediately, spending the night at Uspenskoie six kilometres westwards.

Near the Emperor on this Wednesday night camped troops of Ney's Third Corps. Their experience during these wild hours of darkness proved harrowing in the extreme: when they tried to dig shelter for themselves in the sodden earth they disturbed scores of bodies, half-eaten by wolves, and only then did they realize that their bivouac site stretched on to the battlefield of Borodino. Ségur reached the area with Napoleon next day and provided this haunting description. 'We saw the earth trodden down, naked, devastated; the trees cut down to within a few feet of the ground, and farther on broken hillocks, the largest of which presented the most hideous spectacle. . . . All around, the earth was covered with fragments of helmets and cuirasses, of broken drums and arms, tattered uniforms, and bloodstained standards. Upon this desolate spot lay 30,000 half-devoured bodies. A few skeletons, which remained on the crumbling side of one of these hills, surmounted and looked down upon the whole. It seemed as if Death had there fixed his imperial seat.' Ségur added: 'The Emperor hurried by. Nobody stopped. We were pressed by cold, hunger, and the enemy. . . .'[10]

The battlefield condemned the false hopes of the past and presented a warning of the future. To the Russians the reverse held true. 'I humbly beg you,' wrote Kutuzov during October, 'to leave these fortifications inviolate. May they decay with time, but never be destroyed by the hand of man; may the husbandman, tilling his peaceful fields, never disturb them with his plough; may they be sacred monuments of courage for the Russians of later times; may our descendants on looking at them be inspired with the flame of emulation, and say admiringly: "This was the place where the pride of those beasts of prey fell before the fearless Sons of the Fatherland!" '11

But now, in these last days of October, Napoleon managed to slip through the trap at Viazma. He reached the town at four o'clock in the afternoon, 31 October, after having ridden so fast that his personal guard was still about twenty-five kilometres back down the road. On this Saturday Kutuzov reached Spass-Duvosk about eighty kilometres to the south-east, and although the Russian advance guard under Miloradovich was moving up the tracks ahead, the bulk of Kutuzov's army would clearly be too late to intercept the French. Kutuzov nevertheless felt confident: constant reports revealed the suffering being inflicted on the enemy through the Cossacks, partisans, weather and the precipitate retreat. The Russian commander issued a proclamation to his troops on the 31st describing the French condition in emotional yet reasonably accurate language: 'He is burning his waggons, abandoning his baggage and the treasures his impious hands have snatched from the very altars of the Lord. Desertion and famine spread confusion around him. The murmurs of his soldiers rise behind him like the mutter of threatening waves.'12

Russian troops were also suffering. Wilson wrote on 1 November: 'The army has been without food the whole of this day, and I fear we must march tomorrow without any, as the provision-waggons are left far behind. . . . How lamentable that they [the troops] should have been so commanded!'13

Napoleon stayed in Viazma for forty-eight hours, attempting to catch up on urgent paper-work and to organize his regiments as they marched through the town. He left during the late afternoon of Monday, 2 November; the bulk of the Grand Army had retreated further west but Davout's rearguard was only just departing from Gzatsk about sixty kilometres to the east. The Russian advance guard moved to intercept; Miloradovich first sought to block the enemy rearguard at Czarevo-Zaimishche, the town where Kutuzov had joined the retreating Russian army in August, but Davout pushed this opposition aside before sufficient Russian infantrymen could arrive; the French retreat continued throughout the night. Miloradovich attacked again next morning just east of Viazma, with the assault joined by Platov's Cossacks. Davout's First Corps had already been severely weakened by constant Cossack attacks and through general exhaustion, with manpower having been reduced from 28,000 to 14,000 in the last fourteen days; now the weary, demoralized troops had to fight their way through to the comparative safety of Viazma. They were helped by units hurried back by Eugène, Poniatowski and Ney; Miloradovich, outnumbered by these reinforcements, was unable to prevent the junction of the French rearguard with the remainder of the army, and even Kutuzov admitted that the enemy displayed remarkable cohesion. He wrote later: 'I must say that at Viazma he had still to fall into complete disarray and he had almost all of his artillery.'

The engagement throughout 3 November nevertheless inflicted further heavy casualties on the French. 'The route and the fields were covered with their ruins,' wrote Wilson. 'They could not have lost less than 6,000 men.'[14] By now the Grand Army under Napoleon's direct command had been slashed to about 55,000 men and 12,000 horses fit for active service; Kutuzov's main army numbered at least 90,000 and with the Russians rode 'General Winter': snow began to fall steadily on 4 November and thirty-six hours later the first full blizzard swept across the road between Viazma and Smolensk. 'The cold was icy,' wrote Colonel Griois in Eugène's Fourth Corps, describing conditions on the 6th, 'and the snow had hardened and was all frozen. Winter had just fallen on us with full severity and was not going to leave us.'[15]

Blizzards screamed again on the 7th. Movement for both armies was rendered increasingly difficult, but by now the Russian forces seemed in excellent position to complete the annihilation of the Grand Army. Kutuzov had swung the bulk of his army south-west before reaching Viazma, after realizing that complete interception would be impossible at this town, and he now followed a route parallel to the main Smolensk–Moscow road, thus preventing the French from leaving this highway; Miloradovich and other Russian units continued down the same road as the French to press the enemy from the rear. Meanwhile Wittgenstein's Russian First Army Corps moved to intercept from the north, recaptured Polotsk in mid-October and then veered south towards Vitebsk barely a hundred kilometres from the next French objective, Smolensk. And, to the south of the French escape, lay Chichagov's Danube Army near the Pripet Marshes. Wittgenstein and Chichagov should have been closer, according to instructions sent to them by Kutuzov in mid-

September, but against this Russian threat in the path of the retreating French Army Napoleon could only rely on three French corps, under Oudinot, St Cyr and Victor, which had been left to face St Petersburg while the Grand Army had marched on Moscow.

Daily the horrors of the retreat multiplied, for all forces involved. Miloradovich's rearguard left Viazma in pursuit of the French on 5 November, reaching Dorogobuzh half-way to Smolensk on the 8th. Wilson described the scenes on the road: 'The naked masses of dead and dying men; the mangled carcasses of 10,000 horses, which had, in some cases, been cut for food before life had ceased, the craving of famine at other points forming groups of *cannibals*; the air enveloped in flame and smoke; the prayers of hundreds of naked wretches, flying from the peasantry whose shouts of vengeance echoed incessantly through the woods, the wrecks of cannon, powder-waggons, military stores of all descriptions, and every ordinary as well as extraordinary ill of war combined with the asperity of the climate, formed such a scene as probably was never witnessed to such an extent in the history of the world.' Wilson came across a group of wounded French soldiers sitting over the body of a comrade whom they had just roasted and were now eating.[16]

The worst had still to come. Napoleon's staff reached Smolensk on 9 November, to find that the expected piles of stores were totally insufficient – and to hear, on 10 November, that Vitebsk had been seized by Wittgenstein's forces on the 6th. Napoleon remained in the ruined city for four days, and at one point considered rallying his forces for another battle: he believed he still had about 50,000 effective troops, and claimed that the Russians must be in a far worse state than the Grand Army. Napoleon's assessment might well have been accurate if any other commander than Kutuzov had been directing Russian operations. Kutuzov's critics demanded that his regiments should be driven harder despite inevitable losses from exhaustion; Wilson moaned in his diary on 13 November: 'Our main army has kept aloof; has suffered an enemy so situated, so distressed, so feeble, to gain his communications and resources. Nay, the Russian *main army* fled, or rather was made to fly, from this enemy. . . . Our marches were studiously made to avoid the enemy.'[17] But Kutuzov remained true to his principle: the army must be preserved, ready for the essential and decisive battle. Napoleon might yet attempt to establish winter quarters against which the Russian army must be able to employ superior forces. Meanwhile the retreat would continue and the weather, the Cossacks and the partisans could continue their murderous business. Even Wilson, who had now begun to criticize Kutuzov openly of being in league with the French, admitted in mid-November that 'the regiments were nearly as effective as when they set out'. The main Russian army strength still totalled about 80,000 men plus over 600 cannon, according to contemporary assessments – although the latter varied considerably. This figure represented a drop in Russian manpower of about 10,000 troops in the previous ten days, through sickness and desertion as well as from enemy action, but the French casualty rate was running at an even higher daily loss.

Moreover the march of the Russian army proceeded steadily with Kutuzov averaging about twenty-five kilometres each day despite the weather. By 13 November the regiments had crept far closer than Napoleon realized – the French Emperor was even lulled into thinking that the Russians may have abandoned the principal pursuit. Instead Kutuzov and his army lay to the south – and the advance corps under Miloradovich was curving round Smolensk to block the road further west towards Krasnyi. Kutuzov wrote in a letter dated 13 November: 'It would be very desirable if the enemy stopped if only for a short time in Smolensk. That would make it easier for us to cut him off.'[18]

Napoleon followed his advance guard from Smolensk on the 14th. 'All along our way we were forced to step over the dead and dying,' wrote a French sergeant, François Bourgogne.[19] By nightfall Napoleon managed to reach a tumbled-down hut in the village of Korynia, twenty-five kilometres west of Smolensk. And there he heard that the road ahead seemed blocked.

Kutuzov's headquarters remained some eighty kilometres south-east of Smolensk near Elnya, but Miloradovich had succeeded in his movement to outflank the French, supported by Cossacks. French attempts to break through during the 14th had already been beaten back near Krasnyi; it seemed as if Napoleon must now be trapped. Freezing fog swirled across the desolate road; each time the French vanguard tried to move forward into this murk, Russian muskets flashed vivid in the mist and drove the enemy back again.

Napoleon rode forward to the front early on the 15th. He stood beside the road, his greatcoat collar almost hiding his face, while the officers reported on the situation further up the road; then he called his corps commanders together and told them their troops must make one more effort – salvation lay beyond, soon the border of the Russian Fatherland would be reached, the Russians blocking the road must be battered away. Once again the French regiments drove forward, and once again they succeeded after fighting which lasted throughout the 15th in the muffling mist and sudden snow flurries. The main Russian forces were still too far away to lend effective help to Miloradovich's ambush – over fifty kilometres on the 15th. But in order to escape Napoleon had to sacrifice Ney's gallant rearguard, left behind to protect the retreat, and the fate of Ney's troops served as the epitome of the whole tragic saga.

Over 6,000 combatants left Smolensk under Ney's command on the morning of the 17th, plus several thousand camp-followers. The leading detachments clashed against Miloradovich's defences during the following afternoon, with the Russian guns raking the road with grape and roundshot. Ney was asked to hand over his sword but replied: 'A Marshal of France does not surrender,' and he ordered his men into suicidal attack.

'It was a conflict of heroes,' wrote Wilson, 'and even the vanquished have acquired honour. The carnage was tremendous; the ground was covered with the dead and dying; the Russian bayonets were dripping with the crimson torrents. . . .'[20] Ney's survivors took to the woods hoping to find a way round the Russian defences; they blundered through the drifts and then followed a small stream, breaking the ice to see which way the water flowed to give them the direction down to the Dnieper. At last they reached this river, which they found covered with a thin coating of ice. Ney led the way across; the ice broke, drowning many of his men, but the rest struggled over to the far bank and then through the woods towards Orsha, harassed by Cossacks, dropping from exhaustion and from the terrible cold. At last they reached the temporary safety of Orsha, which Napoleon had entered the day before and where he still kept his headquarters. Of the 6,000 combatants in Ney's corps, only 900 remained.[21]

Kutuzov's failure to intercept with his full army at Krasnyi marks the biggest personal mistake of his career. Although not as near as Wilson maintained in his account, the main army could have been pushed to a greater extent during the preceding few days in order to administer the final blow. Kutuzov's failure probably stemmed from three main reasons: his over-caution in wishing to preserve his army should Napoleon turn back on him – as indeed Napoleon contemplated for a while at Smolensk; secondly, the continued lack of an effective staff system; and thirdly, Kutuzov's own exhaustion. By now the 67-year-old commander was suffering intense weariness combined with fever and constant headaches.[22]

Another reason has been put forward to explain Napoleon's escape: the wily Russian commander may never have wished to engage his army in full battle against the French. According to this theory Kutuzov saw his task as simply to push the enemy from the Fatherland, considering whatever happened afterwards to be none of his concern. Meanwhile, the weather would complete the destruction of the Grand Army. 'Our young hotheads are angry with the old man for curbing their desire,' Kutuzov is reported to have said to Würtemburg after Krasnyi. 'They do not reflect that the circumstances alone are achieving more than our weapons. However, we ourselves must not knock at the frontier like haggard tramps.'[23] Wilson claimed that Kutuzov told him: 'First and foremost I am Russian. I want my country to be liberated. As for Europe, let France and England decide between themselves who will dominate it.' And, also according to Wilson, the marshal even declared: 'I am by no means sure that the total destruction of the Emperor Napoleon and his army would be such a benefit to the world.'[24]

Wilson's words are not to be trusted, but neither are those spoken by Kutuzov to Würtemburg. Kutuzov indeed realized that the weather would prove a greater enemy to the French than the Russian army, yet it is also highly probable that had the opportunity arisen he would have used this army in a decisive battle. His movements and his orders show that he intended to intercept at Viazma, and failed, and the same failure was repeated at Krasnyi. Now another opportunity existed, the greatest so far. Ahead of the retreating French remnants lay the swirling waters of the Berezina river, and converging on the crossing were the forces of Chichagov and Wittgenstein, with Kutuzov still pushing the stumbling French from the rear. Once again Kutuzov's orders reveal that he sincerely hoped the French would be caught at the Berezina. The Russian army commander, soon to hear that Alexander had named him 'Prince of Smolensk' after the action near the city, wrote to Wittgenstein on about 15 November: 'Our main army and the army of Admiral Chichagov are using all means to get as near as possible to destroy the chief enemy army. If Napoleon should retreat towards Orsha I suggest that you occupy some strong position or defile in that direction.'[25]

Napoleon left Orsha on 21 November, rushing to cover the 100 kilometres to the Berezina at Borisov before the Russians arrived. On that same day he had heard confirmation that Chichagov had seized Minsk on the 16th, west of Borisov and nearer to this objective than the French.[26] And, also on the 21st, unknown to Napoleon, Chichagov's advance guard in fact reached the Berezina and seized the vital Borisov bridge. Wittgenstein with the Russian First Army Corps had pushed back Victor at Smoliantsi on the 15th and was believed to be lurking just to the north. It seemed impossible that the French could escape.

'You will see,' wrote Kutuzov to Wittgenstein after Krasnyi, 'what extraordinary losses the main enemy army has undergone in the course of the last five days, during which he has lost almost all his artillery and cavalry. His previous warlike spirit has entirely evaporated. It therefore follows that one central action by our armies on the remaining strength of the enemy, with the help of God, threatens Napoleon with new defeat and complete destruction of his army.'[27]

Kutuzov moved his army slightly northwards to join the same route as the retreating French: now his main regiments marched directly behind the enemy although some distance away; Wittgenstein and Chichagov must be approaching in front; the decisive moment has at last arrived. 'A dark rumour had spread that two new enemy armies were threatening our line of retreat,' wrote a Grand Army officer, Captain Johann von Borcke. 'We approached the Berezina, but on the march these rumours steadily gained substance, and the names "Chichagov" and "Berezina" passed from mouth to mouth. . . . Gloomy, silent, and with downcast gaze, this rabble of dying men walked from Orsha to the Berezina like a funeral procession. . . . We listened with half an ear, answered curtly or not at all, and were without hope or fear. Indifference to everything, to death, even if one had escaped it at that very moment, dominated everybody's dulled spirits. We had sunk to the level of animals.'[28]

But critical flaws existed in the structure of Kutuzov's strategy causing the whole to collapse. The situation proved a throwback to those days of March 1811 when Chichagov had ousted Kutuzov as commander of the Danube Army and when his feeling of dislike for his rival had matched those of the Czar; the Admiral's opinion of Kutuzov had remained unchanged, and so far throughout the 1812 campaign he had conducted an independent role, deploying his army near the Pripet Marshes despite Kutuzov's requests for him to move into closer contact. Chichagov, still a favourite of Alexander, had neglected to cooperate with the commander-in-chief; his own subordinates had urged closer liaison but Chichagov had ignored their pleas, content in the knowledge that the Emperor supported him.

Now, in the tense third week of November, Kutuzov clearly lacked knowledge of Chichagov's whereabouts: the Admiral had failed to send any despatch, and Kutuzov certainly had no idea that he had moved so close to the Berezina. The Russian commander-in-chief sent a message to the Admiral seeking his cooperation, and his words revealed his absence of information. 'Your Excellency can see that as the enemy forces join in the vicinity of Borisov our forces approach closer and can deliver a strong and possibly final blow. If Borisov is occupied by the enemy, then after crossing the Berezina he will probably head straight for Vilna. . . . I therefore order Your Excellency to occupy the defile near Zembin in which it is possible to hold back a very much superior enemy.'[29] Nor was Kutuzov well informed on Wittgenstein's position, this time through the interference of Alexander and the bad communications caused by the weather. Clausewitz, now serving with Wittgenstein, described how the Czar had sent instructions for his northern commander to deploy his forces on a wide line against both Victor at Smoliantsi and Oudinot towards Vilna – a distance of over 150 kilometres stretching over foul roads.[30] This extended deployment prevented close cooperation with Kutuzov's main army, and the lack of concentration within the corps itself resulted in a disastrous delay in orders reaching Wittgenstein. Kutuzov now instructed him to pay special attention to Borisov, where it should be possible to strike the decisive blow. 'Your Excellency can see from this how disastrous Napoleon's position is. The one aim of all our actions is the destruction of the enemy to the last limit of possibility.'

These words reveal Kutuzov's determination to eliminate the Grand Army in a decisive battle at the Berezina. Yet the fatal flaw is revealed by referring to the dates of these two messages from Kutuzov, denied of information, to Chichagov and Wittgenstein – respectively 25 and 27 November. On the first of these two days, when Kutuzov believed he was in the act of arranging the interception at Borisov, Napoleon's army was almost ready to cross the Berezina having completely outwitted Chichagov by luring him out of Borisov, and by the 27th the French operation to pass over the Berezina had reached its final stage.

Napoleon's old energy returned at the Berezina; the Emperor's skill, combined with Chichagov's stupidity, ruined Kutuzov's last chance of a decisive battle. Chichagov's troops had burnt the bridge at Borisov but were then sent scurrying southwards by a French feint in that direction. Napoleon darted twelve kilometres north and his engineers began to throw two pontoon bridges across the snow-swollen river at Studianka, from which the French could reach the narrow gap at Zembin, the defile which Kutuzov's instructions sent this very day specified should be held. The French began to cross during the afternoon of the 26th, with Wittgenstein still over fifty kilometres away to the north, Chichagov still chasing foolishly south, and with Kutuzov's main regiments at Staroselbe over eighty kilometres to the east. Not until the 27th could Wittgenstein reach Studienka; the French continued to cross hour by hour despite Russian artillery bombardments, and Napoleon himself reached the western bank at noon on the 28th. Chichagov, at last returning to the scene, launched an attack on the 28th in combination with Wittgenstein, but the French rearguard under Victor managed to fend off the enemy for another few precious hours. The bridges were destroyed on the morning of the 28th, with Napoleon having managed to save about 40,000 troops. Cossacks drove in amongst the stragglers, camp-followers and wounded left stranded on the eastern bank.

Once again, and for a final time, the Grand Army had escaped. Kutuzov's efforts had been defeated by factors almost entirely beyond his control: Chichagov's incompetence, Alexander's interference with Wittgenstein, the weather, the increasing exhaustion of his own troops, and the continued unsatisfactory relationship between himself and his subordinates at the Russian headquarters which prevented an effective staff system.

'If Bennigsen will but wait a little,' wrote Wilson in his diary, 'the Marshal's age and infirmities will oblige him to resign. They say that "Fortune is blind," but I pretend that "Glory" in this war is less capable of discrimination in her choice.'[31]

Kutuzov finally turned against his chief of staff at the beginning of December. By now he had received from Alexander the letter which Bennigsen had sent to the Czar after Maloyaroslavets complaining against his commander; Alexander had despatched this to Kutuzov together with an award for Bennigsen for his operations at Tarutino. Kutuzov entered the officer's mess, handed the award citation to his chief of staff and asked him to read the words of praise aloud to the assembled officers. Bennigsen obliged, with pleasure. Then Kutuzov passed him the despatch which he had sent the Czar and asked him to read it likewise. Bennigsen declined and stormed from the room. Kutuzov immediately dismissed him as chief of staff; a few days later, after Bennigsen had remained at headquarters constantly opposing his superior, Kutuzov threw him out of the camp with a warning that if he returned he would most probably have him hung.[32]

'The Emperor must now express his opinion as to the merits of the rivals,' wrote Wilson. 'I remained the whole day with Bennigsen. . . . The next morning we parted with mutual regrets.'[33]

The final stage of the retreat had begun. It became the most horrific of all. The extent of Kutuzov's disappointment at the enemy's Berezina escape is impossible to determine, but soon the French deliverance at the river amounted to a mockery: half those who survived the crossing failed to reach the next objective, Vilna, with the vast majority falling victim to the weather and to exhaustion. The truth of an earlier remark by Kutuzov became fully apparent: 'They will all fall to pieces without our intervention.'[34] Kutuzov may have missed his decisive battle, but other essential features of his strategy emerged successful: the enemy had been kept on the move, unable to rest, unable to gain provisions or make a stand, and now Kutuzov's 'General Winter' completed the annihilation of the French. The marshal reached the Berezina in the last days of November and witnessed the torment inflicted on the stragglers and wounded who had been unable to cross the river – trampled by horses, slaughtered by bullet or cannon fire, frozen to the ground, drowned in the icy black waters. Another eye-witness, Clausewitz, wrote to his wife: 'What ghastly scenes have I witnessed here. If my feelings had not been hardened it would have sent me mad. Even so, it will take many years before I can remember what I have seen without feeling a shuddering horror.'[35]

Napoleon left the shambles of his Grand Army on 5 December, heading for Paris to deal with the threat to his political authority caused by the attempted takeover by General Malet on 22 October, and to organize forces to face the military threat to his Empire. Forty-eight hours earlier, 3 December, the French leader had issued his 29th Bulletin, in which he fully admitted the disaster of the retreat but laid all blame upon the weather; he refused to allow Kutuzov credit for the Russian victory, and in conversation with Caulaincourt he even attempted to use Kutuzov's appointment as Russian commander as justification for the French advance on Moscow. 'As the Russians had not been able to defeat us, and as Kutuzov had been forced on the Czar in place of Barclay, who was the better soldier, I imagined that a people who allowed a bad general to be foisted on them would certainly ask for terms.'[36]

Command of the remaining remnants of the French army was entrusted to Murat. He proved unable to maintain any vestige of discipline in the shattered regiments; every man sought simply to survive, and the Russians following behind observed the appalling results.

'The corpses of Frenchmen obstruct the road,' wrote Xavier de Maistre, serving in Kutuzov's army. 'When one approaches any villages which are usually burnt, the spectacle becomes even more terrible. . . . I have seen houses in which more than fifty corpses lay together, and among them three or four men were still alive, stripped to their shirts in fifteen degrees of frost. . . . On every side and along every track one comes across these wretched men who still drag themselves along, dying of hunger or cold.'[37]

For almost a week Kutuzov remained ignorant of Napoleon's exact location. Starved of information from Chichagov he waited at the Berezina to mop up surviving French in the area and to prevent a possible counter-attack: he had written to Chichagov on the 28th: 'I cannot cross the Berezina because I cannot leave Count Wittgenstein alone.' Then the situation became clear: the

French were only concerned with their retreat to Vilna and to the border of Russian territory at the Niemen. Pursuit was resumed. Kutuzov criticized Chichagov strongly in a letter to Alexander dated 1 December, and on the same day ordered Wittgenstein to lead his army north-west to prevent any junction between French forces under Napoleon and those under Macdonald deployed near Riga.[38]

Four days later, on the same Sunday that Napoleon fled from his army, Kutuzov left the forces under his direct command and hurried across country to join Chichagov on the road between Minsk and Smorgoni. As was to be expected, the meeting between the marshal and the admiral proved bitter and extremely hostile; Kutuzov virtually dismissed Chichagov, assuming control of the Danube Army himself. He reached Smorgoni on the 7th; already his forward regiments were approaching the last destination, Vilna.

By now Kutuzov's troops were suffering from the weather almost as acutely as the French. The country had been devastated by the retreating enemy; villages had been set alight and drinking water was often found polluted by corpses. 'The soldier had no additional covering for the night bivouacs on the frozen snow,' commented Wilson, 'and to sleep longer than half an hour at a time was probable death. . . . Firing could scarcely ever be obtained; and when obtained the fire could only be approached with great caution, as it caused gangrene of the frozen parts; but as water itself froze at only three feet from the largest bivouac fires, it was almost necessary to burn before the sensation of heat could be felt.' Wilson noted that one of the chief causes of mutilation arose from 'the trowsers becoming worn by the continued marches in the inner part of the thighs, exposing the flesh, so that the frost struck into it'.[39]

If Kutuzov had forced his men to march harder during the earlier period of the pursuit, and if his army had still failed to halt the French after such extra exertion, then it is doubtful that the Russians would have still been strong enough to press the enemy to the distant border. As it was, Kutuzov drove with the advance guard during these last days persuading the staggering soldiers to continue the march. The method of his persuasion was typical of his character. On one occasion he approached troops sitting miserably by the side of the frozen road apparently unable to continue through hunger. Kutuzov listened sympathetically to their complaints and then shouted angrily: 'I'll order the cursed provisioners to be hanged. Tomorrow you'll have bread, wine, meat, and you will rest.' The soldiers clustered round him, weeping with relief at this promise of food and rest – which Kutuzov knew would be impossible. Then he suddenly frowned, as if a thought had struck him. 'But what about this lads. While you relax the villain will get away, without waiting for you.' The soldiers looked at one another. One said: 'We don't need anything. We'll chase after him without food and wine.' The rest mumbled their agreement. Kutuzov lifted his face to heaven and wiped away tears. 'Great God,' he cried. 'How can I thank you for your kindness when I have the honour to command such fine lads?' He climbed back into his droshky and his 'children' cheered as they continued their march.[40]

Kutuzov suffered with his soldiers. He travelled in the small cart weakened by fever and from the cold; the frost burnt the skin on his facial scars into livid weals, and the tears from the dead eye socket froze as they trickled on his cheek. The icy wind which rushed at him as the droshky careered down the road constantly caused blotches of frost-bite on his face, and every five minutes or so he had to stop and rub snow into his flesh in an effort to prevent congelation. The agony of his rheumatism drummed through his body, and pain pulsed inside his battered head.

Each hour Kutuzov witnessed the hell which both French and Russians were having to endure. He stayed with the forward troops despite his own illness; Clausewitz, riding close behind, described the trail these soldiers left. 'I saw the road, which had only been passed by the advance guard, already marked out by bodies of Russians who had collapsed under the cold and fatigue.'[41]

'Ravages of cold,' wrote one eye-witness, 'were equalled by those of hunger. No food was so rotten or disgusting as not to find someone to relish it. No fallen horse or cattle remained uneaten, no dog, no cat, no carrion, nor indeed the corpses of those that died of cold or hunger. It was not unknown even for men to gnaw at their own famished bodies.'[42] And Wilson jotted in his diary: 'Yesterday I saw four men grouped together, hands and legs frozen, minds yet vigorous, and two dogs tearing at their feet.'[43]

But on Sunday, 13 December, the Russian advance guard reached Vilna. Miloradovich, commander of these forward units, was out of action with a frozen eye and Kutuzov probably directed the troops himself. Vilna, which he remembered with so much affection as a peaceful Polish town, had been transformed into a hell. Wilson, riding close behind, wrote: 'I . . . came into Vilna along a road covered with human carcasses, frozen in the contortions of expiring agonies. The entrance of the town was literally choked with dead bodies of men and horses, tumbrils, guns, carts, etc., and the streets were filled with traineaus carrying off the dead that still blocked the way.'[44]

At the same time as Kutuzov's droshky manoeuvred a way between the corpses in the Vilna streets the last survivors of the French rearguard were crossing the Niemen into Prussia sixty kilometres to the west. The pursuit and the campaign had ended. Kutuzov wrote to his daughter: 'Perhaps I can call myself the first general before whom Napoleon fled. But God humbles the proud.'[45] French units left to guard the Niemen watched with horror as the survivors of the Grand Army struggled towards them; Count Ségur provided this terrible description:

'Instead of the 400,000 companions who had fought so many successful battles with them, who had swept so masterfully into Russia, they saw emerging from the white, ice-bound wilderness only 1,000 infantrymen and troopers under arms, nine cannon, and 20,000 stragglers dressed in rags, with bowed heads, dull eyes, ashen, cadaverous faces and long, ice-stiffened beards. This was the Grand Army.'[46]

XV

In Death, Vindication

(13 December 1812–June 1813)

'Sire,' wrote Ney, commanding the French rearguard, in his last report to Napoleon, 'the army is no more.' The French Emperor lost almost half a million men in the 1812 campaign; about 160,000 horses and 1,000 guns were also left behind in Russia. Kutuzov's army lost about 30,000 men during the pursuit, bringing Russian casualties for the whole campaign to about 200,000 including the initial retreat and the battle of Borodino.[1] Napoleon had now to face the problem of other European nations joining Russia for the final destruction of his Empire: Austria might be persuaded to take up arms; Prussia, always an unreliable ally, might march. Against these combined forces Napoleon would only be able to muster the 40,000 troops which had acted as the southern wing of the Grand Army and the 25,000 under Macdonald outside Riga. Napoleon immediately began to herd recruits into his regiments and succeeded in swelling his ranks to a remarkable extent, but these raw newcomers would need to be trained. Losses in cavalry, harder to replace, would be especially damaging.

Yet France's potential allies had still to form an alliance. In the meantime the Russian forces were exhausted and disorganized, and Kutuzov considered that many urgent preparations needed to be undertaken before any campaign could be opened. Alexander believed otherwise. Now, in the midst of victory, fresh dissension broke out between these two irreconcilable figures.

Alexander left St Petersburg on 19 December to join his army – Napoleon had reached Paris just twenty-four hours earlier. The Russian Emperor's troika slid smoothly over the

225

snow-covered roads; despatch riders hurried ahead to warn of his Imperial approach, and Alexander arrived in Vilna just before dawn on Wednesday, 23 December. Kutuzov stood in the freezing cold to meet him at the entrance to the castle. The two men walked to one another in the flickering lamp-light beside the guard of honour, and Alexander flung his arms round the Marshal's neck, weeping profusely; Kutuzov presented his Emperor with blood-stained, tattered colours torn from the French. The scene was emotional, theatrical and totally false, and both men knew it.[2]

The charade continued next day, 24 December, which happened to be the Emperor's birthday. Kutuzov duly instructed his aides to organize the festivities expected of him. These began with a morning parade, the soldiers attempting to march smartly despite their weariness, shabby uniforms and twenty-five degrees of frost. Afterwards Kutuzov acted as host at a state dinner, during which the Marshal made a gracious speech expressing gratitude for the Order of St George First Class which the Emperor bestowed upon him. In the evening the chandeliers were lit in the Episcopal Palace, and Alexander and his magnificent entourage graced Vilna society with their presence at a birthday ball. The occasion lacked the glitter of similar functions in St Petersburg, and outside the corpses were still heaped high in the streets, but Alexander nevertheless appeared to enjoy himself.

'You will be surprised . . . to find me here at a ball,' he confided to his partner the Countess Tiesenhausen. 'But what could I do? I had to please that old fellow.' A few moments later he declared: 'The old fellow ought to be contented. The cold weather has rendered him a splendid service.'[3]

After a moment's hesitation Sir Robert Wilson also enjoyed himself, prompted by the Czar. 'I danced the Polonaise, Parade, Promenade, and one country dance.' Wilson also commented in his diary that the ball 'was attended by about thirty ladies, several very handsome; and those who were not so had all the attractions of their country – variety, figure, taste in dress and grace of movement.'[4]

Alexander chatted with the Countess de Choiseul-Gouffier, a maid-of-honour at the Russian court who had a personal knowledge of the French Emperor. She wrote afterwards: 'The Czar wished to know what impression Napoleon had made on me. I said that . . . His Majesty's presence inspired more fear in me.

' "Oh!" replied Alexander in a tone of mild reproach. "How can I possibly inspire fear in you?"

' "Yes, Sire, a fear of displeasing you." '

Later the Czar remarked to the countess: 'Have you noticed Napoleon's eyes? Light-grey eyes which gaze at you so piercingly that you cannot withstand them? . . . What a career he has ruined! Having gained so much glory, he could bestow peace on Europe, and he has not done so! The spell is broken.'[5]

Earlier in the day, immediately after the morning parade, Alexander had honoured Wilson with a long private conversation. Wilson's account reveals a remarkable statement by Alexander, in which the Russian Emperor took this foreign general into his full confidence, explaining his true feelings concerning the Russian commander-in-chief so much responsible for shattering Napoleon's 'spell'.

'General, I have called you into my Cabinet to make a painful confession,' declared Alexander. 'But I rely on your honour and prudence. . . . You have always told me *truth* – truth I could not obtain through any other channel.

'I know that the marshal has done nothing he ought to have done – nothing against the enemy that he could avoid; all his successes have been *forced* upon him. He has been playing some of his old Turkish tricks, but the nobility of Moscow support him, and insist on his presiding over the national glory of this war. In half an hour I must therefore decorate this man with the great Order of St George, and by so doing commit a trespass on its institution; for it is the highest honour, and hitherto the purest, of the Empire. But I will not ask you to be present – I should feel too much humiliated if you were; but I have no choice – I must submit to the controlling necessity. I will, however not again leave my army, and there shall be no opportunity given for additional misdirection by the marshal.'[6]

Alexander now considered he had a glorious mission to perform: Europe must be rescued from Napoleon. The Russian regiments must sweep forward to even greater victory. The Emperor noted with approval that forces under Wittgenstein still seemed active to the north, and believed that the main Russian army must soon resume the advance. He wrote to Saltykov at St Petersburg: 'Thank Heavens everything here is going well.

It is proving a little difficult to dispose of the Prince Marshal, but it is absolutely essential to do so.'[7]

Kutuzov himself urged Wittgenstein forward, declaring in a despatch on 28 December: 'Decisive blows must be struck at the enemy upon which depends not only the prosperity of the Russian people but of all the peoples of Europe.'[8] But Wittgenstein's corps had been relatively inactive in comparison with the main Russian regiments, and the ghastly chaos at Vilna continued to reinforce Kutuzov's belief that reorganization was urgently required before a full offensive.

'Sickness has made a very serious progress in this city,' noted Wilson on 30 December. 'In fifteen days 9,000 prisoners have died, and in one eighteen hours seven hundred. The mortality has extended of course to the inhabitants. . . . In spring Vilna must be a complete charnel-house. All the carcases which are removed from the streets and hospitals are laid at a short distance from the town in great masses; and then such parts as the wolves have not devoured during the winter will throw pestiferous miasmata back upon the city, which, from its position, is always shrouded in vapour.'[9] Wilson's description was confirmed a few days later by the German poet Ernst Moritz Arndt. 'The town looked to me like some Tartar hell. Everywhere frightful dirt and smells; greasy Jews; some unfortunate prisoners, most of them wounded or convalescent, crept miserably around; every street was wreathed in acrid smoke and steam, because people had set fire to all sorts of inflammable materials, even dungheaps, in front of each house, in order to disperse the pestilential air from the many hospitals and infection-centres.'[10]

In the midst of this misery Czar Alexander presided over his court and urged Kutuzov to greater efforts. Kutuzov replied that his troops were sick, exhausted, without equipment, no plans had been prepared, winter still lay thick over Prussia, Russia had still to gain allies. But on 4 January the Czar received further encouragement when a messenger arrived from Wittgenstein: on 30 December General Hans David von Yorck, commanding the Prussian contingent which had served with the French in conjunction with Macdonald, concluded a military convention at Tauroggen with the Russian General Diebitsch: this specified that Yorck's troops would withdraw from their alliance with the French and would remain neutral.

The Convention of Tauroggen marked the first step in the War of Liberation. Massive patriotic movements inside Prussia against the French overlords obtained greater momentum; the Prussian warhorse General von Blücher pestered his monarch to sign a full alliance with the Russians; so, too, did influential figures such as Gerhard von Scharnhorst and August Gneisenau. Alexander added his weight, despatching aides to the hesitant and fearful Frederick William. In the first week of January 1813 the Russian Emperor's agitation and excitement increased at an alarming rate: he envisaged grandiose schemes for driving the French out of Prussia and back beyond the Elbe. Kutuzov continued to insist upon adequate preparations: an advance was one thing, consolidation of territory gained would be another; the allies would be vastly extended and would become increasingly so, while Napoleon, for all his present weaknesses, would gradually become more concentrated.

'We can cross the Elbe easily enough,' declared Kutuzov, 'but before long we shall have to cross it again with a bloody nose.'[11] The Emperor was impossible to restrain. On 9 January the Russian headquarters left Vilna, despite Kutuzov's reluctance, and established a temporary base at Meritz on the Niemen. Three days later the Russian regiments began to cross the river into Prussia: the 1813 campaign had begun. Kutuzov issued an optimistic proclamation to his 'children': 'We will . . . make Europe exclaim with astonishment. The Russian army is invincible in war and inimitable in generosity and good deeds. Here there is an ideal worthy of heroes. Let us aim towards it, brave warriors!'[12]

Kutuzov's plan, forced on him by Alexander, entailed an advance into Prussia and Poland in three main columns. The principal army would head towards Kalisch; Wittgenstein would proceed via Königsberg to Marienberg on the Vistula; to the south Chichagov would also converge on Kalisch. Total Russian strength numbered about 100,000 men, although many of the regiments were ill-organized and badly equipped. Wilson commented: 'The wreck is powerful from moral energy, but it is only a wreck.'[13] Moreover, Frederick William had still to declare allegiance, and instead issued a proclamation on 19 January declaiming the Tauroggen Convention; he had already sent an officer to arrest Yorck but this individual was detained *en route* by the Russians. Nevertheless the outnumbered French fell back, increasing Alexander's optimism: this move had been fully expected by Kutuzov – he knew the French to be merely shortening their lines in order to concentrate behind the Elbe.[14]

By 20 January the Russian headquarters had reached Lyse, about 150 kilometres north-east of Warsaw. And there, on the Prussian-Poland border, Kutuzov's illness suddenly increased. His health had seemed to improve for a short while after his arrival at Vilna: at one dance he had seemed in his old form, flirting outrageously with a 16-year-old Polish beauty despite his rheumatism and his sixty-seven years. But now, on campaign again, his strength began to give way. Wilson jotted in his diary on the 20th: 'Marshal Kutuzov is very unwell. . . . Whether the marshal lives or dies, I believe the Emperor will make very good arrangements for the executive army.'[15] The war-weary Russian commander remained with the headquarters, and the advance continued. The overall situation seemed more optimistic, although Kutuzov's misgivings were undiminished. Frederick William escaped from the French influence at Berlin on 22 January, driving for Breslau, and Alexander increased his pressure on the Prussian monarch. Yorck summoned a special session of the East Prussian states on 4 February, and demanded the immediate formation of militia forces, the *Landwehr*, totalling 20,000 men with 10,000 reserves; East Prussia thereby became committed to the liberation struggle and events threatened to move beyond Frederick William's control.

Kutuzov reached the Vistula at Plock, north-west of Warsaw, on 5 February. His health had continued to deteriorate; so too had his relations with Alexander, who seemed to be experiencing a religious ecstasy bordering on hysteria. To the Emperor the campaign was a crusade. 'My faith is sincere and warm with passion,' he wrote to St Petersburg. 'Every day it grows firmer and I experience joys I have never known before. . . . All my glory I dedicate to the advancement of the reign of the Lord Jesus Christ.'[16] Wilson wrote in his diary on 5 February: 'Yesterday, General Barclay de Tolly rejoined the army. All is hocus-pocus in the Russian counsels. Russia, however, has a very brave officer again in employ. She will need every hand very soon to repair the want of a head.'[17]

A thaw set in on 10 February. The climate improved for the

troops, but the melted snow coated the roads with slimy mud as the Russian regiments moved towards Kalisch. Then, in the last week of February, excellent news reached headquarters from Breslau: Frederick William had finally been persuaded to fight. On 26 February Prussian and Russian delegates meeting at Kalisch signed an offensive and defensive alliance, with Russia undertaking to provide 150,000 men and Prussia at least 80,000. Blücher would command the Prussian Army of Silesia; to Kutuzov went the honour of being allied commander-in-chief. Frederick William sent the ailing marshal a snuff box decorated with his portrait in brilliant stones, together with the Order of the Black Eagle and the promise of a handsome Prussian estate.[18] Russian and Prussian advance forces joined on 28 February, and in the first week of March Kutuzov reached Kalisch. Tense discussions took place over the allied plans, with Alexander writing to Catherine on the 7th: 'These last few days I have felt my head going round in circles under the burden of work that has fallen on me all at once.'[19] Kutuzov still urged caution. He believed Napoleon's downfall to be inevitable but feared a 'bloody nose' would still result from a premature allied advance across the Elbe; men should not be wasted through undue eagerness. Yet Alexander received support from leading Prussian generals, anxious for revenge. 'My fingers itch to seize the sabre,' declared Blücher, and many of his colleagues agreed.

Despite the tension and bustle, combined with Kutuzov's ill-health, the marshal and the Emperor's entourage nevertheless found time for social activities at Kalisch. Two balls were held in the first days of March, one organized by the Emperor's court and the other by Kutuzov on behalf of the army. The first proved a failure through a shortage of females. Wilson commented that it was 'very thinly attended, and if there was much fashion there was very little beauty'. The second seemed more successful: Kutuzov had lost none of his influence with the ladies, and when he invited the leading women of the town to come they flocked in response. The admission of the 'town ladies' improved the evening, wrote Wilson, although he sniffed that they 'presented no remarkable model for admiration'. Alexander danced with delighted zeal on both occasions.[20]

Prussia officially declared war against France on 13 March, with Napoleon receiving the news three days later – 'better a declared

231

enemy than a doubtful ally,' he commented. An allied plan of campaign gradually emerged. Wittgenstein would advance in the north, using Berlin as his base – the French had evacuated the Prussian capital on 4 March. Blücher would thrust forward in the south, marching from Silesia to Dresden in Saxony. Kutuzov would lead the main Russian army in the centre. And the initial objective was to be the Elbe, defended by Napoleon's Army of the Elbe under Eugène de Beauharnais.

Blücher began his advance on 23 March, impatient for battle as always, and Wittgenstein moved at about the same time, entering Berlin at the end of the month amidst magnificent celebrations. The main Russian army under Kutuzov started to march at the beginning of April. The overall advance seemed to be extremely satisfactory, and contrary to Kutuzov's advice the allies now pushed over the Elbe: Wittgenstein crossed successfully at Rosslau on 2 April, and Blücher at Möckern three days later to reach Colditz on the 12th. Kutuzov's attitude remained unchanged. He feared that these early successes might generate exaggerated optimism, with the enemy merely falling back and allied communications lengthening. The French army was being compressed like a coiled spring, ready to burst forward when Napoleon released the catch.

'Allow me once more to repeat my opinions of your attacking operations,' wrote Kutuzov to Wittgenstein. 'Now I am in Prussia everyone is complaining about our slowness, supposing that each of our moves ahead is equivalent to victory and each day lost is equivalent to defeat. . . . I find it necessary to consider the distances dividing our western armies from the Elbe and the forces which the enemy might oppose to us. If we keep a small superiority over the minor advanced detachments of the enemy, then after their defeat they [the survivors] will retreat to their main forces and will accumulate as they go back like a snowball. I must compare the constant losses we suffer through attacking quickly and the continually lengthening distance from the sources of our strength. . . . Believe me, one defeat of our detachments will puncture the faith which they have in us in Prussia. I beg you to convey my thoughts to Blücher.'[21]

On 15 April Napoleon left St Cloud to join his armies. And by now the French Emperor had managed to assemble forces totalling 226,000 men and 457 guns, including regiments summoned from Spain. Many of the troops were woefully inexperienced, and the French still suffered from severe cavalry shortages; Kutuzov believed that the allies should seize on these deficiencies through careful, coordinated manoeuvring, and that the advantage could be thrown away if the allies blundered forward in headlong fashion.

But Kutuzov could take no further part in the campaign. The weather suddenly deteriorated in mid-April and the roads became even more boggy. One night Kutuzov's carriage stuck in the mud and he continued on horseback through showers of sleet, after which he suffered a cold which aggravated his recurrent bouts of fever; his strength seeped steadily away. On 18 April he was forced to take to his bed at Bunzlau in Silesia. 'The marshal has had a glimpse of the enemy,' sneered Wilson in his diary, 'and is taken ill very *opportunely*.'[22] Alexander and Frederick William stayed with Kutuzov until 21 April, then left to follow the troops. According to one story the Czar approached the marshal's bed to say farewell and to seek forgiveness for their past quarrels; Kutuzov replied: 'I forgive you Your Majesty, but Russia never will.'[23] Alexander nevertheless left his personal doctor although the patient refused treatment.

Kutuzov died on 28 April, still at Bunzlau. The news was kept secret for several days for fear of upsetting the morale of 'his children' now marching against Napoleon on the far bank of the Elbe. The report allowed Wilson to make one last unworthy remark in his diary: 'He died most opportunely for his fame.'[24]

'A great and painful loss has been caused not only to you but to the whole Fatherland,' wrote Alexander to Kutuzov's wife, whom the marshal had not seen since the previous August. 'I weep with you and all Russia weeps. However, God comforts you with the fact that his name and his acts will remain immortal. A thankful Fatherland will never forget his worthiness. Europe and the whole world will not cease to be amazed by him and will include his name in the number of famous commanders.'[25]

Doctor's cut open Kutuzov's body to remove his heart, which they found to be much larger than normal; they also reported his internal organs were so distorted that it seemed a miracle he had lived so long. His embalmed body was carried back to St Petersburg, with frequent stops *en route* to allow mourners to pay their respects, and rumours circulated of an enormous eagle wheeling slowly over the procession – the same eagle which had soared over Kutuzov when he joined the Russian army for the 1812 campaign. The body reached Petersburg on 11 June and was interred in Kazan Cathedral; his heart was buried after a quiet ceremony in a simple churchyard near Bunzlau, on the highroad from Silesia to Saxony along which his 'children' marched in their attempt to liberate Europe.[26]

Alexander appointed Wittgenstein to be Kutuzov's successor as allied commander-in-chief. Napoleon released the catch restraining the compressed French spring. On 2 May, just four days after Kutuzov's death, the allied armies clashed with Napoleon's concentrated forces at Lützen, 100 kilometres over the Elbe, and by nightfall were in retreat leaving 15,000 dead and wounded. Russian and Prussian troops were forced back over the Elbe on 10 May suffering from their 'bloody nose'; they lost again at Bautzen on the 20th, and were obliged to retreat further into Silesia. Napoleon threatened to retake Berlin. Barclay replaced Wittgenstein as commander-in-chief on the 26th; on 1 June the panicked allies agreed to an armistice and the campaign had to begin all over again.

The armistice allowed the allies time to undertake those preparations which Kutuzov had urged six months earlier, and Napoleon later admitted that the truce turned out to be one of his gravest mistakes. With plans firmly established and with armies strengthened, the allies could take to the field in August for the campaign which would lead to Napoleon's defeat at Leipzig in October, the occupation of Paris on the last day of March 1814, and the abdication of Napoleon Bonaparte.

Kutuzov has never received sufficient credit for his part in bringing about this downfall and in the final ending of Napoleon's rule. Greater glory has gone to Wellington, even though he would only clash with Napoleon once, at Waterloo, and by then both Napoleon and his army were but pale reflections of the enemy against whom Kutuzov had fought and had defeated. Few military commanders in history have enjoyed Kutuzov's facility as a commander, and in many ways his abilities were unique. Throughout his military career Kutuzov had repeated his fascinating strategic concepts, relying heavily upon the power of manoeuvre combined with the deadly effect of striking at the crucial moment. Not even Napoleon could match Kutuzov's clarity of strategic vision and his awesome tactical coolness in putting this perception into practice. His achievements in this respect would have been even greater if he had enjoyed a suitable staff system, similar to Blücher's partnership first with Gerhard von Scharnhorst and then with August Gneisenau, or Wellington's relationship with his quartermaster-general, Sir George Murray.

Beyond Kutuzov's talent as a commander lay another: the highly sophisticated attitude displayed towards battle itself. Kutuzov saw far further than lesser commanders who considered the battle to be the core of a campaign; he realized that this core centred upon the army. The army must be allowed to continue functioning even at the expense of apparently running away, even at the cost of losing Vienna or Moscow; the army which remained intact was undefeated – and ready for the last, decisive battle. The latter might not even be needed. By remaining as commander of a viable army, Kutuzov revealed that he could exert a psychological advantage over his enemy which might be sufficient to bring victory. So it proved in 1812; so it proved in 1811–12 against the Turks; similar success might easily have resulted in 1805, if Kutuzov had been given his way. In this respect Kutuzov's principles provided valuable material for Clausewitz: this great Prussian military philosopher, who studied closely Kutuzov's actions in the 1805 and 1812 campaigns, agreed that battles should not be regarded too highly: if the army remained in being, then threat of battle might suffice. Clausewitz might well have been voicing Kutuzov's own thoughts when he wrote in *On War*: 'We look upon a great battle as a principal decision, but certainly not as the only one necessary for a war or a campaign. . . . The decision may be either a battle, or a series of great combats – but it may also consist of the results of mere relations, which arise from the situation of the opposing forces. . . . Possible combats are on account of their results to be looked upon as real ones.' Military commanders would have benefited from a closer study of Kutuzov's principles in 1914–18: instead they marched their troops out to senseless slaughter.

By contrast with this inhuman, mechanical attitude to war, Kutuzov represented the spirit and feeling of his troops, of his 'children', and he used this transfusion of power to overcome the enemy's will. He acted on behalf of his soldiers. This was an attribute which foreigners like Wilson, Barclay and Bennigsen could never appreciate; nor could Alexander. Kutuzov, a true Russian, represented the Fatherland; his troops, most of them simple peasants, responded in superb fashion. Other commanders might have avoided the mistakes which Kutuzov undoubtedly made: perhaps they would have fought a decisive battle during the Grand Army's retreat, and they would then have been assured a more spectacular place in history. But their actual achievements could not have risen higher than Kutuzov's. His success was that of Russia herself.

Tolstoy, speaking through Prince Andrei in *War and Peace*, described Kutuzov with these words: 'He knows that there is something stronger and more important than his own will – the inevitable march of events, and he has the brains to see them and grasp their significance, and seeing that significance can abstain from meddling, from following his personal desire and aiming at something else.' Clausewitz displayed his own perception when he commented: 'Of all the generals contemporary with Napoleon, two army leaders were perhaps worthy of being compared with him: Archduke Charles and Wellington. But, nevertheless, the prudent and wily Kutuzov was his most dangerous adversary.'

'The glory of Kutuzov,' declared Alexander Pushkin, 'is inseparable from the glory of Russia, from the memory of the greatest event in our contemporary history. His title: The Saviour of Russia.' Kutuzov himself shrugged off his critics. He continued regardless with the inevitable march of events, concerning himself neither with the opinions of the present nor those of the future. 'The longer I live,' he said to his daughter Ekaterina, 'the more strongly I am convinced that fame is mere smoke.'[27]

Sources

Full details of the books listed below are to be found in the Bibliography.

I. Mother Russia

1. Tolstoy, Translator's Intro.
2. Gerhardi, 219
3. Palmer, *Russia in War and Peace*, 98
4. *Russkii Biograf.*, 639, 641
5. Palmer, *op. cit.*, 45
6. Herold, 410
7. Bragin, 3
8. Palmer, *op. cit.*, 75
9. *Russkii Biograf.*, 628
10. Gerhardi, 104–105
11. Bragin, 3
12. *Russkii Biograf.*, 628
13. Gerhardi, 120

14. Longworth, 26
15. Gerhardi, 311
16. *Russkii Biograf.*, 696
17. ib. 629
18. Bragin, 6
19. *Russkii Biograf.*, 629
20. Longworth, 141
21. *Russkii Biograf.*, 629
22. Palmer, *op. cit.*, 117
23. Bragin, 6
24. *Russkii Biograf.*, 630
25. Bragin, 6; *Russkii Biograf.*, 631
26. Bragin, 6
27. *Russkii Biograf.*, 631

II. Suvorov

1. *Russkii Biograf.*, 631
2. Gerhardi, 170
3. ib. 177, 185
4. *Russkii Biograf.*, 628
5. ib. 631
6. Longworth, 102–103
7. ib. 107
8. ib. 317
9. *Russkii Biograf.*, 632; Longworth, 134
10. Gerhardi, 178–179
11. *Russkii Biograf.*, 632
12. ib. 632

13. ib. 632; Bragin, 8
14. Longworth, 150
15. Bragin, 9; Longworth, 152
16. Bragin, 11; Longworth, 168
17. Bragin, 12
18. Smitt, I., 530–531
19. Longworth, 174
20. *Russkii Biograf.*, 634; Bulatov, 18–19
21. Beskrovnyi, *Kutuzov*, 43
22. *Russkii Biograf.*, 634–636
23. Bragin, 13–14
24. *Russkii Biograf.*, 639

The Fox of the North

III. 'Mad' Paul

1. *Russkii Biograf.*, 639
2. Bragin, 14
3. *Russkii Biograf.*, 639
4. ib. 640
5. Bragin, 14
6. *Russkii Biograf.*, 640
7. Longworth, 177–178
8. *Russkii Biograf.*, 640
9. Palmer, *Alexander*, 27–29
10. Bragin, 15
11. Masson, 111
12. Longworth, 227
13. Bragin, 16
14. Anon, *A Cursory View*, 89
15. *Russkii Biograf.*, 641
16. Longworth, 296–297
17. Palmer, *Alexander*, 41; *Russia in War and Peace*, 37–38
18. Palmer, *Alexander*, 43
19. Gerhardi, 213; Palmer, *Alexander*, 45

IV. Alexander and Exile

1. Palmer, *Alexander*, 218
2. Cronin, 303
3. Gerhardi, 213
4. Strakhovsky, 22
5. *Russkii Biograf.*, 641
6. Hodgetts, 30
7. ib. 31
8. ib. 31
9. Gerhardi, 219
10. ib. 326
11. Palmer, *Alexander*, 66
12. *Russkii Biograf.*, 642
13. Bragin, 17
14. ib. 17–18
15. ib. 17
16. *Russkii Biograf.*, 647
17. Thompson, 114

V. Duel Along the Danube

1. Thompson, 129
2. Manceron, 96
3. ib. 121
4. Beskrovnyi, *Kutuzov*, 54, 56
5. Palmer, *Alexander*, 90
6. Beskrovnyi, *Kutuzov*, 56
7. Bragin, 29
8. Beskrovnyi, *Kutuzov*, 56
9. Palmer, *Alexander*, 91
10. Burton, 42; Bragin, 20
11. Bragin, 20–21
12. Burton, 41
13. Bragin, 20
14. Thompson, 131
15. Burton, 56
16. Beskrovnyi, *Kutuzov*, 57
17. Palmer, *Alexander*, 92–93
18. Beskrovnyi, *Kutuzov*, 60
19. ib. 61
20. Manceron, 114
21. Burton, 56, 57
22. Bragin, 21
23. ib. 21
24. ib. 21
25. Hodgetts, 7; Palmer, *Alexander*, 193
26. Burton, 57; Manceron, 117
27. Burton, 58
28. Bragin, 22
29. Burton, 59
30. Palmer, *Alexander*, 93
31. Longworth, 241; Palmer, *Russia in War and Peace*, 119–120
32. Bragin, 23
33. Burton, 59
34. Manceron, 125–126

238

35. Thompson, 132
36. Manceron, 126; Burton, 61
37. Beskrovnyi, *Kutuzov*, 67
38. Burton, 62; Manceron, 127
39. Burton, 62–63; Manceron, 127
40. Manceron, 130–131
41. Beskrovnyi, *Kutuzov*, 73
42. Manceron, 133
43. Bragin, 26–27
44. *Russkii Biograf.*, 648
45. Beskrovnyi, *Kutuzov*, 75

46. Manceron, 141
47. ib. 142
48. Beskrovnyi, *Kutuzov*, 79
49. Manceron, 142; Burton, 66
50. Bragin, 28–29; Burton, 66
51. Bragin, 29–30
52. Palmer, *Alexander*, 95
53. *Russkii Biograf.*, 79
54. Beskrovnyi, *Kutuzov*, 80
55. ib. 81

VI. Austerlitz

1. Palmer, *Alexander*, 98
2. Bragin, 32; Palmer, *Alexander*, 99
3. Burton, 78
4. Manceron, 159
5. Burton, 82
6. Bragin, 33
7. Manceron, 180
8. *Russkii Biograf.*, 691
9. Burton, 82
10. *Russkii Biograf.*, 652; Bragin,

32–33; Manceron, 181–186; Burton, 86
11. Burton, 83–85
12. Manceron, 215–217
13. Manceron, 228, 301–302; Shilder, II, 140; Bragin, 36–37; Mazade, I, 407–409; Palmer, *Alexander*, 108–112; Chandler, 431
14. Manceron, 152

VII. Into the Shadows

1. London *Times*, 31 December, 1805
2. Palmer, *Alexander*, 112–113
3. ib. 113–114
4. *Russkii Biograf.*, 656
5. Palmer, *Alexander*, 117
6. *Russkii Biograf.*, 656
7. *Russkii Biograf.*, 656; Bragin, 39
8. *Russkii Biograf.*, 691
9. *Russkii Biograf.*, 656; Bragin, 39
10. Chandler, 535–545, 554–555
11. *Russkii Biograf.*, 656–657
12. Palmer, *Alexander*, 134–140; Cronin, 303–304; Gerhardi, 372–378
13. *Russkii Biograf.*, 657
14. Cronin, 304–305; Palmer, *Alexander*, 159–162
15. *Russkii Biograf.*, 657
16. ib. 657

17. Brett-James, 35–36
18. Waliszewski, I, 274
19. Palmer, *Alexander*, 186
20. ib. 188
21. ib. 199
22. *Russkii Biograf.*, 657
23. ib. 658
24. Bragin, 42
25. Beskrovnyi, *Kutuzov*, 86
26. ib. 97
27. Bragin, 43
28. ib. 45
29. Palmer, *Alexander*, 231; Bragin, 45
30. *Russkii Biograf.*, 691
31. Brett-James, 6
32. Palmer, *Alexander*, 221
33. ib. 223
34. Brett-James, 41–42

VIII. Invasion

1. Brett-James, 42–43
2. Caulaincourt, I, 280
3. Brett-James, 21
4. ib. 7
5. Clausewitz, 5–9
6. ib. 15; Duffy, 54–55
7. Duffy, 55
8. *Russkii Biograf.*, 670, Olivier, 16
9. *Russkii Biograf.*, 671
10. ib. 672
11. Brett-James, 51
12. Clausewitz, 110
13. Vossler, 50–51
14. Tarle, 75
15. Palmer, *Alexander*, 233
16. Clausewitz, 123
17. Clausewitz, 139; Tarle, 109
18. Brett-James, 77
19. Palmer, *Alexander*, 238
20. Olivier, 201
21. Bragin, 59
22. Wolzogen, 132
23. Tarle, 112
24. Palmer, *Alexander*, 235
25. Bragin, 59
26. Olivier, 201
27. Shilder, III, 98
28. Brett-James, 111–112
29. *Russkii Biograf.*, 673
30. Beskrovnyi, *Kutuzov*, 181
31. *Russkii Biograf.*, 673; Duffy, 66

IX. Back to Borodino

1. Wilson, *Journal*, 1, 153
2. Wilson, *Narrative*, 131
3. *Russkii Biograf.*, 673
4. ib. 674
5. Clausewitz, 138
6. *Russkii Biograf.*, 674
7. Alt'shuller, 343
8. *Russkii Biograf.*, 691
9. Beskrovnyi, *Kutuzov*, 182
10. Clausewitz, 139
11. Beskrovnyi, *Kutuzov*, 184
12. Alt'shuller, 26
13. Beskrovnyi, *Kutuzov*, 180
14. Ségur, I, 279
15. ib. 283, 285
16. Duffy, 68
17. Beskrovnyi, *Kutuzov*, 185
18. Clausewitz, 139
19. Beskrovnyi, *Kutuzov*, 186
20. ib. 194
21. Alt'shuller, 318
22. Duffy, 81
23. ib. 74
24. Labaume, 127
25. Alt'shuller, 383
26. Beskrovnyi, *Kutuzov*, 247
27. Duffy, 77
28. ib. 83–84
29. Wilson, *Narrative*, 139
30. Duffy, 86
31. Bragin, 60
32. Alt'shuller, 90
33. Brett-James, 123
34. Bragin, 69
35. Brett-James, 119–120
36. Bragin, 68
37. ib. 70

X. Borodino

1. Alt'shuller, 386
2. ib. 386
3. Duffy, 74
4. Bragin, 70
5. Alt'shuller, 184
6. Ségur, I, 307
7. Alt'shuller, 137
8. Kircheisen, 164
9. ib. 166
10. Bragin, 72; Duffy, 103

Sources

11. Alt'shuller, 342
12. Bragin, 78
13. Alt'shuller, 381
14. Bertin, 92
15. Wolzogen, 141
16. Alt'shuller, 333
17. Duffy, 109
18. ib. 115
19. Clausewitz, 159; Duffy, 120
20. Beskrovnyi, *Kutuzov*, 219
21. Clausewitz, 166
22. Alt'shuller, 343
23. Duffy, 111
24. Bragin, 81

25. Alt'shuller, 388
26. Clausewitz, 166
27. Ségur, I, 313
28. Bragin, 74
29. Wolzogen, 145-146
30. ib. 146
31. Alt'shuller, 95-96
32. Duffy, 138, 140
33. Chandler, 807
34. Beskrovnyi, *Kutuzov*, 241, 242; Alt'shuller, 141
35. Palmer, *Russia in War and Peace*, 167
36. Palmer, *Alexander*, 244

XI. Moscow

1. Ségur, I, 330-333
2. Duffy, 138
3. Brett-James, 139
4. Beskrovnyi, *Kutuzov*, 245
5. Brett-James, 140
6. Thompson, 273
7. Clausewitz, 182
8. Beskrovnyi, *Kutuzov*, 261
9. ib. 261
10. Olivier, 35
11. Palmer, *Russia in War and Peace*, 168
12. Wilson, *Journal*, I, 162
13. Schnitzler, 141
14. Olivier, 36
15. Brett-James, 153-154
16. Schnitzler, 141-142
17. Bragin, 91-92; Schnitzler, 142
18. Bragin, 92
19. Schnitzler, 148; Bragin, 92; Brett-James, 155-156
20. Bragin, 92-93; Beskrovnyi, *Sbornik Dokumentov*, IV, part 1, 221; Schnitzler, 146-148; Beskrovnyi, *Kutuzov*, 262

21. Olivier, 111-112
22. Tarle, 152
23. Clausewitz, 142
24. Beskrovnyi, *Kutuzov*, 263
25. Palmer, *Russia in War and Peace*, 109
26. Brett-James, 157-158
27. Bragin, 93
28. Clausewitz, 188
29. Brett-James, 160
30. Olivier, 24
31. ib. 37
32. Brett-James, 165
33. Ségur, II, 26-27
34. Cronin, 319
35. Clausewitz, 190
36. Brett-James, 172
37. ib. 165
38. Olivier, 189
39. Clausewitz, 191
40. Olivier, 189
41. Brett-James, 166
42. Beskrovnyi, *Kutuzov*, 264
43. ib. 265
44. Ségur, II, 43

XII. The Tomb of an Army

1. Beskrovnyi, *Kutuzov*, 268
2. Beskrovnyi, *Kutuzov*, 262; Schnitzler, 321
3. Olivier, 98

4. Wilson, *Journal*, I, 158
5. Olivier, 98; Palmer, *Alexander*, 246
6. Brett-James, 186-187

The Fox of the North

7. ib. 189
8. Beskrovnyi, *The Patriotic War*, 86
9. Olivier, 92
10. ib. 98
11. ib. 109
12. Thompson, 274
13. Olivier, 93
14. Olivier, 94–95; Wilson, *Narrative*, 170
15. Ségur, II, 61
16. Wilson, *Narrative*, 169
17. Schering, 116
18. Palmer, *Napoleon in Russia*, 166; Olivier, 93
19. Olivier, 96
20. Wilson, *Narrative*, 174–175
21. Olivier, 96–97; Beskrovnyi, *Kutuzov*, 283
22. Palmer, *Alexander*, 246
23. Olivier, 114
24. Beskrovnyi, *Kutuzov*, 347
25. ib. 281
26. ib. 269
27. Olivier, 154
28. Ségur, II, 65–69
29. Wilson, *Narrative*, 182–189
30. Olivier, 133
31. Wilson, *Journal*, I, 186
32. Olivier, 135–138; Wilson, *Journal*, I, 183–186; Remizov, 20
33. Ségur, II, 71
34. ib. 86–87
35. Beskrovnyi, *Kutuzov*, 279
36. ib. 97
37. ib. 387
38. ib. 387
39. ib. 351
40. Brett-James, 217–218
41. Beskrovnyi, *Kutuzov*, 353
42. ib. 384–386
43. ib. 279–280
44. Bragin, 91
45. Wilson, *Journal*, I, 181–182
46. Palmer, *Alexander*, 251
47. Olivier, 141
48. ib. 147
49. ib. 147–148
50. Wilson, *Journal*, I, 178
51. Olivier, 182
52. Palmer, *Napoleon in Russia*, 185

XIII. Maloyaroslavets

1. Wilson, *Journal*, I, 177
2. Wilson, *Narrative*, 207–210; *Journal*, I, 197
3. Olivier, 155
4. Beskrovnyi, *Kutuzov*, 295
5. *Russkii Biograf.*, 400
6. Olivier, 153
7. Beskrovnyi, *Kutuzov*, 292
8. Brett-James, 207–208
9. Palmer, *Napoleon in Russia*, 182
10. ib. 188
11. Olivier, 167
12. ib. 142
13. ib. 168
14. Wilson, *Journal*, I, 202–203
15. ib. 203
16. Beskrovnyi, *Kutuzov*, 303
17. Wilson, *Narrative*, 299
18. Ségur, II, 102
19. Olivier, 177; Bragin, 113
20. Palmer, *Napoleon in Russia*, 199

XIV. Retreat

1. Wilson, *Journal*, I, 207–208
2. Olivier, 156
3. Beskrovnyi, *Kutuzov*, 308
4. ib. 306
5. ib. 307
6. ib. 311
7. Vossler, 71
8. Wilson, *Journal*, I, 208–209
9. Ségur, II, 126
10. ib. 128

242

11. Duffy, 174
12. Palmer, *Napoleon in Russia*, 210
13. Wilson, *Journal*, I, 209
14. ib. 211
15. Brett-James, 220
16. Wilson, *Journal*, I, 214–215
17. ib. 217–218
18. Beskrovnyi, *Kutuzov*, 315
19. Palmer, *Napoleon in Russia*, 222
20. Wilson, *Journal*, I, 225
21. Palmer, *Napoleon in Russia*, 227–229
22. *Russkii Biograf.*, 684
23. Brett-James, 236
24. Olivier, 173; Wilson, *Narrative*, 234
25. Beskrovnyi, *Kutuzov*, 318
26. Palmer, *Napoleon in Russia*, 231
27. Beskrovnyi, *Kutuzov*, 320

28. Brett-James, 242–243
29. Beskrovnyi, *Kutuzov*, 324
30. Clausewitz, 205
31. Wilson, *Journal*, I, 230
32. Bragin, 121
33. Wilson, *Journal*, I, 232
34. *Russkii Biograf.*, 684
35. Schwartz, I, 493
36. Cronin, 330
37. Brett-James, 281–282
38. Beskrovnyi, *Kutuzov*, 329
39. Wilson, *Narrative*, 352–353
40. *Russkii Biograf.*, 692
41. Clausewitz, 216
42. Vossler, 92–93
43. Wilson, *Journal*, I, 252
44. ib. 252–253
45. Remizov, 27
46. Vossler, Introduction

XV. In Death, Vindication

1. Brett-James, 264
2. Bragin, 129; *Russkii Biograf.*, 687
3. Palmer, *Alexander*, 258
4. Wilson, *Journal*, I, 255–256
5. Brett-James, 282
6. Wilson, *Narrative*, 356–357
7. Shilder, III, 137
8. *Russkii Biograf.*, 332
9. Wilson, *Journal*, I, 256–257
10. Brett-James, 285
11. Shilder, III, 142
12. *Russkii Biograf.*, 688
13. Wilson, *Journal*, I, 265
14. Beskrovnyi, *Kutuzov*, 439

15. Wilson, *Journal*, I, 268–269
16. Palmer, *Alexander*, 260
17. Wilson, *Journal*, I, 275
18. *Russkii Biograf.*, 688
19. Palmer, *Alexander*, 262
20. Wilson, *Journal*, I, 298
21. Beskrovnyi, *Kutuzov*, 439–440
22. Wilson, *Journal*, I, 349
23. Bragin, 131
24. Wilson, *Journal*, I, 356
25. *Russkii Biograf.*, 690
26. Bragin, 131
27. *Russkii Biograf.*, 691

Select Bibliography

Only one English language publication specifically on Kutuzov has so far been printed: Mikhail Bragin's *Field Marshal Kutuzov*, issued by the Foreign Languages Publishing House in Moscow in 1944. This wartime pamphlet extols Kutuzov in idealistic fashion; the result is informative but flimsy and unreliable if read without close reference to other sources. The principal Russian works on Kutuzov are those by the historian L. G. Beskrovnyi, and his *Polkvodets Kutuzov*, which he edited in 1955, has been used extensively in this book. Also useful is the detailed section on Kutuzov in *Russkii Biograficheskii Slovar*, which has the additional value of being written before the Russian Revolution. Among biographies of those connected with Kutuzov is Alan Palmer's recent and excellent study of Alexander, which again has been especially valuable. Works on the 1812 campaign and on Borodino are numerous: I have chiefly relied on the collection of documents edited by R. E. Alt'shuller and G. V. Bogdanov; Christopher Duffy's *Borodino* was also particularly useful, as were the eye-witness accounts compiled by Antony Brett-James. These and other books consulted or quoted are listed below:

Alt'shuller, R. E. and Bogdanov, G. V. (Ed.), *Borodino Dokumenty, Pis'ma Vospominaniya* (Moscow 1962).

Anon., *A Cursory View of Prussia, from the death of Frederick II to the Peace of Tilsit* (London 1908).

Bernradi, T. von, *Denkwürdigkeiten aus dem Leben des Kaiserl. Russ. Generals von der Infanterie Carl Friedrich Grafen von Toll* (Leipzig 1865).

Bertin, G., *La Campagne de 1812* (Paris 1895).

Beskrovnyi, L. G. (Ed.), *Kutozov M. I. Sbornik Dokumentov* (Moscow 1950–56). Specified in source lists as *Sbornik Dokumentov*.

Beskrovnyi, L. G., *The Patriotic War and Kutuzov's Counter-Offensive* (Moscow 1951).

Beskrovnyi, L. G. (Ed.), *Polkvodets Kutuzov* (Moscow 1955). Specified in source lists as *Kutuzov*.

Bragin, M., *Kutuzov* (Moscow 1944).

Brett-James, Antony (Ed. and Trans.), *1812: Eyewitness Accounts of Napoleon's Defeat in Russia* (London 1966).

Bulatov, N., *Suvorov v Narodrykh Pesmyakh i Rasskazah* (Moscow 1942).

Burton, R. G., *From Boulogne to Austerlitz* (London 1912)

Caulaincourt, Armand de, *Mémoires* (Paris 1835).

Chandler, D. G., *The Campaigns of Napoleon* (London 1967).

Chichagov, P. V., *Mémoires* (Leipzig 1862).

Choiseul-Gouffier, Comtesse de, *Historical Memoirs of the Emperor Alexander I* (London 1904).

Clausewitz, Carl von, *Campaign of 1812 in Russia* (London 1843).

Cronin, Vincent, *Napoleon* (London 1971).

Duffy, C., *Borodino: Napoleon against Russia, 1812* (London 1972).

Faber du Faure, C. W. von, *Campagne de Russie, 1812* (Paris undated).

Gerhardi, William, *The Romanovs* (London 1946).

Golubov, S. N. and Kuznetsov, F. E. (Ed.), *General Bagration: Sbornik Dokumentov* (Moscow 1945).

Herold, J. C., *Mistress to an Age: A Life of Madame de Staël* (London 1959).

Hodgetts, E. A. Brayley, *The Court of Russia in the Nineteenth Century* (London 1908).

Holmes, R., *Borodino* (London 1971).

Jenkins, M., *Arakcheev, Grand Vizier of the Russian Empire* (London 1969).

Kircheisen, F. M., *Napoleons Untergang* (Stuttgart undated).

Korobkov, N., *Generalissimus Suvorov: Sbornik Dokumentov* (Moscow 1947).

Labaume, Eugène, *Circumstantial Narrative* (London 1815).

Langeron, L. A. A., Comte de., *Mémoires* (Paris 1902).

Longworth, Philip, *The Art of Victory: the Life and Achievements of Generalissimo Suvorov* (London 1965).

Manceron, Claude, *Austerlitz, The Story of a Battle* (London 1966).

Masson, F., *Memoirs of Catherine II and the Court* (London 1895).

Mazade, Charles de (Ed.), *Mémoires du princ Adam Czartoryski* (Paris 1887).

Meshcheryakov, G. P, (Ed.), *A. V. Suvorov: Dokumenty* (Moscow 1949–53).

Select Bibliography

Olivier, Daria (Trans. Michael Heron), *The Burning of Moscow, 1812* (London 1966).

Palmer, Alan, *Alexander I, Tzar of War and Peace* (London 1974).

Palmer, Alan, *Napoleon in Russia* (New York 1968).

Palmer, Alan, *Russia in War and Peace* (London 1972).

Porter, Robert Ker, *Travelling Sketches in Russia and Sweden* (London 1808).

Remizov, C. P., *Osvoboditel Moski Mikhail Larionovich Golenishchev-Kutuzov-Smolenskii* (Moscow 1867).

Russkii Biograficheskii Slovar (St Petersburg 1898–1918).

Schering, W., *Carl von Clausewitz, Geist und Tat* (Stuttgart 1941).

Schnitzler, M. J. H., *La Russie en 1812: Rostoptchine et Koutousof* (Paris 1863).

Schubert, F. von, *Unter dem Doppeladler. Erinnerungen eines deutschen in russischen offiziersdienst, 1789–1818* (Stuttgart 1962).

Schwartz, Karl, *Lebens des Generals Carl von Clausewitz* (Berlin 1878).

Ségur, General Count Philip de, *History of the Expedition to Russia* (London 1825).

Shilder, N. K., *Imperator Aleksandr I* (St Petersburg 1897).

Smitt, F. von, *Suworow und Polens Untergand* (Leipzig 1858).

Strakhosvky, Leonid I., *Alexander of Russia* (London 1949).

Strokov, Colonel A. A., *Istoriya Voennogo Iskusstva* (Moscow 1965).

Tarle, E., *Napoleon's Invasion of Russia, 1812* (London 1942).

Thompson, J. M. (Ed. and Trans.), *Napoleon's Letters* (London 1954).

Tolstoy, Leo (Trans. and introduced by Rosemary Edmonds), *War and Peace* (London: Penguin Classics Edition 1957).

Vossler, Heinrich, *With Napoleon in Russia, 1812* (London 1969).

Waliszewksi, K., *La Russe il y a Cent Ans, La Règne d'Alexandre* (Paris 1923).

Wilson, Sir Robert, *Narrative of Events During the Invasion of Russia* (London 1860).

Wilson, Sir Robert, *Private Journal* (London 1861).

Wolzogen, Ludwig Freiherrn von, *Memoiren* (Leipzig 1851).

Index

Index

Index

Index